D1180858

Churchill and the
Norway Campaign
1940

Churchill and the Norway Campaign 1940

GRAHAM RHYS-JONES

Pen & Sword
MILITARY

First published in Great Britain in 2008 by
PEN & SWORD MILITARY
An imprint of
Pen & Sword Books Ltd
47 Church Street
Barnsley
South Yorkshire
S70 2AS

ISBN 978-1-84415-753-2

A CIP catalogue record for this book is
available from the British Library

Typeset by Concept, Huddersfield, West Yorkshire
Printed and bound in England by CPI UK

FSC
Mixed Sources
Product group from well-managed
forests and other controlled sources
Cert no. SGS-COC-2953
www.fsc.org
© 1996 Forest Stewardship Council

Pen & Sword Books Ltd incorporates the Imprints of Pen & Sword Aviation,
Pen & Sword Maritime, Pen & Sword Military, Wharncliffe Local History,
Pen & Sword Select, Pen & Sword Military Classics, Leo Cooper,
Remember When, Seaforth Publishing and Frontline Publishing

For a complete list of Pen & Sword titles please contact
PEN & SWORD BOOKS LIMITED
47 Church Street, Barnsley, South Yorkshire, S70 2AS, England
E-mail: enquiries@pen-and-sword.co.uk
Website: www.pen-and-sword.co.uk

To William, Anna and David

Contents

List of Maps

Preface

In a speech to the Central Committee of the National Union of Conservative and Unionist Associations on Thursday, 4 April 1940, Neville Chamberlain, seventy-one years old, man of peace but war leader by necessity, declared that Hitler had 'missed the bus'. It was an ill-chosen phrase and one that he would come to regret but it contained a germ of truth. Seven months of 'Twilight War' had passed without any significant move against the Western Allies and his government had begun, bit by bit, to fill the more important gaps in the nation's defences. The time of greatest danger was past. He was, he told his audience, ten times more confident of victory than he had been at the beginning.

At dawn on the following Tuesday, German forces overran Denmark and, in an operation of extraordinary precision and daring, occupied six principal ports and population centres along a thousand miles of Norwegian coastline from Narvik in the arctic north to Oslo in the approaches to the Baltic. So wildly improbable did the operation appear that it was late evening before London was certain of its full extent and could decide how best to respond.

The countermoves launched by the Chamberlain Government became a byword for ineptitude. Three small expeditionary forces were ashore in Norway within the week but of these, one was quickly reduced to passivity by the Norwegian climate and by unbridgeable differences between the naval and military commanders, while the others (both lightly equipped and seriously under-trained) found themselves under immediate pressure from German forces which seemed able to call on every appliance of modern war. Downing Street was soon smarting under gibes, passed back by a dutiful Minister in Stockholm, that the British had treated Norway as a punitive expedition against the Zulus but had ended up as the Zulus themselves. By the end of the month the Government was preparing its supporters for an embarrassing withdrawal. A week later it was fighting for its survival in the celebrated Commons Debate that marked its passing.

ix

This book began some years ago as a case study for the US Naval War College. If it concentrates on the higher levels of politico-military decision-making at the expense of the battlefield perspective it is merely betraying its origins. It looks firstly at the making of grand strategy in a Cabinet of reluctant warriors as they searched for ways to throttle a German war industry, heavily dependent on Scandinavian raw materials, without provoking a major offensive in the West and without losing what would now be called the moral high ground. (It was the inability of the Allied governments to square this circle that allowed Hitler to strike first and present the Allies with a fait accompli.) Unwilling to grant Hitler yet another bloodless victory the Chamberlain Government prepared to inter-vene.

The shadow of Churchill looms over the brief campaign that followed. As a lone voice warning of dangers to come, and now as the single 'hawk' in a Cabinet of 'doves', his reputation in the country at large stood high. But in these early months of war he had been viewed with suspicion by a Whitehall establishment still committed to the deliberative and cautious policies adopted by the Chamberlain Government. He was verbose, bel-licose, mercurial, 'a difficult colleague'. People close to the Government were alarmed at his growing influence and were quick to see in Norway worrying parallels with Gallipoli, that disastrous product of his first term as First Lord of the Admiralty twenty-five years before. No study of this new adventure on the European periphery can be complete without a look at Churchill's role as the main (and most persistent) advocate of action against German interests in Norway. Nor is it possible to ignore the disastrous consequences of his attempts in the immediate aftermath of the German coup to take over the direction of the campaign and, in his quest for instant results, to ride rough shod over the opinions of military commanders. This study is not a critique of Churchill's role and it has no 'revisionist' pretensions. It is too easy for historians with seventy years of scholarship to fall back on and, with the leisure to weigh one small factor against another, to condemn decisions made in the fog of war and under the pressures of the clock. It will have served its purpose if it casts a little more light on Churchill's defects as a war leader as well as on his virtues.

The 'Twilight War' had already seen naval actions of considerable savagery but nothing so far between Allied land forces and the German Army. This first encounter was to provide an early foretaste of what was to happen on a far larger scale in Flanders and on the Meuse a few weeks later. Soldiers had sometimes comforted themselves with the thought that Hitler's armies would not compare with the Kaiser's men and that, however good the German might be in the carefully planned 'set-piece', he would come unstuck when challenged by the unexpected and the un-familiar. In a remote and undeveloped country like Norway the British gift for improvization would come into its own. They were to be sadly dis-illusioned. The book goes on to examine the difficulties faced by British commanders as they tried to adjust to the twists and turns of government policy, fought against the handicap of a sclerotic administrative tail and struggled to grasp the methods of a new kind of enemy, one who seemed willing to take extraordinary risks and who seemed to have regained levels of tactical mobility not seen since Napoleonic times. Norway was eclipsed by the far larger convulsion in the West but its lessons were enduring.

Histories of failed campaigns do not always make attractive copy. I am thus grateful for the support of Henry Wilson of Pen & Sword without whose support this project might never have reached completion. I must thank Chris Page of the Naval Historical Branch for his advice on the loss of the *Glorious* and for help with sources, James Peat for adding a gloss of professionalism to my untidy maps, Roni Wilkinson of Pen & Sword and Martina Caspers of the Bundesarchiv for help with photographs, and the unsung heroes of the National Archive at Kew on whose patience and dedication any researcher ultimately depends. To these I must add the staff of Dorset County Library who have never failed to track down the pub-lished documents that I have asked for. But most of all I must acknowledge my debt to the minute-takers, diarists and letter-writers, official and private, known and unknown, who recorded their impressions of these events as they unfolded. It is their words not mine which give life to the narrative. My final tribute must go to my wife; she has suffered a good deal over the course of this project but has borne my obsession with her usual tolerance and good humour.

Graham Rhys-Jones
Charminster

Abbreviations

AA	Anti-aircraft
AS	Anti-submarine
AT	Admiralty Telegram
BCS	Battle Cruiser Squadron
BdU	*Befehlshaber der U-boot* (Admiral Dönitz)
BEF	British Expeditionary Force (in France)
CAS	Chief of the Air Staff
CIGS	Chief of the Imperial General Staff
DCNS	Deputy Chief of Naval Staff
DMQ	Director of Military Quarters (War Office)
GC & CS	Government Communications and Cipher School (Bletchley Park)
GHQ	General Headquarters
GOC-in-C	General Officer Commanding in Chief
GQG	*Grand Quartier Général*
HMG	His Majesty's Government
JPS	Joint Planning Staff
KOYLI	King's Own Yorkshire Light Infantry
MCC	Military Co-ordination Committee
NOIC	Naval Officer in Charge
OIC	(Admiralty) Operational Intelligence Centre
OKW	*Oberkommando der Wehrmacht*
QMG	Quartermaster General
RA(D)	Rear Admiral (Destroyers)
RD/F	Radio Direction Finding (Radar)
ROP	Report of Proceedings
SIS	Secret Intelligence Service
SOE	Special Operations Executive
SWC	(Anglo-French) Supreme War Council
VCIGS	Vice Chief of the Imperial General Staff
W/T	Wireless Telegraphy (Morse)
Y & L	York and Lancaster Regiment

Chapter 1

A Divided Cabinet

On 5 April 1940, the Chamberlain War Cabinet put its fears and scruples aside and gave its reluctant consent to Operation 'Wilfred'. That evening, Allied ministers delivered tersely worded notes to the neutral governments in Oslo and Stockholm, and on the following morning, the Saturday, two minelaying groups sailed for the Norwegian coast to mine the approaches to Narvik, the Atlantic outlet for the Swedish iron-ore trade, and to block the Norwegian Leads off Stadlandet, a prominent headland some 500 miles to the southward. The mine lay was to begin at dawn on the Monday morning. Considered in isolation, 'Wilfred' was a modest and tentative escalation in a conflict that had yet to come to the boil. Its main sponsor, Winston Churchill, had sometimes presented it in that light when seeking the support of more cautious colleagues.[1] But it had the potential to open up a new and unfamiliar theatre of operations, and to carry the war to new levels of violence.

During the months of circumspection and restraint that had followed the Allied declaration of war, the Western powers had seen maritime blockade as their principal offensive weapon. The British Government had enforced its belligerent rights from the first and had quickly established a stranglehold on Germany's ocean trade. It had then embarked on the more delicate task of persuading Germany's neutral neighbours to limit their exports to pre-war levels or, better still, to reduce them. The Scandinavian region had been among the first to come under the Whitehall spotlight for, with the loss of established sources of supply in France and Spain, German industry had become more than usually dependent on the import of iron ore from the mines of northern Sweden. And the dependence of that trade during the four winter months on a single ice-free outlet within easy reach of British bases had seemed to present London with a unique opportunity to inflict critical damage on Hitler's war potential.

Churchill had first raised the matter in Cabinet on 19 September.[2] (It had been one of his earliest initiatives as First Lord of the Admiralty.) He had stressed the importance of reaching a decision before the winter trade

1

started in earnest and he had hinted at the need to mine Norwegian waters if diplomatic measures failed. His colleagues had been uneasy. Heavy-handed treatment of inoffensive neutral states was at odds with the Government's deepest instincts and incompatible with Britain's wider international and economic interests. When towards the end of November he had raised the subject again, he had run into concerted opposition. Lord Halifax, Foreign Secretary in the Chamberlain Government and a man of strict principle, had outlined the legal and moral objections and raised the question of German retaliation. He had carried the majority with him. The Cabinet had called for reports on Germany's likely response and on what the military and economic penalties might be.[3]

Believing that his colleagues had failed to appreciate the full scope of the opportunities before them, Churchill responded with a detailed paper in which he presented his proposals as part of a comprehensive plan which, by the summer of 1940, would extend to Luleå – the main summer outlet for Swedish iron – and the Baltic routes as well. Narvik was to be a mere preliminary. A success at Luleå, he claimed, would amount to 'a first class victory in the field'. A sustained blockade might even prove decisive. He went on to urge his colleagues to dismiss fears of German retaliation. The strategic advantage lay with the Allies. There was no reason why they should not 'meet the German invader on Scandinavian soil'. As for the legal and moral objections that had been raised in Cabinet, the Allies had taken up arms in support of the principles of the League of Nations. They should not allow 'technical infringements of international law' to stand in their way.[4]

Churchill found himself pushing at an open door for, as the end of the year approached, a new and quite separate question had started to shape the strategic debate. British reactions to the Russo-Finnish crisis in the autumn of 1939 had been characteristically phlegmatic. The Chiefs of Staff had advised that Allied interests were not directly threatened and that military resources were already stretched to the limit. Attitudes had hardened following Stalin's brutal attack on Finland at the end of November, but the Government's response had been muted and its stance at the League of Nations equivocal. French reactions had been much more volatile. In Paris, the anti-Communist Right had whipped up a storm of popular outrage and the Daladier Government, smarting under accusations of weakness and inertia, had made the defence of Finland a matter of national honour.[5] At a meeting of the Anglo-French Supreme War Council on 19 December, the two strands in Allied policy became inseparably linked. The Council recommended giving all possible help to the Finns and, in order to secure the active co-operation of the Norwegian and Swedish governments, suggested the offer of military support in the event that either of them got into trouble with their powerful neighbours. If accepted, the Council concluded, this guarantee 'might be developed into the dispatch of an expeditionary force ... to occupy Narvik and the Swedish iron ore fields as part of the process of assisting Finland and defending Sweden'.[6]

The ideas set out at this meeting of the Supreme War Council found a powerful champion in Edmund Ironside, Chief of the Imperial General Staff, and the dominant personality on the Chiefs of Staff Committee. Ironside returned from Paris, convinced that the opportunities in Scandinavia were important enough to justify a departure from existing strategic priorities. He had come to question the prevailing emphasis on Flanders and the Rhine frontier, and to see it as dancing to the German tune. Here was an opportunity for the Allies to seize the initiative and upset Hitler's timetable. An expedition to northern Scandinavia, he told the Military Co-ordination Committee on 20 December, would be a 'legitimate sideshow'. It need not mean a large commitment. In this remote and mountainous region, the advantage would lie with the man who got there first; it would be very difficult to turn him out.

The War Cabinet met on 22 December sensing that it faced decisions of critical importance. Churchill saw no inconsistency between the Council's ideas and his own. He threw his weight behind the proposed guarantee and urged a simultaneous warning to Norway about German shipping using the Narvik route. Chamberlain spoke of an historic turning point and referred to the prospect of delivering a 'mortal blow'. But decisions remained cautious and deliberate. The War Cabinet accepted the new proposals in principle but instructed the Chiefs of Staff to consider the military implications of a strategy directed against German ore supplies, and to report on what could be done in practice to protect Norway and Sweden from attack. The Admiralty, meanwhile, was to take no action until the Chiefs of Staff had reported back and until the Cabinet had assessed the reactions of the Swedish and Norwegian authorities.[7]

In the days that followed, some of the obstacles that would face a military expedition in the far north came into sharper focus. Ironside remained convinced that the Allies had stumbled on an idea which had a real prospect of upsetting German plans. But the advance on the Swedish mining areas was going to depend on the single-track electric railway that wound its way from the ore terminal at Narvik upwards through twenty-three tunnels to the Swedish border and on through the mountains to the mining areas round Kiruna and Gällivare. There were no alternative routes; and the use of this essential rail link was going to depend wholly on Norwegian and Swedish co-operation. For Ironside and those who shared his vision, premature adventures on the Norwegian coast which inflamed Scandinavian opinion and alerted Germany to British intentions risked everything. When they came back to Cabinet on 31 December, the Chiefs of Staff gave their full backing to the northern expedition and told Ministers that they could see no prospect of an equivalent opportunity elsewhere. But they warned that a major operation aimed at the Swedish mining areas could not be ready for two months and that, if the Cabinet wanted to adopt the idea, it would be unwise to initiate any smaller projects beforehand.

Churchill fought his corner with his usual determination. The 'larger project', he suggested, was based on a false premise. Norwegian and Swedish co-operation would never be forthcoming since helping the Allies would expose both countries to the threat of invasion. Far from jeopardizing the larger project, his plans provided the only realistic way forward since a strike at German shipping on the Narvik route would provoke a violent reaction, force the Norwegians to take up arms in self-defence and turn to the Allies for help. He nearly carried the day. On 3 January 1940, the Cabinet gave qualified support to Churchill's plans and authorized the necessary diplomatic preliminaries. But it withheld a final decision until it had studied the Norwegian reply. And it instructed the Chiefs of Staff to draw up plans for the occupation of key ports and airfields on the west coast of Norway so that, if the need arose, it could forestall a German retaliatory move.

On 6 January, Halifax informed the Norwegian ambassador that Britain would act to prevent the misuse of neutral waters by German ships. The interview was an awkward one, a foretaste of trouble to come. The Norwegian Government's response was uncompromising. It was clear that co-operation was the last thing on Scandinavian minds. Churchill urged his colleagues to 'brace themselves for the hazards of action', but to no avail. On 12 January, the Cabinet decided to postpone action against the Narvik traffic since it would 'imperil the success of the larger project'.[8] Instead, the Foreign Secretary was to work on plans for a high-level mission to Oslo and Stockholm to explain the Allied case. Churchill, with the weight of Cabinet opinion against him, bowed to the inevitable and, on 19 January, the War Cabinet authorized the Service departments to begin detailed preparations for major land operations in northern Scandinavia.

A report by the Chiefs of Staff issued towards the end of January provides a convenient summary of the pros and cons of the northern expedition as seen at the time.[9] The Chiefs of Staff thought it unlikely that the Germans would launch a major offensive in the West without first securing the economic basis for a lengthy campaign. A pre-emptive move on the Swedish mining areas would throw the German timetable into confusion and possibly alter the course of the war. They made it clear that the stakes were high. The necessary forces could only be found at the expense of the build-up in the West; the strain on shipping and escort forces would be heavy and, given the lack of suitable airfields in central and northern Norway, there would be a worrying imbalance in the air, but they were in no doubt that, if the opportunity presented itself, the Allies should 'seize it with both hands'.

Yet the essential condition of Scandinavian consent was still unsatisfied. There had been no progress on the diplomatic front and the Scandinavian governments were asserting their neutrality as firmly as ever. Early enthusiasm for a ministerial mission to the Nordic capitals had waned and nothing had come to take its place. The Prime Minister was at a loss, certain only that tough talking and threats of naval action were unlikely to help the situation. The only hope was that the plight of the Finns might eventually bring about a change in Scandinavian attitudes. As the end of the month approached, the dangers of drift became plain for all to see. In London, Finland might be little more than a pretext; in Paris, it was an urgent political imperative. During a flying visit to the French military headquarters at Vincennes, Ironside found General Gamelin, the French military supremo, under intense pressure to develop plans for a landing at Petsamo in the Finnish Arctic, a scheme which sidestepped the question of Scandinavian neutrality but which risked confrontation with the Soviet Union, and did nothing to solve the problem of Swedish iron. He thought the idea 'a military gamble without a political prize'.[10] But the warning signs were unmistakeable. The continuing uncertainties surrounding the British project risked divisions within the alliance.

On 5 February the Prime Minister travelled to Paris to explain British plans and reconcile differences. He took Halifax, Churchill and the three Chiefs of Staff with him. In deference to French sensibilities, he accepted that a Finnish collapse would represent a major defeat for the Allies. But he wanted to reassert the original (economic) motive for intervention and reminded his French colleagues how an Allied occupation of the Swedish mining areas 'ostensibly and nominally designed for the assistance of Finland' could be made to 'kill two birds with one stone'.[11] He got Daladier's full agreement. On the vexed question of Scandinavian consent, it was decided that, when all was ready, the Allied governments would get the Finns to make an urgent appeal for help. They would respond with a demand for immediate free passage and an offer of armed support to Norway and Sweden in the event that either of them came under attack. Daladier, less sanguine about the chances of Scandinavian co-operation, asked for the Petsamo plan to be reconsidered if the neutral governments declined to fall in with Allied proposals. This was accepted.[12]

Immediately following this meeting the British 42nd and 44th Divisions, which had been due to leave for France within the week, were held back to prepare for operations in the far north. There was little time to lose. The Baltic sea routes would open in early April. If the Allied expeditionary force was to beat the Germans to the northern ore fields, it would have to start loading stores at the beginning of March.

Churchill had accepted the collective will of the War Cabinet during these weeks and had resisted the temptation to press the case for naval action against the Narvik traffic. (His uncharacteristic silence at the Supreme War Council on 5 February had been the subject of comment.) But, his decisive handling of the *Altmark* incident a fortnight later served to strengthen his hand.[13] Spurred on by the public acclaim that had followed the sensational boarding of the 'prison ship', and armed with unassailable evidence of German duplicity and Norwegian weakness, he had again urged the War Cabinet to mine Norwegian waters and, on 19 February, had gained its hesitant agreement. But he had not been able to move forward. Despite mounting criticism of British inertia from across the Channel, Halifax had maintained a principled opposition. The legal grounds for action against Norway were, he thought, slender. Churchill's proposals would damage Britain's standing in the United States, Italy and the smaller neutrals. The risks to British economic interests in the Scandinavian region were incalculable and the Cabinet might decide in a few months time that it had gained a little but lost much more.[14] Halifax provided a rallying point for those who remained unconvinced. The Prime Minister conceded that the step could not be taken lightly. Britain had entered the war on 'moral grounds' and had to preserve that advantage. He needed to carry the Dominions with him and he needed to canvas the views of opposition leaders.

Chamberlain gave his ruling on 29 February. His soundings among the opposition parties and among the Dominion high commissioners had been mostly negative. He favoured Churchill's plan in principle; but he was not convinced that it 'would be opportune at the present moment'. He acknowledged the difficulty of getting help to Finland but he did not want to prejudice the chances that remained. And, like the Foreign Secretary, he was concerned about international opinion and the risk to Britain's economic interests. He was thus unable to recommend the measure to his colleagues.[15] Churchill withdrew his proposals as gracefully as he could.

It was possible by now for the Chamberlain Cabinet to glimpse something of the scale and complexity of the plans being drawn up in the War Office. Under Operation 'Avonmouth', a British infantry brigade and a demi-brigade (three battalions) of Chasseurs Alpins would land at Narvik and move forward by rail to occupy the Swedish mining areas and Luleå on the Gulf of Bothnia. An international force of two or three brigades would then operate in support of the Finns. Under 'Stratford' the 49th (Territorial) Division would occupy Stavanger, Bergen and Trondheim and take control

6

of the railway leading eastward to the Swedish frontier. Three further divisions previously assigned to the BEF, one regular and two territorial, would move forward to help the Swedish Army counter a German invasion. Estimates ran to 100,000 men and 11,000 vehicles, totals that would put scarce shipping space under severe strain and overwhelm port facilities at the far end. The whole move was expected to take eleven weeks and occupy an escort force of forty Royal Navy destroyers. To his considerable annoyance, Ironside found himself defending his figures in Cabinet against Churchill's hostile probing.[16]

As the end of February approached, Cabinet decisions on 'Avonmouth' and 'Stratford' were becoming urgent. The earliest date for the landing in Narvik had been put at 20 March. (Troops would have to sail on the 15th and the slower stores ships on 12th.) The latest date for the landing if Allied forces were to establish themselves before the Baltic opened and the Germans mounted a counter-offensive was put at 3 April. Embarkation would have to begin in a matter of days. Yet there was little evidence that Scandinavian attitudes were softening; rather the reverse for, on 16 February, the Swedish Government had stated emphatically that it would not allow foreign troops to cross its soil. The Cabinet remained divided. Chamberlain still nursed the hope that public indignation and World opinion might induce a change of heart.[17] Churchill wanted to put the Scandinavian governments to the test. Ironside was demanding talks with the Swedish General Staff. Flexible minds searching for a way round the impasse were beginning to accept that, in the absence of formal consent, some degree of force might be inevitable. By 20 February, the Prime Minister was taking a personal interest in the instructions that were being drafted for the Force Commanders.[18]

Events on the ground, however, were making all such considerations academic. When Chamberlain and Daladier had put Finland at the top of the Allied agenda it had been assumed that the Finns could hold out until May. But, at the beginning of February, the Red Army, reinforced and reorganized after its early failures, had renewed its attack on the Mannerheim line and had quickly breached the Finnish defences. By mid-month, Helsinki's appeals for aircraft, artillery and ammunition were becoming desperate. Ironside was gloomy. After their 'rash guarantee' to Poland, Allied promises carried little weight. The Scandinavian neutrals, he thought, felt the burden of war bearing down on them; they would never accede to Allied demands. The fate of Finland was certain. The Allies faced another bloodless defeat to match those in Abyssinia and Poland.[19] By the end of the month, it was becoming clear that the entire house of cards that the Allied governments had created was on the point of collapse.

On 22 February, the Finnish President asked the Allies to lend their weight to a diplomatic settlement. It was soon evident that Stalin would not retreat from his pre-war demands. In a forlorn attempt to keep the Finns in the field and to preserve the mechanism that would trigger the northern expedition, the British Government authorized its Minister in Helsinki to reveal the plans agreed by the Supreme War Council and to promise a force of 20,000 men by the middle of April. (The move had little effect; the Finnish Government was already considering other options.) On 1 March the Finnish Minister in London presented Halifax with a stark choice. If the Allies could not increase their offer to 100 bombers and 50,000 men before the end of the month, his government would be forced to negotiate. And he had asked pointedly how the Swedish and Norwegian stance would affect London's ability to honour its pledges. The Foreign Secretary had replied that the Allies would do everything that lay in their power but he had given no definite assurances.

Next day, the Cabinet agreed to make its plans known to the Norwegian and Swedish governments. The diplomatic note, a request for co-operation rather than a robust statement of intent, was again firmly rejected. Recognizing that the tide of events was running against it, but unwilling to be cast in the role of scapegoat for another strategic defeat, the War Cabinet began to steel itself for a landing at Narvik without the formal consent of the Norwegian Government. The expeditionary force would test the strength of Norwegian resolve; but it would withdraw if it encountered stiff resistance. Churchill seems broadly to have accepted this formula. Norway and later Sweden, he told Admiral Pound who was to represent him in Cabinet on 7 March, 'ought to be put to the proof'. He doubted that the Norwegians would resist; if they did, commanders should be prepared to lose a few men but they should press on, infiltrate and 'Get Narvik by nightfall by force or persuasion'.[20]

On 11 March the French ambassador called at the Foreign Office and delivered what Cadogan, the acerbic Permanent Under Secretary, described as a 'grand remonstrance' about British inertia. He hinted that Britain's policy towards Finland was a sham and warned of political crisis in Paris. With the future of the alliance at stake, the War Cabinet at last committed itself to a landing at Narvik; and that evening Chamberlain revealed to the House of Commons that Britain and France were acting together to help the Finns. According to Ironside, next morning's Cabinet was 'dreadful'. The Prime Minister had seemed surprised when told that troops were embarking. He had peered at a chart of Narvik and asked about the effect of heavy shells on naval transports. There had been more inconclusive discussion about how much force might be permissible. In the end, the Prime Minister had been persuaded to meet the commanders of the expedition and satisfy himself that the Cabinet's orders were fully understood.

Major General P.J. Mackesy[21] and Admiral Sir Edward Evans (a colour-
ful rogue with strong Norwegian ties)[22] had presented themselves at
Downing Street that evening. The PM had seemed ill at ease but he had
approved instructions allowing the landing force to test the strength of the
Norwegian opposition and to use force as an 'ultimate measure of self-
defence'.[23] Halifax had been dubious about the whole enterprise saying
that, if it involved taking Norwegian lives, he was against it, ore or no ore.
In the end, Chamberlain had said, 'Good luck ... if you go.' No one had
seriously believed that the landing would take place. General Mackesy
thought that the chances were a hundred to one against.[24]

Next day it became clear that the Finnish Government had accepted
terms. Chamberlain put Operation 'Avonmouth' at forty-eight hours'
notice. When it later became clear that the ceasefire was holding he stood
the forces down.

The Finnish armistice generated mixed emotions among British leaders.
Cabinet members had seemed despondent when they met on 14 March
and exchanges had been ill tempered. Churchill, who had quickly found a
new pretext for intervening in the far north, had been 'particularly annoy-
ing'.[25] The Prime Minister's response to the turn of events was part relief
and part irritation, for he was now certain that the Gallic ally would try to
pin the blame on him. But, in the Commons, he defended his government's
record with vigour, pointing to the twists and turns in Finnish policy and
to the failings of the Swedish and Norwegian authorities. His speech was
well received and did much to quell the anxieties of a restless House.[26] As
the shock of events receded, many expressed unease about mechanisms of
government that seemed better suited to scrutiny than to decision-making.
In a private letter to Halifax, Churchill referred to a 'critical and obstructive
apparatus' that had thwarted action at every turn and to a Cabinet that
had never done anything but 'follow the line of least resistance'.[27] But the
administrative reforms adopted in the wake of the Finnish debacle were
confined to a modest pruning of War Cabinet numbers and to Churchill's
appointment as Chairman of the Military Co-ordination Committee, an
arrangement that allowed him unprecedented influence over the full scope
of British strategy but which, under the pressure of events, would become
at best unworkable and at worst dangerous.[28]

In France, the collapse of Finnish resistance brought political crisis.
Faced with wholesale defections in the Chamber of Deputies, Daladier
resigned on 20 March and was replaced as President of the Council by an
arch enemy, Paul Reynaud. But his power to shape the course of events
remained significant. He retained the post of Minister for War in a coalition
paralysed by personal animosity and political infighting.[29]

9

The change of administration did little to improve relations between the Allied governments. Recognizing that it needed to strengthen Allied cohesion and demonstrate a new commitment to the war against German revanchism, the Chamberlain Cabinet began to review a range of operations consistent with the broad thrust of existing strategy and which could be put in hand without delay. They settled on two that appeared eye-catching and at the same time realistic – the much-maligned and often-postponed Operation 'Wilfred', and that other product of Churchill's fertile imagination, Operation 'Royal Marine', a scheme to lay fluvial mines in the Rhine as a deterrent to a German offensive in the West. Both operations were ready or nearly so and both had the imprimatur of the Chiefs of Staff.

But on 22 March, the incoming French Premier circulated an alternative set of proposals designed to show that a new and more decisive hand had taken the helm. His paper advocated robust treatment of the minor neutrals, immediate action to assert control over Norwegian waters and the occupation of strategic positions on the Norwegian coast. It also revealed a longstanding French preoccupation with German oil supplies, and with the danger of Nazi-Soviet collusion by proposing attacks on Russian tankers in the Black Sea and the bombing of Caucasian oil installations, operations which the British considered misconceived and wholly unrealistic. Chamberlain had bridled at the implied criticism of his war leadership and had dismissed the paper as the work of a novice.

On 27 March, Reynaud brought a posse of military advisers to London for a meeting of the Supreme War Council. Chamberlain, determined to curb all signs of visionary excess, handled the plenary sessions with consummate skill, providing a lucid exposition of the strategic situation and successfully spiking French guns. There was no defence against his cold logic and forensic skill. In Ironside's memorable if barbed description, Reynaud sat there nodding 'for all the world like a little marmoset'[30] while his delegation, lulled by a good lunch at the Carlton, dozed peacefully. The day belonged to Chamberlain. The Council accepted the need for a more virile war policy and agreed a detailed timetable for the days ahead. On 1 April (the Monday following) Allied ministers in Oslo and Stockholm would deliver a joint warning about the trade in strategic raw materials. On the evening of 4th April, and subject to the approval of the French Comité de Guerre, Churchill's naval parties would initiate 'Royal Marine' with the release of fluvial mines into the Rhine. (The operation would be extended to German inland waterways ten days later.) And, on 5 April (the Friday) the Royal Navy would mine the Norwegian Leads. The question of later operations against Narvik and Luleå was referred to the military staffs for further study.[31]

10

The following day, the War Cabinet endorsed the Council's recommendations. Churchill briefed the Cabinet on 'Wilfred' and on the procedures to be adopted in the event of a confrontation with the Norwegian Navy. And he reintroduced a topic which had been set aside under the pressure of events, but which had always been of special concern to the Cabinet – the issue of German reprisals and the measures necessary to forestall them. He expressed the hope that the German response to 'Wilfred' would open the way to a landing in Norway with the consent of the Norwegian authorities; and he reminded his colleagues that, at the very least, they would have to be ready to secure the Norwegian ports. The Cabinet seems to have taken this new shift of policy in its stride. There was no possibility of reconstituting Operation 'Stratford'. Oliver Stanley, Secretary of State for War, made it clear that the divisions set aside for that task had already been sent to France. But the brigade intended for Narvik and the battalions earmarked for Stavanger were still available and, on 1 April 1940, the War Cabinet endorsed what was, in effect, a hasty rehash of what had gone before. The plan was known simply as 'R4' and was summarized by the Chiefs of Staff as follows:

The moment the Germans set foot on Norwegian soil or there is clear evidence that they intend to do so, our object should be (a) to dispatch a force to Narvik to secure the port and, subsequently, the railway inland as far as the [Swedish] frontier, and to pave the way to the Galivare ore fields; (b) as a defensive measure, to dispatch forces to occupy Stavanger, Bergen and Trondheim, in order to deny their use to the Germans as naval and/or air bases.[32]

The initiative was to rest with the Germans. It was accepted that the landings would be impossible if the Norwegians were hostile. A German invasion of Sweden was considered unlikely; there was little that could be done about it in the short term but options for the future including full restoration of the original plan were under study.

The final days before the launch of 'Wilfred' proved far from easy. The French attitude to 'Royal Marine' had always been lukewarm and on Reynaud's return to Paris, the Comité de Guerre had vetoed the proposal on the grounds that it would provoke reprisals against the vulnerable French aircraft industry. Inevitably, opposition had centred on Daladier who had demanded a three-month delay while defences were improved and facilities dispersed. The French Ambassador had called on Chamberlain on 31 March to express Reynaud's deep regret and to pass on the suggestion that the Prime Minister might visit Paris to use his persuasive powers on the Minister for War. An exasperated Chamberlain had

11

declined the invitation and replied 'No mines – No Narvik'. The two men had then parted agreeing to discuss the conversation with colleagues.

The linkage between Operations 'Wilfred' and 'Royal Marine' had not been explicit before this moment and came as a surprise to Churchill, the main sponsor of both projects. But there was an element of logic behind it since the mining of the Rhine would give the lie to any suggestion that the Allies were prepared to bully weak neutral states but not to take effective action against their principal enemy. The Cabinet thus agreed to delay the start of 'Wilfred' until Monday, 8 April in the hope that the French might still be open to persuasion. And after another failed attempt to set up some kind of dialogue between the Prime Minister and Daladier, it was eventually decided that the First Lord would make a flying visit to Paris at the end of the week to talk the obdurate Minister round. Churchill dined with Reynaud at the British Embassy on the Thursday evening. He found the French Premier unwilling to overrule his Minister for War on a matter of strategy and thus to risk further political crisis. A meeting with Daladier on the Friday morning convinced him that further attempts to get the French to act against their better judgement risked permanent damage to the alliance. He informed London accordingly.[33]

On Friday, 5 April, the War Cabinet accepted the postponement of 'Royal Marine' and gave its final approval to the launch of 'Wilfred'. It was hardly a unanimous decision. The Foreign Office had continued to look on the operation with lofty disdain; Halifax, it was said, had only agreed out of loyalty to the Prime Minister.[34] Many in Whitehall shared his views. 'Wilfred' came too late to have a significant impact on the German war economy; the Baltic trade routes would reopen in a matter of weeks. Nor could the operation be presented as the first step in a diversionary campaign that would upset the smooth progress of German plans; the Chamberlain Government had looked that spectre in the face and quailed. 'Wilfred' was action for action's sake; it was military theatre, staged to save the reputation of a divided Cabinet and to preserve relations with a fractious ally.

Chapter 2

Against All Precedent

It is one of the ironies of history that the Kriegsmarine, the branch of the German armed forces least adapted to the task ahead, should have directed Hitler's attention to the dangers on his northern flank and played the leading part in the development of operational plans.

The British declaration of war on 3 September 1939 had hit Naval Headquarters 'like a bombshell'.[1] Grand Admiral Erich Raeder, disciple of Tirpitz and architect of the Navy's revival during the Hitler years, had abandoned plans for a world-class surface fleet in favour of a programme which put overwhelming emphasis on short-term needs and on a rapid expansion of the U-boat arm. There had been little alternative.

The broad outline of his strategy was already clear. (Again, there had been little choice.) Following the Czechoslovak crisis of summer 1938 when the possibility of war with England had first entered the naval reckoning, the Navy had rethought its operational doctrines and rewritten its Battle Instructions. If it was to pursue an active strategy and demonstrate its utility as an instrument of state, it would have to avoid a direct confrontation with the British fleet (still the world's most powerful despite two decades of official neglect) and launch its offensive against Britain's Achilles heel – her critical dependence on overseas imports. Raeder's first priority was now to sell this concept to a sceptical Führer. In his early wartime conferences, he dwelt on the importance of the Navy's strategic mission (its war against the British economy), on the restrictions that Hitler had imposed on the operations of the U-boat flotilla and on the resources that he needed for his expanded U-boat programme. If this was going to be a 'fight to the finish', he would need to put Britain under a state of siege; indeed it seemed likely that 'the entire burden of the war against England' was going to fall on the Navy and particularly on his submarines.[2]

In the early months of war, the protection of economic interests in the far north had not loomed large in Raeder's thinking. He had seen the coast of Norway through the prism of his maritime campaign. He had wanted to establish U-boat bases in the far north but the Army had shown little enthusiasm and the question of base defence had never been resolved. He had hoped that the Norwegian authorities might be open to persuasion and, during a meeting with Hitler on 10 October, he had offered the suggestion that Russian help might be invoked.[3] He had later become concerned at the volume of Scandinavian trade being routed through Norwegian ports (notably Trondheim) for onward shipment to Britain and it was in this context that he had first hinted at the need to occupy Norway.[4]

The Soviet attack on Finland at the end of November provided the catalyst for a more radical shift in naval thinking. Regional tensions were running high and it was becoming possible to see how fears of Soviet encroachment might propel nervous Scandinavian governments into the orbit of the Western Powers. A well-timed intervention by Alfred Rosenberg, the Party official responsible for developing relations with kindred parties abroad, seems to have tipped the scales. In early December, this self-styled 'philosopher' of Nazi-ism presented Raeder with a memorandum pointing to dangerous trends in Norwegian policy and commending a Norwegian protégé, Vidkun Quisling, leader of the far-right Party of National Unity, and one-time War Minister in the Norwegian Government, as a promising candidate to head a military coup.[5]

Raeder met Quisling on 11 December. The Norwegian, a driven personality with a deep and personal hatred of Bolshevism, saw the new Germany as an essential bulwark against Soviet domination. According to the records of this meeting, he claimed that the Norwegian Government was engaged in secret negotiations with the British and that Carl Hambro, the influential Speaker of the Storting, had started a deliberate campaign to shift Norwegian opinion in favour of the Western Allies. And he seems to have painted a convincing picture of how a military presence in Norway would extend British influence throughout the Scandinavian region and turn the Baltic into a theatre of war. For his own part, he wanted to counter Russian influence by putting bases at Germany's disposal. He was approaching Raeder because months of discussion with Rosenberg had produced nothing concrete.[6]

Raeder reported this conversation to Hitler the following day. He was cautious about Quisling's reliability but he stressed the absolute necessity of preventing Norway from falling into British hands. Hitler agreed. The C-in-C Navy went on to warn the Führer that a German occupation of Norway would provoke strong countermeasures, put Narvik traffic at risk and result in bitter fighting along the Norwegian coast, something that the German Navy in its present state of development would find it hard to sustain. This was a definite risk. But he urged Hitler to task OKW to prepare contingency plans for the putsch that Rosenberg and Quisling had been working on and for a full-blooded military alternative.[7] Having first taken the precaution of meeting Quisling himself, Hitler gave orders accordingly.

OKW issued its preliminary thoughts to the Service Staffs on 10 January 1940 in a paper entitled *Studie Nord*. This claimed that the political situation in Norway favoured a British intervention, that the coming offensive in the West ('*Fall Gelb*') gave the British the pretext that they needed and concluded that the only realistic solution was for Germany to strike first. Although the tough-minded Chief of Naval Staff, Vice Admiral Otto Schniewind, gave full backing to the OKW analysis, the paper got a mixed reception in Naval Staff circles. The influential Operations Division was openly critical and their war diary for 13 January set out their reservations in some detail. There was little evidence, they suggested, that the British were capable of so decisive a move. The Western Allies, they thought, could hardly afford to antagonize Russia and they would have to consider the very powerful countermeasures open to Germany. The idea that Britain could dominate Sweden from bases in Norway was, they thought, fanciful; German military power would be the deciding factor in Swedish thinking. Germany, on the other hand, had much to lose by upsetting the status quo. Norwegian territorial waters would no longer offer immunity to German shipping, ore shipments from Narvik could no longer be guaranteed and a valuable access route to the Atlantic and to Base North, the newly acquired naval base on the Murman coast, would be lost. Schniewind made no attempt to counter these arguments. He simply ruled that the course of events in Norway was unpredictable and that the Navy had to be ready to meet the call if it came. The Naval Staff began, therefore, to consider its military options.[8]

It was clear from the first that an invasion of southern Norway, the simplest and the most obvious solution, would leave the north of the country exposed to British attack, putting vital economic interests at risk and leading, in all probability, to a lengthy and inconclusive campaign. If, instead, German forces could seize all major ports and population centres in a single surprise move, they would prevent all possibility of concerted resistance and make outside intervention difficult, if not impossible. The concept was an ambitious one; plans would have to be prepared and executed in the strictest secrecy. And they would have to involve carefully synchronized attacks on up to seven objectives spread over 1,000 miles of Norwegian coastline from Tromsø in the far north to Oslo in the Baltic approaches. Although airborne and air-landed troops would have a key part to play, prime responsibility for delivering troops to Norway would rest with the Navy. Early proposals included the covert use of merchant ships to get the assault troops to their objectives, but the risk of discovery during the long passage of the Norwegian Leads was judged too great. Nor did it seem likely that merchant ships could act with the precision that the operation so obviously required. The delivery of assault units would be a job for the warships of the German surface fleet. The number of men and the volume of materiel in this first wave would inevitably be small but, with the ports and airfields in German hands, the necessary reinforcements and materiel support could follow quickly behind.[9]

Staff thinking had got no further than this when Hitler recalled *Studie Nord* and put planning in the hands of a small tri-service working group under the direct supervision of OKW. His stated aim was to bring the military planning process into the 'closest conjunction with general war policy'; but it seems likely that his decision reflected worries about security and a growing distrust of the large service bureaucracies.[10] For the moment the project, now codenamed *'Weserübung'*, went forward slowly within the confines of the Führer headquarters. And for the moment the Service Staffs found themselves excluded from the planning circle. When they were next invited to consider the question of Norway, they did so against the background of a strategic directive and in the aftermath of several important decisions.

For some weeks Hitler's intentions towards his Scandinavian neighbours had remained unclear. Fears about anti-German sentiment and British meddling had been largely forgotten and, in a meeting with Raeder at the end of January, Hitler had treated Norway as a peripheral matter. Despite his recent postponement of *'Gelb'*, a decision prompted by extreme winter weather and disagreements with the General Staff, his mind had remained fixed on the West where France had to be defeated and Britain expelled from her base on the Continent. The *Altmark* affair seems to have tipped the scales. The boarding of this German auxiliary, under the noses of its Norwegian escort, brought final proof of Britain's contempt for Norwegian neutrality and of Norway's inability to defend it. A volley of decisions followed. Hitler abandoned ideas for a putsch and decided on a strictly military solution. He called for plans to be completed as a matter of urgency and, at Jodl's suggestion, brought in General Nikolaus von Falkenhorst, GOC XXI Corps and a veteran of the 1918 Finnish intervention, to reinvigorate the planning process and to command the operation.[11] And where once it had been assumed that political pressure would be sufficient to ensure access through Danish waters and to obtain forward air bases in northern Jutland, he now approved plans to occupy Denmark as well.

Hitler issued his *'Weserübung'* directive on 1 March, citing as his objects the need to forestall British action in Scandinavia, the protection of

Swedish ore supplies and the provision of 'expanded bases for operations against England'. 'The basic aim,' he said:

> is to lend the operation the character of a *peaceful* occupation designed to protect by force of arms the neutrality of the Northern countries. Demands in this sense will be made to the Governments concerned at the beginning of the occupation and the necessary emphasis will be given, if required, by naval and air demonstrations. Any resistance which is nevertheless offered will be broken by all means available.[12]

The Naval Staff found out what would be required of them later the same day. The main points arising from the briefing by Captain Theodor Krancke, head of the *'Weserübung'* planning cell, were that the occupation of Norway and Denmark would take place simultaneously and, if need be, at the same time as *'Gelb'*. The movement of the initial landing forces would, with minor modifications, follow the scheme already outlined by the Naval Staff with support and logistics following as soon as 'the situation in the ports is under control'.[13] A Naval Staff working group would now have to carry the plans forward. And it would have to work quickly; no date had been set for the operation but Hitler had indicated that he might demand its execution at short notice.

The Naval Staff recognized straight away that they had been handed a task of epic proportions. It was going to involve the whole Navy – nothing that could float and move could be excluded. Raising the necessary number of ships was going to put the Navy and the dockyards under intense pressure and demand the most careful husbanding of resources. On 4 March, the Naval Staff took the decision to suspend all other operations including the long-cherished Atlantic sortie of the pocket battleship *Lützow*, the mining campaign on the east coast of England and the replacement of U-boats in the war against commerce.[14] And it had seemed inevitable that naval participation in *'Fall Gelb'* would be severely curtailed. Schniewind felt 'in duty bound' to tell the Führer of the likely penalties; he warned him that the naval campaign was coming to a complete standstill, something that was only tolerable if *'Weserübung'* is an absolute necessity and takes place soon'. Referring directly to Hitler's stated objectives, he warned that ore imports from Narvik would be suspended for an indefinite period and that, in its current state of material weakness, the Navy would gain little from improvements in strategic position.[15]

That said there could be no question of the Navy's failing to meet the demands placed on it. Whatever the attitude of the Army and the Luftwaffe – both continued to look on *'Weserübung'* as a side issue and to resent the intrusion of the OKW into their affairs – the Navy now threw itself wholeheartedly into the project. There was to be no more argument

17

about the pros and cons. The time for 'military scruples' was over, Schniewind warned former sceptics in the Operations Division during a meeting on 2 March; it was necessary to conform 'at lightning speed to political conditions and necessities'.[16]

The task given to the staff planners was a broad one, covering embarkation, outward passage, penetration of the fjords, landing phase, consolidation and withdrawal, but the debate within Naval Headquarters and with authorities outside it quickly centred on a handful of key issues. An amphibious operation across waters controlled by the enemy was at odds with 'all the precepts of naval warfare' but, given the factor of surprise and a decision to move before the arrival of spring weather, planners were in little doubt that they could deliver the Army safely to its objectives.[17]

The far more difficult question was how to recover the invasion flotillas to German waters once the landings were over. It seemed imperative that ships should leave the fjords as soon as their mission was accomplished and before the enemy could bring the weight of his sea and air power to bear. Ships destined for southern ports presented no great difficulty – they could break back individually under cover of darkness. But the ships assigned to the northern ports would face a lengthy passage home, this time without the benefit of surprise. Some delay would be inevitable while ships refuelled from a tanker group timed to arrive within hours of the assault. But, at the earliest possible moment, the ships would have to spring the trap and make for home. The future of the Navy as a fighting force depended on it.[18]

The admirals soon discovered that their views ran counter to those of OKW and to those of the Führer himself. The scattered landing forces on the coast of Norway would remain vulnerable to counter-attack until their support had arrived and until a favourable air situation had been established. Schniewind had conceded this point during a meeting with Hitler on 5 March, when he had called for the early seizure of Norwegian coastal defences and for a rapid build-up in air strength. But Hitler had wanted ships held back in Narvik and Trondheim to provide artillery and anti-aircraft support; and OKW had quickly followed up with a supplementary directive. The Naval Staff was prepared to deploy U-boats off the Norwegian ports in large numbers but not to leave key surface ships exposed to the enemy's counter offensive. Admiral Raeder made the point with unusual force when reporting to Hitler on 9 March. He had explained the hazards of the return voyage and the merits of a combined breakout by the northern groups. 'Not one destroyer may be left behind, let alone a cruiser,' he told the Führer, 'when the fate of the German Fleet is hanging in the balance.'[19]

Compared to the hazards of the return voyage, the penetration of the Norwegian fjords appeared as a minor challenge. Opposition from the paltry Norwegian Navy could be discounted; the *Altmark* affair showed that it would bow to superior force. The coastal defences, manned or at least part-manned, had seemed a more serious obstacle, but careful enquiry had suggested that local commanders would refer to Oslo before opening fire. Even if they acted on their own initiative, their window of opportunity would be extremely narrow. Again, security, surprise and tempo would be the keys to success. The Norwegians wouldn't make the decision to fire quickly enough, Raeder assured Hitler, even if they decided to do so at all.[20] Time would show him half right and half wrong.

Two further issues raised hackles in Naval Headquarters as the planning process continued – the reluctance of operational commands to accept an active role for the battleships *Scharnhorst* and *Gneisenau*, the only capital ships as yet completed under Raeder's rearmament programme, and the totemic nucleus round which the Navy hoped to rebuild a battle fleet when victory was won; and the growing demands of the Army and the Luftwaffe for merchant shipping to carry heavy weapons, ammunition, fuel, horses and motor transport to Norwegian destinations.

The Naval Staff had been confident that their assault groups could avoid contact with major elements of the British Fleet during their outward journey, but they had been unable to rule out chance encounters with convoy escorts in the North Sea or with cruiser patrols off the coast of Norway. They had thus insisted on heavy cover for the northern groups. The battleships would not seek action for its own sake; but they would escort the Narvik and Trondheim groups to their destinations and fight off any opposition that barred their way. While landing operations were in progress, they would make a diversionary sweep to seaward to draw the enemy away from the Norwegian coast and, when the critical breakout phase began, combine with the forces emerging from the fjords and fight their way back to Germany. To its desk-bound authors, the plan was entirely in line with staff doctrine on the employment of the 'nucleus battle fleet'. To operational staffs in Kiel and Wilhelmshaven, it smacked of academic strategy and a wilful disregard of risk. This squabble, essentially a domestic one, would emerge into the open on the eve of operations.

The second issue was even more contentious because it threatened the key principle on which the success of *Weserübung* depended. In their preliminary discussions the Naval Staff had ruled out the early movement of merchant ships on the grounds that it was likely to attract the scrutiny of the Norwegian authorities and risk the loss of surprise. But they had not considered questions of reinforcement and resupply in any depth. When, following Hitler's Directive of 1 March, they had found themselves restored to the planning circle, they had been dismayed to find that OKW expected a score of ships to reach their destinations on *Weser*-day and that the first of these ships (the so-called 'Export Group') would have to leave

Germany on W-6. The planners had at once expressed the strongest reservations. By 6 March, they were warning that the early movement of merchant shipping could 'endanger the whole operation'.[21] As preparations continued, worries about premature disclosure became more and more acute.

While the Naval Staff were wrestling with these problems, rumours of an Allied intervention in support of Finland reached fever pitch. On 6 March, sources in Oslo reported that the Allies had demanded the right of passage across Norwegian territory and that French and British officers had been seen looking at unloading facilities in the Norwegian ports; Stavanger, Trondheim and Narvik had been mentioned and so had Kirkenes. All this was happening, it was said, with the knowledge of the Norwegian Government.

On 8 March the Luftwaffe reported an unusual concentration of heavy ships in Scapa Flow. It was not immediately clear whether this was a routine move by the British Home Fleet or whether, perhaps, the Admiralty was expecting an Atlantic breakout to coincide with the new moon period in the middle of the month. But coupled with critical developments in Finland, the news from Norway and the general excitement in the European press, the concentration acquired a special significance. An Anglo-French landing supported by the entire strength of the Home Fleet appeared imminent. But '*Weserübung*' was not ready. Although preparations in the North Sea bases were progressing well, ice was still blocking the embarkation ports in the Baltic and the Navy's trials programme had been seriously disrupted. If the call came now, the Kriegsmarine would be found wanting.

The Finnish armistice brought worries of a different kind. On 13 March, Hitler declared that the Scandinavian crisis had eased and that preparations for Norway could continue 'without excessive haste' – it now seemed possible that the Navy's war against the British economy, already suspended since the beginning of the month, might remain on hold indefinitely while Hitler tried to adjust his decisions to the ebb and flow of international events.[22] After a further week of frustration and uncertainty, the Naval Staff sought permission to examine what operations could be reinstated without serious risk to the Navy's state of readiness. The options were few. If they resumed mining operations on the east coast of Britain or authorized attacks on North Sea convoy traffic, they risked compromising the readiness of the destroyer flotillas. If they sent U-boats to the Western Approaches, they risked failing to meet their commitments in Norway. The only reasonable possibility was to reinstate plans for the breakout of the *Lützow* and of one or more of the auxiliary cruisers. They thus sought OKW approval to delete the *Lützow* from the order of battle for Norway and to replace her with the *Blücher*, a brand new cruiser that was just completing sea trials.[23]

But this modest compromise was not enough and Raeder went into his next meeting with the Führer determined to bring matters to a head. He accepted that the threat of an Allied invasion had receded but asserted that Britain would soon begin to harass German traffic in Norwegian waters and eventually take action to suppress it altogether. At some point, he told Hitler, '*Weserübung*' would become a matter of necessity. It would be best to order it sooner rather than later and certainly before the arrival of spring weather and shorter nights put the enterprise at serious risk. He gave 15 April as the latest acceptable date and offered 7 April (the date of the new moon) as his personal preference.[24] The Führer agreed to initiate the operation at 'about the time of the new moon' and later named 9 April as *Weser*-day and 0515 (German Summer Time) as *Weser*-hour.

The final shape of '*Weserübung*' was now becoming clear. Group XXI aimed to paralyse the Norwegian state and stifle signs of incipient resistance by seizing Oslo, and by occupying as many other centres of population as the carrying capacity of the German surface fleet allowed.[25] Apart from Oslo, Norway's first city and seat of government, they settled on Narvik for its access to the ore fields; Trondheim, the ancient capital and main port of central Norway; Bergen, the country's second city and a place deserving special attention as the closest port to British bases; Stavanger for its well-placed airfield; and Kristiansand, the port commanding access to the Baltic. A number of subsidiary objectives were included as well: Arendal, a minor port on the Skagerrak within easy reach of Kristiansand; and Egersund, the terminal for the cable to England.

Three lightly equipped divisions would be used in the initial landings. Their function was to secure the beachheads and hold them until relieved; they were not to engage in offensive operations in the interior of the country. Three further divisions would follow close behind; these would be shipped to Oslo to consolidate the hold on the capital and then advance by road and rail though the Norwegian highlands to relieve the isolated garrisons and establish control over the interior. These follow-on divisions would be equipped for major offensive operations with generous armour, artillery and engineering support. The Luftwaffe would provide three parachute companies and three anti-aircraft battalions.

Ten of the Navy's most modern destroyers would deliver three battalions of General Eduard Dietl's battle-tested 3rd Mountain Division to Narvik. The heavy cruiser *Hipper* and four more destroyers would land the two remaining battalions at Trondheim. These task groups (Groups 1 and 2) would be the first to sail and would be escorted northwards by the

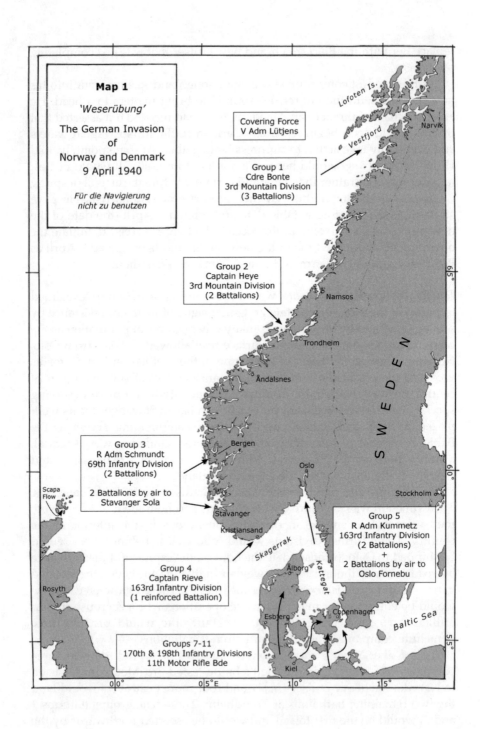

Map 1

'Weserübung'

The German Invasion
of
Norway and Denmark
9 April 1940

*Für die Navigierung
nicht zu benutzen*

Lofoten Is.

Narvik

Covering Force
V Adm Lütjens

Vestfjord

Group 1
Cdre Bonte
3rd Mountain Division
(3 Battalions)

Group 2
Captain Heye
3rd Mountain Division
(2 Battalions)

Namsos

Trondheim

Åndalsnes

S W E D E N

Bergen

Group 3
R Adm Schmundt
69th Infantry Division
(2 Battalions)
+
2 Battalions by air to
Stavanger Sola

Oslo

Stockholm

Scapa
Flow

Stavanger

Kristiansand

Group 5
R Adm Kummetz
163rd Infantry Division
(2 Battalions)
+
2 Battalions by air to
Oslo Fornebu

Skagerrak

Group 4
Captain Rieve
163rd Infantry Division
(1 reinforced Battalion)

Ålborg

Kattegat

Rosyth

Esbjerg

Copenhagen

Baltic Sea

Groups 7-11
170th & 198th Infantry Divisions
11th Motor Rifle Bde

Kiel

0|0°   0|5°E   1|0°   1|5°

65°

60°

55°

acting Fleet Commander, Vice Admiral Günther Lütjens, flying his flag in the *Gneisenau*.

The 69th Infantry Division (no previous battle experience) would take responsibility for the west coast ports. Group 3, a mixed force of torpedo boats, coastal craft and auxiliaries led by the light cruisers *Köln* and *Königsberg* would land two battalions at Bergen. Two additional battalions would be flown to Stavanger during the course of the day and a third on W+1. The rest of the division would be shipped to Oslo on W+2 and W+3, and get to Bergen by train.

The 163rd Infantry Division would seize the capital and take responsibility for the south coast. Group 4, the cruiser *Karlsruhe* and a mixed group of coastal forces and auxiliaries would land a reinforced battalion at Kristiansand and extend along the coast to Arendal. The ships of Group 5, the cruisers *Blücher* and *Emden*, and a force of smaller craft (and in a late change of plan the pocket battleship *Lützow*) would deliver two battalions to Oslo. Two parachute companies would seize the airfield at Fornebu just west of the capital, and the rest of the 163rd Infantry Division would be flown in during the course of the morning. The total strength of the landing teams would be 8,850 men; a further 8,000 would arrive by air during the first three days.

Oil for the naval forces would be supplied by a tanker group, eight ships in all, two for Narvik and two for Trondheim; and one each for Bergen, Stavanger, Kristiansand and Oslo. They were to arrive on *Weser*-day. Urgent supplies for the Army would be delivered by an 'Export Group' of seven ships (three for Narvik, three for Trondheim and one for Stavanger) and by fifteen ships of the 1st Sea Transport Group divided between Bergen, Stavanger, Kristiansand and Oslo. All these ships were to be routed independently via Norwegian coastal waters to reach their ports of destination on *Weser*-day. Thereafter, the movement of shipping outside the Baltic was likely to become problematical and the 2nd and subsequent Sea Transport Groups would be routed to Oslo.

The three follow-on divisions would reach Oslo within the week. The 196th Infantry Division would disembark on W+2 and deploy northwards to seize key positions on the land routes to Trondheim. The 181st Infantry Division would arrive on W+6, occupy the area to the south-east of Oslo and then deploy along the Swedish border to guard against an intervention from that quarter. And the 214th Infantry Division would reach Oslo on W+8, deploy south and west to secure the sector Stavanger to Arendal and relieve the landing teams on that stretch of coast. There was every hope that the Norwegian Government would bow to the inevitable and that the occupation would be peaceful; but if this was not the case, the German High Command would impose its will using all means necessary.

'*Weserübung Süd*', the plan for the conquest of Denmark, was to be a largely separate operation under the command of General der Flieger Leonhard Kaupisch.[26] The order of battle included two infantry divisions (170th and 198th) and the 11th Motor Rifle Brigade, supported by three motor machine-gun battalions, two batteries of field artillery, two tank companies and a number of armoured trains. The Air Force provided a parachute company and two anti-aircraft battalions. The Danish terrain lent itself to mobile warfare and plans provided for a rapid thrust northwards from the German border by the 11th Motor Rifle Brigade with a motorized regiment of the 170th on its left towards the airfields at Ålborg in northern Jutland. These were priority objectives and were to be seized by parachute troops and an air-landed battalion at dawn on *Weser*-day. The northern thrust was to be supported on the left by amphibious landings at Esbjerg and Tyborön while, on the right, three reinforced companies of the 170th Division would land at Middelfart to secure the bridge over the Little Belt and advance across the island of Fyn towards Nyborg. In all, the Navy would provide five additional ship groups, a mixed bag of minesweepers, auxiliaries and harbour craft, but including the elderly battleship *Schleswig-Holstein*, for operations against Denmark.

The task of occupying Sjæland and the Danish capital was given to the 198th Infantry Division. One battalion was to land at Copenhagen and occupy the Citadel; a second was to land at Korsor on the west coast of the island and advance on the capital from that direction. There was to be a further landing (this one at company strength) at Nyborg to secure the crossing of the Great Belt and link up with elements of the 170th Infantry advancing from the west. A third battalion with an armoured train would embark at the ferry terminal at Warnemünde, land at Gedser on the island of Falster and approach Copenhagen from the south. In a late addition to the plan, a parachute company was detailed to seize the key rail bridge linking the islands of Falster and Sjæland. Overall, the scheme was a model of ruthless efficiency.

Air operations in support of '*Weserübung*' were controlled by X Air Corps (Lieutenant General Hans Ferdinand Geisler) operating from his headquarters in Hamburg. X Air Corps, which had specialized in anti-shipping operations, was brought up to a strength of more than 1,000 aircraft including ten medium bomber wings (about 300 aircraft, mostly He-111 and Ju-88), a Ju-87 (Stuka) dive-bomber wing and three fighter wings (ninety aircraft), the majority twin-engined Me-110s.[27] Two medium bomber wings were to be held in reserve at German bases for operations against the British Fleet. The remainder were to make 'demonstrations' over the Danish and Norwegian capitals and over the principal military objectives in southern and western Norway. One medium bomber squadron was to move to Stavanger on *Weser*-day and operate from there. Two dive-bomber squadrons were to move to Ålborg on *Weser*-day and a third to Stavanger; from W+1, the entire dive-bomber force would be based on Norwegian soil.

Five hundred transport aircraft were assigned to the operation, most of them three-engined Ju-52s. Their mission was to deliver parachute companies and air-landed battalions to key objectives (Ålborg, Oslo and Stavanger were the most important) and thereafter to rush in reinforcements and supplies. Like Group XXI, X Air Corps put considerable emphasis on the idea of a 'peaceful occupation' in its orders and hoped that a simple demonstration of German airpower would be enough to ensure compliance. But nothing was to be left to chance. To ensure that the victims were receptive to this kind of threat, Göring summoned the Berlin diplomatic corps to the premier of the film *Baptism of Fire*, which dwelt at some length on the effects of German bombing on Polish cities; this on 5 April, four days before operations against Norway and Denmark were due to begin. And that same evening, the film was shown to invited guests at the German embassy in Oslo.[28]

During the anxious final days, the Naval Staff fought hard to defend its plans against interference from other quarters. The burning issue for OKW and for the staff of XXI Corps was the Navy's plan to recover its ships to Germany as soon as the landings were complete. On 12 March, General Keitel, OKW Chief of Staff and Hitler's military mouthpiece, had raised the matter again, this time with the support of Göring who had claimed that the Navy's ships would be safer if they delayed their return until the Luftwaffe had established control over Norway's coastal waters. Schniewind had questioned the reliability of Luftwaffe guarantees and insisted that a vital matter like this had to be decided on the basis of naval considerations alone.[29] Hitler had returned to the subject on 29 March although, after a 'forcible statement' by the Chief of Naval Staff, he had dropped his insistence on Narvik. But he had wanted the question of Trondheim looked at again. In the end the Navy had accepted the formula that any 'lame ducks' likely to impede the breakout might be sent to Trondheim. But the final decision would be left to the commanding admiral.[30]

For the Navy itself, the employment of the two battleships remained the more sensitive issue and the approach of action saw a reawakening of the simmering disagreement between Berlin and Group West headquarters in Wilhelmshaven. Rear Admiral Kurt Fricke, Head of the Operations Division, had little time for faint hearts in the operational commands. The German Navy would never succeed, he reflected on 31 March, if it did not make a conscious effort to 'free itself from the psychological pressures of a much superior enemy'. It was now being argued that the battleships should be held back to the south of the Shetland-Norway narrows, ostensibly to support the landing force destined for Bergen, the objective closest to British bases. On 1 April, the Führer added his voice to the clamour by suggesting that the early movement of heavy ships would alert the enemy. He had been supported by a number of task group commanders who had questioned the wisdom of directing the enemy's attention towards the north of Norway so early in the operation. The Naval Staff planners stuck resolutely to their case. Without the battleships, the Narvik and Trondheim groups were 'as good as delivered defenceless into the hands of a superior enemy'. The forward movement of the heavy ships was a 'necessary condition' for successful operations in the north. They acknowledged that the movement of the heavy ships might alert the enemy but, in a cogent and prescient appreciation, they argued that, far from disclosing the true nature of German intentions, the movement would be interpreted as an intended breakout into the North Atlantic and make the enemy focus his attention on the line Shetlands–Iceland.[31] The original plan was thus confirmed.

They were less successful in defending their plans for the *Lützow*. When they revealed their scheme for the Atlantic sortie, Hitler insisted that the ship should carry 400 men of the 3rd Mountain Division to Trondheim and make her break from there. The Naval Staff had been obliged, therefore, to reinstate her in the '*Weserübung*' plan. In the event, serious machinery defects ruled out all possibility of a lengthy ocean deployment and, at the eleventh hour, the *Lützow* returned to the Baltic to join the *Blücher* and the Oslo group before starting a recovery programme in Kiel.[32]

From the Navy's perspective, the main threat to the success of the operation, and thus to the survival of the German surface fleet, lay in that mass of merchant shipping assembled to meet Army and Luftwaffe demands. In the tense prelude to action we find evidence of increasing unease. During the night of 2 April, as the first ships of the Export Group left harbour to begin the long passage to Narvik, Admiral Fricke recorded his formal opinion that the early sailing of these ships constituted 'an extremely undesirable risk' and that the slightest incident during their passage of the Norwegian Leads would disclose German intentions. On 4 April, it was reported that ships of the follow-on echelons were loading in Stettin 'exposed to the unimpeded gaze of interested spectators'. On the evening of 6 April as the first of the Navy's landing groups assembled off Wilhelmshaven and as the slower ships of the 1st Sea Transport Unit left Baltic ports with men and material for Bergen and Stavanger, the Naval Staff reflected that it would be 'an extraordinary stroke of luck if this immense transport set-up reached its ports of destination without disturbance ... and without the enemy receiving prior warning'.[33] On the 7th, it was known through telephone tapping that a neutral Naval Attaché had asked for an urgent meeting with the Danish and Norwegian ambassadors to impart information of 'the highest political importance'. When on Monday, 8 April, the eve of the landings, Naval Headquarters got wind of an Allied ultimatum to the Norwegian Government, of British minefields in Norwegian waters, of a troop transport aground off the Danish coast, of the *Rio de Janeiro*, a ship of the 1st Sea Transport Unit, sunk off Kristiansand and of uniformed survivors being brought ashore in Norway, it had seemed that all possibility of surprise had been lost. 'We must now expect', the Naval Staff recorded, 'to meet resistance at all points.'[34]

Chapter 3

One Step Behind

As Cabinet members dispersed for their weekend break, Churchill's mine-layers were making their final preparations for departure. The main force, four converted destroyers of the 20th (Minelaying) Flotilla with four ships of the 2nd Destroyer Flotilla as escort was poised at Sullom Voe, the Navy's forward base in the Shetlands.[1] Their task was to lay the minefield in the approaches to Narvik. Two additional forces were getting ready in Scapa Flow; the first, based on the minelayer *Teviot Bank*, had orders to mine the Norwegian Leads off Stadlandet, while the second was to simulate a minelay off Bud on the same stretch of coast.

Few special precautions had been taken to protect the minelayers from an intervention by German surface forces. Planners had relied on geography and early warning to keep them out of trouble; but they had been unable to rule out a confrontation with the Norwegian Navy. At first, they had seen the cruiser *Birmingham*, already searching the coast of Norway for a German fishing fleet, as providing sufficient cover for the operation; but, on 1 April, they had heard that up to four coast defence vessels might be assembling in the far north to defend Norwegian waters. These were veterans of forty years service but they each mounted two 8-inch and six 6-inch guns, and the Commander in Chief Home Fleet, Admiral Sir Charles Forbes, had felt the need for some extra deterrent weight behind his northern group.[2] As 'Wilfred' began, therefore, Vice Admiral W.J. Whitworth had left Scapa with the battlecruiser *Renown* and a screen of four destroyers to act in support of the Narvik group. He had met the minelayers off the Shetlands on the Saturday morning (6 April) and taken them northwards, planning to make the approaches to the Vestfjord on the Sunday night. The minelay was to begin at 0430 on the Monday morning.

Preparations for Plan 'R4' were by now well advanced. Harassed staff officers had assembled an expeditionary force from the remnants of Operations 'Avonmouth' and 'Stratford' and landing forces for Narvik and Trondheim were now mustering on the Clyde where two large transports awaited them. Admiral Evans, who had hoisted his flag in the cruiser

Aurora on 4 April, had already made his rounds of the ships to bring enthusiasm to fever pitch. The four battalions earmarked for the occupation of Bergen and Stavanger, objectives which lay closer to German bases and which had seemed at more immediate risk, mustered on the Forth where, on the Sunday, they embarked in four ships of the 1st Cruiser Squadron, the *Devonshire, Berwick, York* and *Glasgow*. Also getting ready in the Forth were the cruisers and destroyers of the striking force for use against a German seaborne expedition. Built round Vice Admiral Sir George Edward-Collins's 2nd Cruiser Squadron (HM Ships *Galatea* and *Arethusa*) and an initial force of four destroyers, the C-in-C planned to increase the strength of this formation as other ships were released from convoy duty.

But the first line of defence was to be provided by the submarine arm. As Plan 'R4' was being finalized, the Flag Officer Submarines (Vice Admiral Sir Max Horton) had ordered a special disposition to cover the sea approaches to southern Norway. He had expected a violent reaction to 'Wilfred' and his orders had made troop transports rather than warships priority targets.[3] By the weekend 6/7 April, a total of eighteen submarines (fifteen British, two French and one Polish) were approaching their assigned patrol areas in the Kattegat, Skagerrak and German Bight.

For the British authorities, this was the calm before the storm. Admiral of the Fleet Sir Dudley Pound, First Sea Lord and Chief of Naval Staff, had seized the opportunity to escape from London for a weekend's fishing. Admiral Forbes, anxious to minimize wear and tear on ships and men, had kept his battle group at anchor in Scapa Flow, determined to see how the situation developed before committing it to sea. He was expecting reinforcements in the form of the French cruiser *Emile Bertin* and some French destroyers on the Sunday evening. And for a day or two at least, the busy convoy traffic between the Firth of Forth and the coast of Norway could be allowed to continue. The incoming convoy HN24 was already passing the Shetlands; its successor, HN25 was assembling in Bergen. The outbound convoy ON25 had already sailed from Methil and was making its way slowly northwards. The ships of the 18th Cruiser Squadron were preparing to leave Scapa to cover its passage.

Looking back, one is struck both by the quality of the intelligence reaching London and by the inability of the authorities to recognize what it meant.[4] Reports that Hitler had decided to act against southern Scandinavia had been brought before the War Cabinet as early as January. On 3 February, the Cabinet had examined reports from the Military Attaché in Stockholm that the Germans were drawing up plans to secure the Narvik–Luleå rail link and to occupy the southern provinces of Norway and Sweden. Since then it had become conventional wisdom in Whitehall that Germany would act to secure her economic interests in the far north as soon as the Baltic routes reopened. With the passage of time, reports had become more insistent and more specific. On 26 March the British Minister in Stockholm had warned of shipping concentrations in the Baltic ports and of aircraft massed on north German airfields; and, in the days that followed, Scandinavian capitals had been a-quiver with news of German preparations. On 5 April, Naval Intelligence had warned that Berlin was feeding the Scandinavian press with stories about developments 'fraught with immense danger' for neutral countries which discriminated in favour of the Allies.[5] But as the official history of the Norway campaign observes, Europe was seething 'with rumours of plans and counter-plans making it almost impossible for Governments to separate truth from fiction'.[6]

Professor Hinsley offers other clues to the apparent blindness of the intelligence services. Arrangements for sharing information between departments (SIS, Foreign Office and Service ministries) were still defective; as a result decision-makers often lacked that scrap of corroborating evidence that might just have tipped the scales. It seems clear too that individual Intelligence branches tended to share the strategic and operational preconceptions of their parent departments and to discard material that ran counter to the prevailing consensus. Military Intelligence, for instance, was deceived by the lack of any obvious increase in troop levels in Germany's northern districts. As late as 8 April it felt able to report that dispositions 'did not support any probability of a Scandinavian invasion', although it did not rule out minor operations in response to similar initiatives by the Allies.[7] Naval Intelligence was watching for signs of a new threat to Britain's Atlantic communications. A descent on Narvik across 1,000 miles of hostile sea lay outside its mental compass. The events of the next few days were to reveal a critical failure to draw the correct inferences from the information available and an unhealthy reliance on direct contact with the enemy as the basis for operational decisions.

The first direct evidence that major operations were imminent reached London on 4 April when a reconnaissance aircraft operating over the German Bight reported the presence of *Scharnhorst* and *Gneisenau* in Wilhelmshaven roads. On 6 April, the Saturday, listening stations reported significant increases in the volume of German signal traffic particularly on the minesweeping wave. But neither of these fragments provided the clear evidence of intent required by Plan 'R4'. During the night 6/7 April, aircraft returning from leaflet drops over German territory reported unusual activity in the North Sea and Baltic ports; wharves had been brightly lit and traffic had been moving with unshielded headlights. These reports seemed to justify increased vigilance; they did not justify bringing the Fleet to immediate readiness or taking up a commanding position on the Norwegian coast.

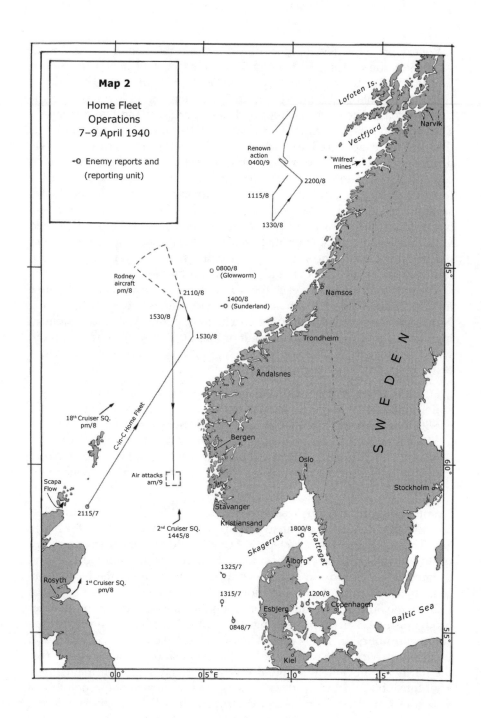

Map 2

Home Fleet
Operations
7–9 April 1940

⊶O Enemy reports and
(reporting unit)

Lofoten Is.

Vestfjord

Narvik

Renown
action
0400/9

'Wilfred'
mines

2200/8

1115/8

1330/8

65°

O 0800/8
(Glowworm)

Rodney
aircraft
pm/8

2110/8

Namsos

1400/8
⊶O (Sunderland)

1530/8

1530/8

S W E D E N

Trondheim

Åndalsnes

18th Cruiser SQ.
pm/8

C-in-C Home Fleet

Bergen

Scapa
Flow

Oslo

60°

Stockholm

Air attacks
am/9

2115/7

Stavanger

Kristiansand

2nd Cruiser SQ.
1445/8

1800/8

Skagerrak

Kattegat

Ålborg

1325/7

Rosyth

1st Cruiser SQ.
pm/8

1315/7

1200/8

Esbjerg

Copenhagen

Baltic Sea

0848/7

55°

Kiel

0 0°

0 5° E

1 0°

1 5°

We can trace the development of events from the records of the C-in-C. At 0848 on the morning of Sunday, 7 April, a Coastal Command Hudson sent to monitor the naval activity in the German Bight sighted a group of warships northbound off the Horn Reef and more than 100 miles from the German coast. The force was reported as two cruisers and two destroyers. The report reached Admiral Forbes at 1120; he was told soon afterwards that the force appeared to consist of a *Nürnberg* class cruiser and six destroyers, but that the German fighter escort was making identification difficult. He was informed that Bomber Command was sending a strike force of thirty-five aircraft, that one group had already left and that a second was on the point of leaving. Home Fleet Staff remained watchful but ordered no increase in Fleet readiness; and their judgement seemed vindicated when, at 1400 on that weary Sunday afternoon, a new report reached the flagship showing that a force of three destroyers had just been found in the same area, evidently homeward bound.

The next information to reach the C-in-C had come from a neutral source in Copenhagen (the US Embassy) and had seemed so far-fetched that Naval Intelligence had suspected a deliberate plant. After discussions at high level about whether to release it or not, the Admiralty had sent it out with a strong caveat.[8] 'Recent reports suggest that a German expedition is being prepared,' the telegram read:

> Hitler is reported from Copenhagen to have ordered the unostentatious movement of one division in ten ships by night to land at Narvik with simultaneous occupation of Jutland. Sweden to be left alone. Moderates said to be opposing the plan. Date given for arrival at Narvik was 8th April. All these reports are of doubtful value and may well be only a further move in the war of nerves. Great Belt opened to traffic 5th April.[9]

Despite London's obvious reservations, Admiral Forbes brought the Fleet to one hour's notice and began to prepare for major operations in the North Sea. That afternoon he took steps to bring his Rosyth-based striking force up to full strength, gave it a position off the southern tip of Norway and ordered it to be ready to start a sweep northward along the Norwegian coast by 0700 on the following morning.[10] An urgent message issued at 1720 on the Sunday evening and reaching the flagship seven minutes later brought these leisurely proceedings to an end. The telegram revealed that, some four hours earlier, Bomber Command's strike group had attacked a German force in 56° 48' North, 06° 10' East, a position showing clearly that the northerly movement reported early in the day had been maintained. The force had included two cruisers and a heavy ship, possibly a *Scharnhorst*, and as many as ten destroyers; it had been steering to the north-west. The implications were serious – this was clearly a major

32

operation. And the inexplicable delay in reporting the incident meant that the Germans could reach open waters north of the Shetland–Norway narrows before the heavy ships of the Home Fleet could be in a position to intercept them.[11] The C-in-C ordered his ships to raise steam. By 2050 he was clear of the land and with the battleships *Rodney* and *Valiant*, the battlecruiser *Repulse*, the cruisers *Penelope* and *Sheffield* and a screen of ten destroyers, set course to the north-eastward in hot pursuit.

We can get a glimpse of the mood in the Admiralty at this critical time from the diaries of Captain Ralph Edwards who, as Director of Operations (Home), was a party to the high-level debate in the Operations Intelligence Centre. For much of the weekend, the naval hierarchy had been reluctant to attach any great significance to signs of activity in the German Bight and had rejected the suggestion that 'Wilfred' should be postponed until German intentions became clear. (Churchill had been in no mood to see his hard-won Cabinet victory put at risk.) Pound had returned late from his weekend's fishing and was 'dead beat'. His deputy, Tom Phillips, who had held the fort in his absence, was close to exhaustion too and the First Lord 'well dined'.[12] There had been no clear consensus on the meaning of the German moves. Pound had seen the early signs of an Atlantic break-out and had squashed warnings (from Edwards) that the C-in-C's movements were leaving the coast of Norway dangerously exposed. Churchill, who had been in the thick of these professional discussions, had seen parallels with the sorties of the High Seas Fleet during the First World War and had been looking for a second Jutland. The only common ground between them was the assumption that this was a purely naval problem calling for purely naval solutions. The Admiralty's first priority was to ensure that the C-in-C had the cruisers and destroyers that he needed for what might well become a wide-ranging and protracted operation. The 2nd Cruiser Squadron had already sailed; and the 18th would become available as soon as the safety of the Norwegian convoys could be assured. The cancellation of the Stadlandet minelay would free up yet more assets and orders were issued accordingly. But the Admiralty had to look beyond the short term. Late that evening, Pound gave instructions that the 1st Cruiser Squadron (poised in Rosyth for the occupation of Bergen and Stavanger) should march its troops ashore and sail to join the C-in-C. And he stripped the Narvik expedition of its escort force by moving the *Aurora* and her destroyers forward to Scapa Flow. These decisions spelt the end of Plan 'R4' and were made by the Admiralty alone; although conclusive evidence is lacking, it is an odds-on certainty that Churchill was a party to them.

With the return of daylight, a chance meeting between the British destroyer *Glowworm* and the *Hans Lüdemann*, a straggler from the Narvik group, provided British participants with the first fresh information on the whereabouts of the German task force since the sighting by Bomber Command Blenheims more than eighteen hours earlier.

The *Glowworm* had sailed on the Friday night as part of Admiral Whitworth's screen but she had been detached on the Saturday to search for a man overboard and since then she had spent many hours hove to, riding out the heavy weather that was affecting the Norwegian coast. Early on the Monday morning, she had told Admiral Whitworth that she was coming to join him but that she was uncertain of her position since she had been unable to obtain a recent fix. Her next signals had indicated that she was in action with an enemy destroyer and then with a second. She had been about 200 miles north-west of Trondheim. Towards 0900, she had reported a new contact closing from the north at a range of 6 miles. Her transmissions had then faded. On receiving her signals, Admiral Whitworth, who had detached the 'Wilfred' mine layers the evening before and who, with the *Renown* and a single remaining escort, had taken up a covering position off the entrance to the Vestfjord, turned southwards towards the *Glowworm*'s position and worked his ships up to the best speed they could manage against a heavy head sea. He estimated the distance to run as 140 miles. And far to the south-west, Admiral Forbes, then approaching the latitude of Stadlandet where the trend of Norwegian coast turns from north to north-east, detached a fast division consisting of the *Repulse*, the *Penelope* and four destroyers to close the reported position.[13]

This encounter with the enemy forces, well to the northward and on the route to Narvik, provided new clues to German intentions. The Germans were in a position to reach the Vestfjord in a matter of hours and the Admiralty's first thought was to correct what it saw as a dangerous dispersal of force in the far north. In mid-morning, it instructed the eight destroyers that were patrolling the Vestfjord minefield to leave their station and rejoin the *Renown*. (The effect of this instruction would become apparent later.) It then released a signal conceding that the information received from Copenhagen might, after all, be true.[14]

At 1130 that Monday morning, an exuberant Churchill coming straight from the Admiralty map room put the whole matter before the War Cabinet. (Ironside was astonished at his boyish enthusiasm.[15]) There was a good deal of speculation about what the Germans were doing. Some suggested that a seizure of Narvik might be the prelude to a general move against the Swedish mining areas; others favoured the breakout theory. In either case, this seemed 'a most hazardous venture'. The Germans could not get to Narvik without meeting the *Renown*. 'It is impossible to forecast the hazards of war,' Churchill told his colleagues in an extraordinary piece of circumlocution, 'but such an action should not be on terms unfavourable

34

to us.'[16] The mood in Cabinet remained overwhelmingly positive. No one asked why the Navy's response had come so late or why 'R4', a plan proposed by the Chiefs of Staff and approved at the highest level, had been set aside on the unilateral say-so of the Admiralty. There had been an awkward moment when the Prime Minister had asked about the cruisers in Rosyth. According to one witness, Churchill had looked 'decidedly sheepish'.[17] But it had soon passed.

The C-in-C learned about these developments in the early afternoon. He found the Admiralty's orders surprising since he felt that he had enough ships for the task at hand without drawing on assets that had been earmarked for 'R4'. But time for reflection was short. The afternoon brought a new sighting and one that seemed to offer a genuine prospect of action. At 1400, a Sunderland flying boat searching the sea areas ahead of the C-in-C sighted a group of ships in 64° 12' North, 06° 25' East, a little north of the latitude of Trondheim and now only 120 miles ahead of the Fleet. The group included a battleship. The course given was west – an unexpected direction but one which suggested that an interception might be possible. An amplifying report reaching the *Rodney* an hour later showed the composition of the force as a battleship, two cruisers and two destroyers. At 1600, Admiral Forbes turned north to intercept and, soon afterwards, to 340°. What he needed now was a period of uninterrupted shadowing so that he could verify the enemy's course and speed and adjust his movements accordingly. Luck was against him. The Sunderland, which had blundered into the German squadron in stormy conditions, had been damaged by anti-aircraft fire and had been forced to turn for home; a relief aircraft had failed to find the enemy.[18] With evening approaching, Forbes sent out the *Rodney*'s Walrus aircraft in the vain hope that he could relocate the German force and bring about a meeting before darkness set in. It was a bold decision for it was now blowing hard from the north-west and the chances of recovering the aircraft at the end of the sortie were slim. But Forbes was now certain that an invasion of Norway was imminent and he had briefed the Walrus pilot accordingly.[19] This was a last chance.

As hopes of action began to fade, the focus of attention shifted from the Norwegian Sea to the Baltic approaches. Soon after midday, the Admiralty had learnt from the Naval Attaché in Copenhagen that a *Blücher* or a *Gneisenau* with two cruisers and three destroyers had entered the Great Belt (the narrow waterway leading northwards from Kiel) at dawn that morning, and that a similar group had been seen entering the Kattegat towards noon.[20] The possibility that these ships might round the Skaw and turn westwards into the Skagerrak came to dominate the thoughts of Admirals – ashore and afloat – as evening approached. By 1930, Forbes was sure that his interception had failed. He thought it probable that the force he had been chasing was still to the north of him bound, in all liklihood, for Narvik. He still needed to reinforce Whitworth. But there was now a battleship on his southern flank making, he had to assume, for the North Sea. The 1st and 2nd Cruiser Squadrons were sweeping northwards from Rosyth and there were no heavy ships in a position to support them. Forbes left the *Penelope* and the *Repulse* to continue northward to join Whitworth and, at 2100 on the Monday evening, turned southwards towards the narrows with the *Rodney*, *Valiant* and *Sheffield* to bring the second group to action. There would be plenty of cruisers to the southward to act as his eyes and ears.

The Admiralty's assessment had been broadly similar. Seeing the need for a clear division of responsibility in a situation of increasing complexity, it instructed Whitworth to concentrate on preventing the enemy from reaching Narvik, and gave the C-in-C the dual task of preventing this enemy's return to German waters and of bringing the southern group to action if, as appeared possible, it was bound for Bergen or Stavanger. At 1800 the submarine *Triton* had reported the German group off the Skaw and earlier suspicions had been confirmed. It was possible, the Admiralty told Forbes, that the two German groups might try to affect a junction off Bergen by about 0500 on the following morning.[21]

At 2258 Forbes signalled his intentions for the coming hours. By midnight he would be in 63° 15′ North, 03° 00′ East, course south, speed 18 knots. Admiral Layton's 18th Cruiser Squadron was to meet him in the narrows at 0700 in the morning. By 0500, the cruisers of the 1st and 2nd Cruiser Squadrons were to form a search line south of Bergen and sweep northwards along the Norwegian coast until they met the Fleet. The plan was never implemented. In the early hours of Tuesday, 9 April (*Weser*-day) the Admiralty vetoed the C-in-C's directions on the grounds that they placed a weak and dispersed cruiser formation in a position where it might be caught between two enemy fires while the Fleet was still more than 100 miles away. Instead, the 1st and 2nd Cruiser Squadrons were to rendezvous 80 miles off the Norwegian coast and steer to meet the C-in-C.[22] There were thus no British ships on the Norwegian coast when the German invasion groups entered the fjords.

Although by the Monday evening, the Admirals had begun to grasp something of the purpose and scope of German plans, their decisions were still based on the reported movements of German heavy ships. This was the response of a Navy brought up in the shadow of Jutland. It was a cautious and prudent response. But the obsession with the movements of the enemy's heavy ships, a less-than-reliable guide to the unfolding of German plans, prevented the one tactic which might, even at this eleventh hour, have put serious obstacles in the enemy's path – a free-for-all in the approaches to the Norwegian ports.

An inshore battle on a treacherous coast was not something that Admiral Whitworth had been willing to contemplate. His first reaction to the *Glowworm*'s signals had been to steer directly for her position but, in response to the Admiralty's warning that Narvik might, after all, be under threat, he had first adjusted his course to cover the southern approaches to the Vestfjord and then, on finding the visibility closing in and the chances of sighting the enemy diminishing, he had turned back to the northward to rendezvous with his destroyers. He had met them off the entrance to the Vestfjord and had at once begun to consider how best to use them during the coming night. He had been following the recent developments off Trondheim but had reached no firm conclusion on the enemy's intentions – he might return to German waters, he might steer for Iceland or he might come north, either to make a landing at Narvik or to take fuel from the base near Murmansk. Time would tell. Whitworth was clear that his first duty was to cover the northern options leaving the rest to the C-in-C. But the wind was in the north-west at storm force and attempts to manoeuvre a large formation in confined waters during the hours of darkness meant considerable risk. Whitworth considered but rejected the option of patrolling the Vestfjord. (In the weather prevailing the enemy would never attempt a landfall in the dark.) He chose instead to set up a line-ahead patrol to seaward, intending to turn back towards the coast at midnight and cover the approaches to the Vestfjord at first light. At 2200, he told the *Repulse* and the *Birmingham* that he was 40 miles south-west of the Skomvær light, on a course of 310° at 8 knots. He gave the wind as north-west Force 10 and said that he intended to patrol the entrance to the Vestjiord when the weather moderated.[23]

The scene was now set for the first and only contact between British and German heavy units during the course of '*Weserübung*', for it was in the early hours of 9 April, and shortly after his turn to close the land, that Whitworth encountered the German battleships which, having released their destroyers in the approaches to an unguarded Vestfjord, were now making their way to seaward to begin the diversionary sweep that their orders required. The wind had dropped a little and veered to the north-north-east but the night was black as pitch and Whitworth, worried that some of his destroyers might lose touch, waited for the first hint of light before making his turn. At 0230, he judged the moment right and led his formation round to the south-east; and it was an hour later in the dim twilight of an arctic dawn that his lookouts made out the shape of a large ship emerging from a snow squall broad on his port bow. It was a ship of the *Scharnhorst* class and it was closely followed by a second, thought to be

37

a *Hipper*. The range was uncertain; the gunlayer could see nothing in his telescope. But the enemy was on an opposite course to the *Renown* and was going to pass well clear down the port side.

As the bearing of the German ships drew aft, the Captain of the *Renown* (Captain C.B.E. Simeon) increased speed and turned inwards to close the range. Ten minutes later when range-takers could see the Germans in their lenses, he turned hard left to parallel the enemy, ending up just abaft the enemy's beam with all guns bearing. At 0405 the *Renown* opened fire on a range of 18,600 yards, using her 15-inch guns on the leading ship and her secondary armament on the other.[24]

The leading enemy ship returned fire at 0411. The *Gneisenau* had seen the *Renown* twelve minutes earlier but had been unable to identify her against the dark western horizon. (The *Scharnhorst* had seen nothing until the *Renown* opened fire.) To the west the Germans could see the gun flashes of Whitworth's destroyers.

The action continued towards the north-west for a further six minutes with courses slowly converging. The *Renown* took two hits but neither penetrated and damage was slight. Then, at 0417, with the range at 14,600 yards, she hit the leading enemy (the *Gneisenau*) in the area of the fore-top destroying the principal fire control position and, for the moment, silencing the main batteries. The target turned away abruptly and her consort crossed her stern laying smoke to cover her retirement.

The *Renown* hauled round to the northward to follow and the chase continued to windward with the ships plunging into the teeth of the gale, the enemy engaging with their after turrets and yawing occasionally to bring all guns to bear. But the wind was rising once again and with wind and sea on the bow, the *Renown* was finding it increasingly difficult to keep her speed. Before long, she was forced to ease back to 23 and finally to 20 knots. She was barely holding the range. Towards 0500, the enemy disappeared in a snowstorm; the *Renown* altered a point or two off wind and sea and increased speed in an endeavour to close the distance. After twenty minutes the weather cleared; the German ships had kept on to the northward but the range had opened still more. The *Renown* adjusted course to put the enemy fine on the port bow and opened fire once again but without effect. She then wound herself up to full speed and achieved 29 knots for a brief spell, but the enemy continued to draw away and when last seen at 0615 was 'far ahead and out of range'. Whitworth continued to the northward until after 0800 but made no further contact.

While this action was taking place in the far north, London was waking to the news that the Germans had seized Bergen. It was scarcely conceivable; there was a risk to the southern ports – that had been recognized. The movements in the Great Belt and the Kattegat had pointed in that direction and since then the evidence had been accumulating. At noon on the Monday, the Polish submarine *Orzel*, patrolling off Kristiansand, had attacked the *Rio de Janeiro*, a ship of the 1st Sea Transport Unit and sent her to the bottom. Soon afterwards, Rear Admiral Tom Phillips, Pound's able and energetic deputy, had told the Press that an invasion of Norway appeared imminent. In early evening the submarines *Triton* and *Sunfish* had both reported major surface units off the Skaw, reinforcing the Admiralty's impression of a threat to the southern ports and leading to the assessment that the Germans could concentrate off Bergen during the early hours of 9 April. Late evening had brought the agency reports from Oslo that had so alarmed the German Naval Staff, of uniformed survivors from the *Rio de Janeiro* being brought ashore in Kristiansand and saying that they had been on their way to Bergen 'to protect it from the British'. After midnight, reports from submarines in the Skagerrak had added to the sense of crisis and, at 0235 on the Tuesday morning, a shaken Norwegian Foreign Minister had admitted to the British Ambassador that his country was under attack. But now it was clear that the Germans had not only launched their attack but that they had seized a number of key objectives as well. Bergen had gone and, what was even more incredible, so had Trondheim.

The Chief's of Staff were summoned to a meeting at 0630 to concert their views. (It was lamentable, thought Ironside, that the Germans should have pulled off this coup while the Government had been 'argle-bargling'.[25]) The Chiefs decided that their first priority was to prevent the Germans from consolidating their gains in Bergen and Trondheim; but they would send a battalion to Narvik as a precautionary measure. The War Cabinet could not be convened before 0830. (Ironside had fumed at these leisurely arrangements and at the 'dreadful exhibition of loose talk' that had followed.[26]) Churchill reported Whitworth's action in the far north but there were few details as yet. There was no denying the German successes at Bergen and Trondheim but, he assured his colleagues, there were British destroyers covering the entrance to the Vestfjord and the C-in-C was massing a large force off Bergen. The CIGS emphasized the need to secure Narvik before the Germans got there; one battalion would be ready to sail at noon and could be there in three days. Meanwhile, it was vital to prevent the Germans from consolidating their positions in Bergen and Trondheim. Their numbers could not be strong at present; it was essential to prevent the arrival of reinforcements so that the Norwegians could retake the towns and hold them as ports of entry for the Allies. The Cabinet authorized Churchill to take immediate steps to clear enemy ships from the fjords and instructed the Chiefs of Staff to prepare expeditions for Bergen, Trondheim and Narvik; but nothing was to move until the naval situation had been cleared up. Meanwhile, the Air Ministry was to establish what

39

was going on at Stavanger and the Foreign Secretary was to assure the Norwegians of all possible help.[26]

That morning the Prime Minister's front office was crowded with people all wanting to know how the Fleet had allowed the Germans to take Bergen and Trondheim, while discussing unconfirmed reports that they had taken Narvik as well.[28] When the Cabinet reconvened at noon, Churchill was unable to deny this latest rumour; he intimated that a German transport might have slipped past British patrols in foul weather. But he had not been idle during the brief interval between Cabinet meetings and he had returned from the Admiralty determined to put a positive interpretation on events. The general strategic situation was, he assured his colleagues, better than before since Britain was now free to apply her overwhelming sea power on the Norwegian coast. It would have been impossible to prevent the German landings without constant (hence wasteful) patrols off the Norwegian ports; and, anyway, the Allies would 'liquidate' the German landing forces in a week or two. He had ordered the Navy to force its way into Bergen and Narvik; he was going to leave Trondheim for the moment since, with German heavy ships still on the loose, isolated detachments might easily be mopped up. And he had sent two telegrams to Paris, the first to Reynaud proclaiming: 'Now is the time for Royal Marine', and the second to Daladier urging a change of heart. He had also decided that now was the time to press for new rules for his submarines. He thus sought and obtained Cabinet authorization for new instructions allowing submarines operating in the Skagerrak to assume that all targets were warships or troop transports and thus to sink them on sight.[29]

But ministerial enthusiasm was not enough. Events were soon to demonstrate that the Fleet massed off Bergen could do little about the German ships lying in the fjords; nor could it defend itself against the powerful strike forces that the German X Air Corps could muster off southern Norway.

At 0620 on the Tuesday morning, Admiral Forbes asked London for information about enemy strength in Bergen. The Admiralty responded with an order to prepare plans for an attack on warships and transports in Bergen and for controlling the approaches to the port. He was to act on the assumption that coastal defences remained in Norwegian hands and prepare similar plans for Trondheim if he had 'sufficient forces for both'. (These instructions were despatched from Whitehall at 0820 and formed the basis of Churchill's initial statements to the War Cabinet.) Forbes gave the job to a reinforced 18th Cruiser Squadron (HM Ships *Manchester*, *Southampton*, *Glasgow* and *Sheffield*) and to a flotilla of seven destroyers; but the plan betrayed something of the Navy's reluctance to commit scarce and valuable resources to an inshore battle when the nature of the threat could not be precisely defined. The destroyers were to carry the fight into the intricate maze of fjords leading to the port of Bergen, while the four cruisers remained outside, controlling the two principal avenues of approach.

The Fleet had continued southward during the forenoon and Admiral Layton had faced an 80-mile transit to his objective with wind and sea on the bow. Progress had been slow. But the Admiralty had been having second thoughts. At 1132 it told the C-in-C to postpone his attack on Trondheim until the enemy's heavy units had been found in order to avoid a potentially dangerous 'dispersion of forces'. Soon after midday it told him he could no longer count on the coastal defences in the approaches to Bergen being in friendly hands and at 1357 it called off the attack. (Admiral Evans who had been obliged to haul down his flag but who had remained at sea in the *Aurora* had wept with rage and frustration when he heard the news.) We can only speculate on the Admiralty's motives; they seem to have reflected a growing sense that risks outweighed potential gains, and that new and more promising attack options lay just over the horizon. Whatever the reasons, Admiral Pound cancelled the operation, breaking the news to the First Lord as he emerged from the midday Cabinet meeting and presenting him with a fait accompli. After a brief review of the facts, Churchill gave his reluctant consent.

In the matter of air defence, Forbes now found himself paying for his and for the Admiralty's failure to prepare adequately for operations within range of German bases. Despite all that had passed in recent months, two of the Navy's principal carriers (the *Ark Royal* and the *Glorious*) were training in the Mediterranean and the only ship available for operations with the Home Fleet, the *Furious*, was completing a post-refit work-up in the Clyde with her air squadrons disembarked. Forbes had thus sailed on the Sunday night without a carrier and nothing had been done until the Monday evening to put the matter right. By then, with one German task force loose in the north and a second reported westbound in the Skagerrak, the need for a carrier had become so urgent that the ship had sailed without her fighter squadron rather then accept further delay.[30] The *Furious* and the battleship *Warspite* had left the Clyde in the early hours of the Tuesday morning and set off northwards to join the C-in-C.

Off the Norwegian coast on the morning of *Weser*-day, the weather had cleared and, from 1030 onwards, the Fleet had been shadowed by German flying boats. In early afternoon radar detected large formations of aircraft to the south and east and the Fleet had then come under sustained attack from X Air Corps bombers flying from bases in Lübecke and Sylt.[31] The first and heaviest attacks fell on Admiral Layton's ships as they returned from their abortive foray against Bergen. The cruisers *Glasgow* and *Southampton* were damaged by near misses though neither seriously, but the destroyer *Gurkha*, which had broken formation and reduced speed in

41

an attempt to improve her gunnery, was hit by dive-bombers and damaged so severely that she later sank. Attacks on the main body of the Fleet began at 1530 when a Ju-88 made a diving attack on the *Rodney* and hit her with a 500kg bomb. The weapon failed to penetrate the armoured deck, however, and damage was slight. Then after a short lull the onslaught started again and included high-level and dive-bombing attacks. Several bombs fell close, the *Rodney, Valiant, Devonshire* and *Berwick* all reporting near misses. Fleet gunfire exacted few penalties from the enemy, only a single bomber being brought down within sight of the main body. Yet rates of ammunition expenditure were unprecedented. That evening, Admiral Layton's cruisers reported that they had used 40 per cent of their 4-inch AA ammunition.

This demonstration of German airpower forced a radical review of Fleet plans. Forbes had intended to use the *Furious* torpedo bombers against naval targets in Bergen and had proposed an attack at dusk next day, 10 April. But in the light of the day's events, the C-in-C decided that it would be better to deploy his offensive capability in an area that was more remote from German bases. He told the Admiralty that the *Furious* could not work in the latitude of Bergen and that he was going to shift his point of attack to Trondheim. His general plan of campaign from now on would be to 'attack enemy forces in north with surface forces and military assistance, leaving southern area mostly to submarines'.[32] That night, Forbes detached the ships of the 18th and 2nd Cruiser Squadrons to sweep southwards as far as Stavanger in search of German reinforcements while, with the rest of the Fleet, he continued to the northward to meet his carrier and prepare for the attack on Trondheim.

Chapter 4

'Weserübung'

Despite the resurgence of German militarism, the Norwegian Government, neutralist and pacifist in its leanings, had done little to prepare for a new and more dangerous age. Norway's tradition of compulsory military service had survived but training commitments had been allowed to wither and the material shortfalls of the armed forces had gone uncorrected. Mobilization, when complete, was expected to generate a force of 100,000 men but equipment stocks were meagre and ammunition reserves sufficient for the briefest of campaigns only. The military developments taking place in the rest of Europe had passed the Army by. Guns were horse-drawn and of 'ancient vintage'. Cavalry regiments (Dragoons) had evolved into motor machine-gun units, but there had been no investment in armour. Units had no anti-tank or anti-aircraft weapons. Of the score of aircraft under Army control (there was no independent air force) only six were fighters; the rest, spread thinly between the six military districts or 'divisions', were observation and reconnaissance types. The Navy, very much the junior partner in this enterprise, was in a similar state of neglect. It had four modern destroyers but the rest of its ships were obsolescent or, like the coast defence vessels of the *Norge* class, survivors from a bygone age. The naval air arm, larger than its army equivalent but equally outmoded, had thirty floatplanes, mostly reconnaissance machines, but including a few torpedo bombers.

The mission of the armed forces in the spring of 1940 was to protect Norwegian neutrality. The Navy had mobilized in September 1939 to police the nation's coastal waters and since then had maintained standing patrols off all major ports. Coastal batteries had been alerted but they remained well short of their war complements and the infantry units tasked with defending them against attack from the land had not been raised. The Finnish war had prompted precautionary moves in the extreme north. The 6th Division, responsible for the security of Norway's Arctic provinces, had mobilized its 'field brigade' (a balanced force consisting of four rifle battalions with cavalry, artillery and engineer support – the standard unit of currency in the Norwegian Army) but in other districts, the military authorities had been content to call up a single battalion for 'neutrality watch' and training. Further precautionary moves meant mobilization and all the social and economic dislocation that went with it.

An account has already been given of the warning signs that might have alerted Scandinavian governments to the fate that Hitler was planning for them. Suffice it to say here that by 5 April (the Friday) Colonel Hatledal, the Norwegian Army Chief of Staff, was sufficiently alarmed by reports coming from Berlin to call for mobilization in the four military districts covering the southern part of the country. But ministers who had placed absolute faith in the principle of neutrality, and who had publicly re-affirmed that principle only days before, were not easily persuaded that their beliefs were mistaken.[1] General Laake, Commander-in-Chief and a man well past his prime, had declined to support the proposal and the Nygaardsvold[2] Government had postponed a decision and turned its attention to more pressing matters.

That Friday the Allies had presented the warning notes agreed at the Supreme War Council and, on the Monday morning (8 April), Allied ministers had informed the Norwegian and Swedish governments that, in retaliation for German violations of international law and neutral rights, they had laid mines in three specified areas along the Norwegian coast. This blatant challenge to Norwegian neutrality had demanded a riposte. The Foreign Minister, Halvdan Koht, had spent much of the morning drafting a note of protest. The text had then been discussed in the influential Parliamentary Committee for Foreign Affairs before being referred to the Norwegian Parliament, the Storting, for further debate during the evening. When these constitutional formalities were complete, the Cabinet had reconvened to agree the necessary measures.

News of German naval movements had been arriving in Oslo throughout the afternoon. The Minister in Copenhagen, keeping in close touch with contacts on the Danish General Staff, had passed on the news that a powerful naval force had moved north through the Great Belt earlier in the day. The evening papers had carried first news of the sinking of the *Rio de Janeiro*, while a later report from the District Commander at Kristiansand had highlighted the remarkable claims being made by the survivors. The story had been greeted with disbelief in political circles and with a hint of amusement; the claims had seemed to illustrate the extraordinary gullibility of the German soldier.[3] A little later, the legation in London had given warning of a possible threat to Narvik and had passed on the latest sightings off the Norwegian coast. The Cabinet had discussed the question of mobilization once again but had not been persuaded that the time for additional precautions (which might themselves inflame the situation) had yet arrived. The Cabinet had dispersed that night unconvinced by the

44

warnings of their military advisers and confident that a sufficient deterrent was already in place.[4]

Shortly after midnight, the city's air-raid sirens went off and Oslo was plunged into darkness. Dr Koht, just reaching home at the time, dismissed the cacophony as a test alert but the sirens persisted and he telephoned the Foreign Ministry to find out the cause. He was told that foreign warships had entered the fjord and that the defences had opened fire. He set out at once to return to his office and, unable to find a taxi, stumbled back through the darkened city to the Victoria Terrasse to find the whole Cabinet assembling there. The scale of the challenge facing the Government was soon clear. The intruders had passed the outer forts and were continuing their advance on the capital. Reports from Bergen told a similar story and had identified the attacking force as German. There had been an incident at Stavanger as well and, a little later, a further intrusion at Trondheim. The Commander-in-Chief was summoned from his home in the country and agreed to the limited measures that Hatledal had urged three days earlier; at 0245 on the morning of 9 April, the Cabinet, shaken by this series of unexpected blows, gave the order to mobilize.

Much is sometimes made of the fact that these amiable and moderate men gave their approval, apparently unwittingly, to a partial and secret mobilization rather than to an immediate and general call to arms. It is not clear that this final oversight made much practical difference for the damage had already been done. All chance of an orderly mobilization process (general or partial) had passed; each military district now had to respond to the crisis as best it could and under the pressure of German arms.[5]

At 0445 that morning, while the Cabinet was still in session, Dr Kurt Bräuer, the German Minister in Oslo, arrived at the Victoria Terrasse and demanded a meeting with the Foreign Minister. The two men met in the library by the light of two small candles. Bräuer presented a lengthy paper claiming that Germany had proof positive that the Allies planned to invade Norway and establish a base for operations against the Reich. Germany was therefore taking responsibility for the defence of Norway for the duration of the war.[6] The paper listed thirteen demands in all, the more important being that the Government should call on the people not to resist, that forts and military establishments should surrender themselves intact and that press, radio, railways, ferries and port facilities should be placed at Germany's disposal. The people of Norway needed to appreciate Germany's predicament, Bräuer told the Foreign Minister; Germany had no wish 'to interfere with the territorial integrity or political independence of the Kingdom of Norway now or in the future'. Koht withdrew to confer with his colleagues. He returned at about 5.30. It was just getting light. He rejected the German demands and replied: 'We will maintain our independence as long as possible.'[7]

Fate does not always provide a man equal to the situation but in this instance it did. Carl Hambro, the widely respected President of the Storting, whose supposed anti-German leanings had already been brought to Admiral Raeder's notice, had been involved all day in discussions about British mining, but had reached home earlier than Dr Koht and gone to bed. He was woken by the sirens and telephoned contacts in the press agencies to find out what was happening. He recognized at once that the King, the Government and members of the Storting were in imminent danger of capture, and promptly telephoned the Clerk to the Storting, telling him to call his staff together, pack the state papers and prepare to leave.[8] He drove to the Parliament building to ensure that all was in progress and went on to the Foreign Ministry, arriving soon after the Government's rejection of the German demands. He proposed the immediate evacuation of the Royal Family, Government and Storting to Hamar, a provincial capital with good rail and road connections, 70 miles north of Oslo. Some members of the Cabinet were hesitant but he calmed their fears and an Order in Council giving effect to the move was issued there and then. After a short discussion about ways and means, the Transport Minister ordered a special train to be ready at the East Central Station at seven o'clock and the Finance Minister took steps to evacuate the gold reserves. Orders were sent to the Army and Navy staffs to prepare to move and the foreign legations notified. Hambro then left for Hamar by car to alert the civic authorities and prepare a new seat of government.

While Bräuer and Koht were still conferring, German assault groups were beginning their carefully synchronized landings along the 1,000-mile front from the Arctic Circle to the Baltic Approaches. Although German commanders had hoped that a mere demonstration of force would be enough, their orders betrayed no hint of the ambivalence that had been so marked a feature of British orders for Operations 'Avonmouth' and 'Stratford'. '[We] must succeed and we will,' wrote Raeder on the eve of *Weserübung*, 'if every leader is conscious of the greatness of his task and makes a supreme effort to reach the objective assigned to him.' Group commanders and captains of ships were to be governed by an inflexible determination to reach their objectives whatever obstacles might lie in their path. They were not to be diverted by the delaying tactics of local commanders, or deterred by the actions of guard ships or coastal fortifications. Resistance, when encountered, was to be 'broken ruthlessly'. 'Faith in the justice of our cause and implicit trust in our *Führer* and Supreme Commander,' the Admiral concluded, 'give us the assurance that in this task, as always, victory will be on our side.'[9]

The destroyers of Group 1 led by Commodore Friedrich Bonte in the *Wilhelm Heidkamp* were released off the mouth of the Vestfjord at 2000 on the Monday night. Their passage northwards had been one of acute discomfort. The high speed ordered (the passage had been planned at 26 knots), the rising gale and the long quartering sea had tested the skill of helmsmen to the limit and left the soldiers of the 139th Mountain Regiment, crammed below decks, suffering the tortures of the damned. The *Bernd von Arnim*, a ship of the 4th Flotilla, had been over on her beam ends while trying to outrun the *Glowworm* and two men who had been washed overboard had been left to their fate. Sheltered water came as a welcome relief. Bonte entered the narrows at 0300 on the morning of *Weser*-day. He left one ship to act as a picket, detached two to seize the batteries at the entrance to the Ofotfjord, and three more to capture the regimental depot at Elvegårdsmoen in the Herjangsfjord about 10 miles north of Narvik (see Map 3 on page 66). With his remaining ships (there were just three of them since the *Erich Giese* was running late) he arrived off Narvik at 0415. There he encountered the *Eidsvold*, one of the veteran coast defence ships whose presence at Narvik had worried Admiral Forbes. The ship had been warned of his approach by a picket in the outer fjord; she made the signal to stop and fired a warning shot.

Bonte sent his operations officer on board the *Eidsvold* with a note demanding surrender. The atmosphere on the ship's quarterdeck was polite but frigid. After a brief consultation with his senior officer, the Norwegian captain rejected the demand, and ordered the officer back to his ship. As the boat cleared the *Eidsvold*'s side, the German fired a red signal cartridge as a warning and Bonte, urged on, it is said, by General Dietl, ordered torpedoes. Two weapons from a pattern of four hit the *Eidsvold* and the ancient ship went down there and then taking all but a handful of her ship's company with her.[10]

The *Arnim*, meanwhile, had slipped into the harbour and made for the Post Pier where she was to discharge her troops. She had found it hard at first to get her bearings for snow was driving across the water and visibility was poor. But as she approached her objective, her decks crowded with waiting troops, she came under fire from the *Norge* (the *Eidsvold*'s sister ship) which had slipped her moorings and taken up the challenge. The range was less than 1,000 yards but the Norwegian salvo went over. The *Arnim* replied with salvos from her 5-inch guns and eventually with a volley of torpedoes. One, perhaps two, of these hit the target and the *Norge* went down in a matter of minutes.[11] The *Arnim*, the *Heidkamp* and the *Thiele* put their troops ashore in quick succession. There was no resistance. The garrison commander, Colonel Sundlo, an alleged Quisling sympathizer, surrendered the town without a fight and when later questioned by city officials replied simply that he had been outnumbered and that, after the sinking of the coast defence ships, resistance had been hopeless.[12] Dietl established his headquarters in the Grand Hotel and at 0810 on the morning of *Weser*-day, reported to Group XXI that Narvik was in German hands.

Despite the conspicuous success of the operation so far, there were enough clouds on the horizon to worry any thoughtful commander. Bonte was relieved to find the tanker *Jan Wellem* (a converted whale factory ship) anchored in the harbour awaiting his arrival, but the second tanker (the *Kattegat*) had not arrived and nor had the ships of the Export Group bringing artillery, anti-aircraft weapons, ammunition and transport for the Army. The *Jan Wellem* carried enough fuel to fill all Bonte's destroyers and to provide for the U-boats deployed off Narvik as well, but her pumping rate was slow and it would be nearly thirty-six hours before all ten destroyers could be ready to leave. And until the ships of the Export Group arrived, Dietl's grip on Narvik and its approaches could hardly be considered secure. The position, already precarious, was made worse by the complete absence of coastal defences. The troops landed at Ramnes and Hamnes (the supposed sites of the coastal batteries) had reported 6 feet of snow and a few empty gun emplacements, nothing more. Seaward defence was now going to depend on a handful of U-boats and what Bonte could provide from his own resources. Although by the evening of *Weser*-day he was aware that British capital ships had been in action off the Lofotens, and that a British destroyer flotilla had been sighted in the Vestfjord, he does not seem to have been unduly worried by the danger to his ships or by the tenuous nature of the Army's hold ashore. He seems instead to have been sunk in lethargy. Some have suggested that the ruthless action forced on him by the Norwegian Navy was weighing heavily on his mind;[13] he may simply have believed that he was safe for the moment and that the real danger lay outside the fjords when he came to leave. He ordered patrols – that seems certain – but his orders were ambiguous and the execution casual.[14] His mind was on fuelling. He put two ships of the 3rd Flotilla alongside the tanker and two more in waiting positions nearby. The rest he dispersed to anchorages within a 10-mile radius of Narvik, two to Ballangen Bay to the west of the town and three to the Herjangsfjord (scene of the recent action against Elvegårdsmoen) to conserve fuel and await their turn in the queue.

At other points along the extended perimeter, the invasion groups found the Norwegian coastal defences manned and ready, though not always equal to their task. At Trondheim, a Norwegian patrol vessel raised the alarm as the ships of Group 2 approached. The *Hipper*, bearing the scars of her collision with the *Glowworm*, rushed the forts at Brettingsnes and Hysnes at a speed of 25 knots, and on reaching safe water used her 8-inch guns to cover the passage of the destroyers following behind.[15] Captain

Heye landed rifle companies to take the forts and continued on to Trondheim. By 0700 on the morning of *Weser*-day he had put his battalions ashore. The town itself had offered no resistance and the landing force had captured the mobilization depot intact. But when night came, the forts were still holding out and so was the vital airfield at Værnes, 16 miles to the eastward. As at Narvik, tankers and Export Group units were missing.

Rear Admiral Schmundt, leading Group 3 (the light cruisers *Köln* and *Königsberg*, the training ship *Bremse*, two torpedo boats and a number of auxiliaries and light craft) had approached Bergen via the Korsfjord. When challenged by a Norwegian torpedo boat he had replied, 'HMS *Cairo*'. He had later responded to a signal station ashore with the message: 'I am proceeding to Bergen for a short visit'. Thereafter he had been illuminated and challenged repeatedly as he neared his objective. He had detached the *Königsberg* on approaching the Byfjord to land troops and storm the Kvarven battery, but he was running late and he had moved on without waiting for the fort to fall. Helped by a series of misjudgements and mishaps on the part of the defenders, the result of inexperience and poor training, the *Köln* had passed the guns unscathed but the *Bremse*, following behind, had taken one 8-inch hit and the *Königsberg*, following later still, three. But all ships had broken through to their objectives and the men of the 69th Infantry Division had occupied the city after overcoming weak resistance. A flight of medium bombers had joined the attack on the forts and, by noon, the batteries were in German hands. Later in the day there were reports that Norwegian troops were still holding positions dangerously close to Bergen. There were new calls for warships to stay behind until the situation had stabilized (calls that the Naval Staff had again firmly resisted), although it was already clear that, for the *Königsberg*, delay was inevitable.[16]

The airfield at Sola, 8 miles south-west of Stavanger was an additional and critical objective for the 69th Infantry Division. At 0845 on the morning of *Weser*-day, a flight of Ju-52 transports with long-range fighters in support had approached at low level and delivered a parachute company with perfect accuracy. The airfield had fallen after a brief engagement and the infantry battalions had started to arrive as soon as the runway had been cleared of obstructions. There was no attempt by Norwegian forces to defend Stavanger; the battalion of the neutrality watch had withdrawn to cover the mobilization of the 8th Infantry Regiment at Oltedal some 20 miles to the south-east. The export units assigned to Stavanger had shared the fate of those elsewhere. The infantry's heavy weapons had gone down in the *Roda*, sunk in the early hours of the Tuesday morning by a Norwegian torpedo boat, while the Luftwaffe's supplies of aviation fuel had been lost in the *Stedingen*, victim of a British submarine. X Air Corps was unable to make full use of Sola until a second tanker arrived forty-eight hours later.[17]

At Kristiansand, success had turned on a knife-edge and Captain Rieve, leading the attack in the light cruiser *Karlsruhe*, had displayed all the tenacity and ingenuity that Raeder had demanded of his group commanders. The fog had been dense on the southern coast of Norway and Rieve had delayed his attack in the hope that it might lift. When, towards six o'clock, he had made his first move, he had emerged from the mist to find the Odderøya batteries fully prepared and had been forced to withdraw under cover of smoke. He had tried again an hour later, this time with the help of a flight of bombers but with the same result. Next he had tried to send his torpedo boats into the narrows while the *Karlsruhe* smothered the batteries with fire, but the fog had rolled in again and the attempt had ended in confusion. He had then tried to approach with the *Karlsruhe* alone and had been saved from grounding only by an alert fog lookout. But, towards 1100, the fog had lifted. Rieve had approached the batteries making the signal 'British and French destroyers coming to help. Do not fire.' His ruse was successful. Three motor torpedo boats slipped past the batteries into safe water and landed men on the unprotected landward side. By noon the batteries were in German hands. The town was not defended – the local battalion had withdrawn northwards to cover the Setesdal where mobilization was taking place – and German forces occupied it during the afternoon.

Nowhere had the mix of boldness, ruthlessness and surprise worked better than in Denmark. The Danish Cabinet had been warned of large-scale troop movements on the southern border but the northward movement of German naval forces during 8 April had pointed to an objective outside Danish territory, and the state of alert had been confined to southern Jutland. The armed forces had been ludicrously ill prepared to counter the German offensive. Mechanized units had crossed the border at 0515 pushing assault parties ahead of them to prevent demolitions on the line of advance and using tanks to break pockets of resistance. At 0700, X Air Corps had launched its airborne operations to take the airfields at Ålborg and to seize the key rail bridge linking the islands of Falster and Sjælland, thus opening Copenhagen to attack from the south. Surprise had been complete. By 0800 both objectives had been in German hands. XXXI Corps amphibious operations had met with similar success. In spite of a pre-dawn mishap in the Great Belt when the pre-Dreadnought battleship *Schleswig-Holstein* had run aground, the key ferry crossings linking Jutland with the Danish islands had been captured according to plan. In Copenhagen itself, an infantry battalion, landed from the mine-layer *Hansestadt Danzig* and the ice breaker *Stettin*, had stormed the Citadel while General Himer, XXXI Corps Chief of Staff, who had arrived incognito forty-eight hours earlier to lend weight to German diplomacy, provided a running commentary to his headquarters over an open telephone line. Hastened to a decision by the threat of bombing, the Danish Government surrendered at 0720.[18]

Only in Oslo, the greatest prize of all, did the *'Weserübung'* plan go seriously awry. To provide the build-up needed to secure the capital and take control of the road and rail networks radiating from it, XXI Corps staff had envisaged a combined operation involving the Kriegsmarine and the Luftwaffe. Group 5, consisting of the heavy cruiser *Blücher*, the pocket battleship *Lützow*, the light cruiser *Emden*, three torpedo boats and a flotilla of motor minesweepers, was to carry two battalions of General Engelbrecht's 163rd Infantry Division into the heart of the city, while X Air Corp's transport squadrons, acting in relays, would lift two more into Fornebu, the airfield on the city's western outskirts. The field (known to be defended) was to be secured by a parachute company twenty minutes before the first of the transports arrived.

Rear Admiral Oskar Kummetz flying his flag in the *Blücher* arrived in the approaches to Oslofjord a little before midnight on 8 April with ample time in hand. Allied submarine activity in the Kattegat and Skagerrak had been intense and his passage northward had been punctuated by submarine alarms. The attack on the *Rio de Janeiro* at midday had been quickly followed by the sinking of the *Posidonia*, an 8,000-ton tanker bound for Kristiansand with fuel for the U-boat flotilla. And Group 5 had itself come under attack soon after passing the Skaw, prompt action by the escorts preventing a disaster.[19]

Kummetz now faced a 50-mile night transit through narrow waters defended by two lines of coastal fortifications, the island forts of Rauøy and Bolærne marking the outer limit of the fjord and the fortress of Oscarsborg guarding the Drøbak narrows about 10 miles short of his objective. Like other group commanders he had been provided with a cover story for use when challenged and his intention, in broad outline, was to bluff his way past the defences and clean up behind him so that the waterway would be open for the reinforcement shipping arriving to exploit his coup.

The first hint of trouble came when the radio intelligence team in the *Lützow* monitoring Oslo radio overheard an order addressed to harbour authorities to extinguish coastal lights and beacons. Captain Thiele saw this as an ominous development and urged Kummetz to press ahead as quickly as possible while the lights were still burning and coastal defences still off balance. But the Admiral held firmly to the published plan. A second incident, following soon afterwards, made it clear beyond doubt that surprise had been lost and that deception would no longer be enough. Just on midnight, there had been an exchange of fire between one of

Kummetz's escorts and what was evidently a Norwegian picket. The vessel concerned, the 200-ton armed whaler *Pol III*, had challenged, fired on and finally rammed the *Albatros* before being overwhelmed. Fourteen seamen had been pulled out of the water but the Captain, a Norwegian reservist, had been killed.[20]

Yet, thirty minutes later, Kummetz had passed the outer forts at Rauøy and Bolærne without serious mishap. The Rauøy battery had swept the channel with a searchlight as the German force approached and fired several shots. But the Norwegian gunners, hampered by low visibility, had found it impossible to identify and hold a target, and their shooting had been wild. When he reached safe water north of the batteries, Kummetz had loitered for more than an hour transferring assault teams to his mine-sweepers, sending them off to mount attacks on the island forts and to capture the naval base at Horten on the western shore before resuming his advance.

The main obstacle between Kummetz and his objective was now the fortress of Oscarsborg in the Drøbak Sound where the channel narrows to a width of two or three cables and makes a 30° turn to the left. The fortress had been constructed during the nineteenth-century hay day of coastal fort building and rearmed at the turn of the twentieth. The main battery (two 11-inch cannon manufactured by Krupp of Essen in 1892 and popularly known as Moses and Aaron) was mounted on the island of South Kaholm on the western side of the channel, while guns of smaller calibre (8-inch Armstrong weapons) were mounted at Drøbak on the eastern shore. A battery of torpedo tubes (of Austrian origin) was mounted on the islet of North Kaholm just beyond the heavy guns.

Visibility remained poor as the *Blücher* approached the forts. There was no sign of life ashore and no searchlights, nothing to raise suspicions until a boat stationed just short of the forts fired flares. But by then Kummetz was committed to the narrows. The Norwegian fire, withheld until the range was point blank, was devastating. A succession of heavy shells slammed into the *Blücher*'s superstructure, destroying the AA gun direction platform, and starting a fierce petrol fire in the hanger. The *Blücher* responded with a barrage of light and heavy flak but her 8-inch guns, unable to find a target, remained silent. Finding that the ship would not answer the helm, Captain Heinrich Woldag put his port shaft astern as the forts came abeam in order to negotiate the left-hand bend. As the ship slowed under the influence of stern power, she was rocked by two heavy underwater explosions. With her engine rooms flooded and her turbines stopped, she drifted clear on the flood tide and, a mile or so beyond the forts, dropped an anchor to arrest her northward progress. After swinging through 180° so that her bows pointed south, she came to rest off Askholmene, burning like a torch and listing heavily.

Captain Thiele who had followed Kummetz into the narrows had applied full stern power and got his ship clear. A heavy shell had immobilized the *Lützow*'s forward turret and she had taken minor damage elsewhere, but her survival had not been threatened. At 0450, Kummetz had passed the command of Group 5 to the *Lützow*, and Thiele, determined that no further attempt on the narrows could be made while the forts remained in Norwegian hands, had landed his rifle companies at Sonsbukten on the eastern shore to attack Drøbak from the landward side and continue the advance on Oslo by road. The *Blücher* had been left to solve her problems alone. By six o'clock, her fires were raging out of control and were threatening a 4-inch magazine. At 0630 there had been another heavy explosion and the ship had lurched to a new angle of heel; and when, twenty minutes later, the ship had turned on her side, paused for a moment and then gone down, most men had been forced to swim for it. Only one boat had survived the fires and that had been reserved for the seriously wounded. Casualties were heavy and included most of General Engelbrecht's staff.[21]

In mid-morning, the X Air Corp's Stuka group was given the task of reducing the forts. The batteries on the eastern shore, attacked from the land and from the air, surrendered during the afternoon (as did the forts at the mouth of the fjord and the naval base at Horten), but Kaholm was not secured until the following morning (10 April) and it was only then that the waterway could be opened to traffic.

Commander Richard Schreiber, the German Naval Attaché, who had gone down to the harbour on the morning of *Weser*-day to welcome Admiral Kummetz, had waited in vain. By 0930, his staff had been burning their secret papers and distributing pistols to defend the mission. And, as he drove around the town trying to assess what was going on, he had slipped a civilian overcoat over his naval uniform.[22] Nor had Dr Bräuer and his senior military advisors been able to call on troops from Fornebu to retrieve the situation. At 0830 that morning, the Ju-52 transport squadron carrying the parachute companies which were to seize the airfield had met a thickening wall of cloud as they approached the Norwegian coast and, after losing some of their number, had turned back for Ålborg. To the dismay of his transport chief, General Geisler had then insisted on re-calling the rest of the transport groups which were following close behind. Only the initiative of a handful of junior officers who had questioned the authenticity of the recall order, continued inland and sighted their objective had saved the day. Supported by a flight of long-range fighters that had been able to loiter long enough to see them safely in, they had put down on an airfield that was still in Norwegian hands and on which the wrecks of two or three Norwegian fighters were still burning. The parachute companies and the rest of Engelbrecht's infantry had started to

53

arrive at noon. The build-up had then been rapid and by early evening a whole regiment had been brought in. Only then had it been possible to take effective control of the capital.

The predominant feeling in Naval Staff circles as the first phase of *Weserübung* came to a close was one of relief. There had been a 'noticeable stiffening' in Norwegian attitudes in the days leading up to the invasion and surprise had been lost, but the landings had succeeded 'thanks to the resolute action of the forces participating favoured by luck.' Losses (the staff diarist was referring mainly to the sinking of the *Blücher*) had been 'grievous' but they had been 'in proportion to the risks run and in no sense excessive'.[23] It was clear, on the other hand, that the unexpected presence of powerful British forces on the Norwegian coast had made the next phase of the operation, the recovery of the surface fleet, even more difficult than anticipated. Every hour counted and the failure of tankers to reach their ports of destination put every ship at risk. Fuel for the destroyers in Narvik seemed to be assured but it would be a further twenty-four hours before all ten were ready to move. (It was assumed that the Commodore Destroyers was doing everything that he could to speed things up.) There were similar problems in Trondheim; the *Hipper* appeared to have enough fuel to reach German waters (albeit with no margin for safety) and could leave immediately, but two of her destroyers would not be ready until next day. That night, the Naval Staff considered relieving the Fleet Commander of his 'obligations regarding the destroyers in Narvik' and recalling the battleships there and then. But Group West persuaded them that the idea was premature and that, for the moment, the decision was best left to the man on the spot.[24] The recovery of the battleships and of the ships still in the Norwegian ports remained, nevertheless, at the top of Naval Staff priorities.

It was clear, finally, that the 'supply situation' had become very difficult. Although the fate of individual ships remained a mystery, the plan to deliver the Army's heavy weapons and ammunition by means of a clandestine 'Export Group' had miscarried. And to make matters worse, the Oslo supply route had come under serious threat from British submarines. Other tasks listed as 'urgent' included the strengthening of U-boat dispositions off Narvik and Trondheim, and stronger anti-submarine measures in the Kattegat and Skagerrak. And in view of the obvious difficulty of supplying German garrisons through the west coast ports, staff officers were beginning to wonder whether supplies could not be delivered via the Swedish and Norwegian railway systems.[25]

Whether the Norwegian Government would accede to German demands or maintain its show of defiance remained for the moment unclear. The Storting, meeting at Hamar during the afternoon of 9 April, had endorsed the Government's initial position but news of the Danish capitulation and gloomy reports from the General Staff had fostered a growing sense of pessimism. Faced that afternoon with new offers of negotiation from Dr Bräuer, and renewed assurances that Germany would respect the 'political independence of the Kingdom of Norway', the Government had wavered and the Prime Minister, Johan Nygaardsvold, had tendered his resignation, advising the King to appoint a government of national unity. A hastily summoned Council of State had discussed the future of the Government and the question of negotiation without reaching a decision and both matters had been referred to the Storting. Here, Hambro's cool courage and solid common sense had stopped the rot. He had argued, persuasively, that this was the wrong moment for the existing Cabinet to let go of the reins – the result had been a unanimous call for the Government to remain in place and for the King to confirm ministers in their posts. He had then compared the case for negotiation as presented by the Prime Minister with the case for resistance, referring to King Haakon's view, clearly and firmly set out during the afternoon council, that Hitler's promises could not be trusted. The question of negotiation was left unresolved, however, for deliberations were interrupted by the news that a column of German troops was approaching Hamar. Hambro suspended the sitting and summoned members to reconvene as soon as possible at Elverum, a provincial town and centre of the Norwegian timber industry some 20 miles to the eastward. King, ministers, deputies, officials, and members of the diplomatic corps who had followed the Government from Oslo, grabbed their belongings and fled once again before the German advance.

The Storting met in Elverum late that night. It was its last meeting. It unanimously adopted a motion drafted by Hambro giving the Nygaardsvold Government plenary powers until such time as it could reconvene 'in full liberty'.[26] Before dispersing, however, it authorized the Government to open negotiations with the German Minister and appointed a small delegation to oversee them.

Bräuer's hopes of reaching a settlement that would preserve an outward semblance of legality and leave Norway with a substantial measure of autonomy had been compromised meanwhile by events in Oslo and Berlin. The flight of the Government had allowed Quisling, backed by Gruppenleiter Scheidt (one of Rosenberg's henchmen), to step forward and present himself and his Nasjonal Samling as the de facto successor. Attempts to block the move proved fruitless for, in Berlin, an edgy Führer had seized on Quisling's proposals as the obvious solution to what had become a vexing political problem. Bräuer, keenly aware of the contempt in which this unstable visionary and his (mostly) juvenile supporters were held, had made his opposition clear during lengthy telephone calls with

Ribbentrop and then with Hitler himself, but in the end he had been instructed to sever all contact with the existing administration and demand the appointment of a Quisling Government in its place. That evening Quisling made a broadcast to the nation saying that he had stepped in to fill the vacuum left by the flight of the Government. He demanded the immediate obedience of the armed forces and the civil authorities and made it clear that the order to mobilize had been based on a misunderstanding. And late that night, Bräuer sent a message to Elverum demanding a personal meeting with the King.

In the small hours of the morning, exhausted ministers were roused from their beds and warned that there was fighting on the road to Elverum. They fled north-eastwards with their retinue of followers towards the remote village of Nybergsund close to the Swedish border, leaving the Foreign Minister and the Storting delegation to conduct negotiations with the Germans. But that night, a scratch force made up of the heavy weapons company of the Guards Battalion from Oslo, and a few local conscripts and civilian volunteers led by Colonel Otto Ruger, a respected soldier and a former Chief of Staff, stopped the German advance in the approaches to the town and inflicted a number of casualties. Among those mortally wounded was Captain Spiller, the German Air Attaché who had been leading the column in his private car.[27] On the Wednesday morning (10 April) Ruger was able to report that his defences were firm and that the enemy had retired. Confident that Elverum was secure, at least for the moment, Koht had felt able to offer Bräuer a meeting with the King and a time had been set for that afternoon.

The negotiations foundered, as Bräuer feared they would, on the question of Quisling. Dr Koht who had been called to join the meeting at the King's insistence described a Quisling administration as 'a puppet government by grace of a foreign power'.[28] Bräuer referred to his conversation with Hitler and replied that there was no alternative. No decision was reached. King Haakon insisted on putting the matter before his constitutional advisors and it was agreed that Bräuer would telephone Koht during his journey back to Oslo to get the answer. Bräuer's telephone call came through at eight o'clock that evening. He was told that the King could not, as a constitutional monarch, appoint a government that had no basis of popular support. He asked whether resistance would continue and was told, 'Yes, as long as possible.'[29] In a broadcast late that evening from the remote hamlet of Nybergsund, the Government called on the people to unite and help to maintain the freedom and independence of Norway. King Haakon associated himself with the call.[30] The Germans responded with a bombing attack. Next day, Laake, the ailing Commander in Chief, was forced into retirement and Ruge, the military man of the moment, was promoted to Major General and charged with the defence of Norway.

Chapter 5

Caught out of Bounds

For much of the Tuesday, the situation in Narvik remained uncertain. During the afternoon Chamberlain told the Commons that the press reports coming from Oslo might refer to Larvik (a minor port in the approaches to Oslofjord) rather than to its near-namesake in the far north. The matter was still in doubt in early evening when the Supreme War Council met in emergency session. Churchill conceded that a single German ship might possibly have slipped through the British net but told the meeting that he was sending some destroyers up to Narvik to establish the facts.[1]

A signal reaching London soon afterwards revealed the shocking truth. Late that afternoon, Captain B.A.W. Warburton-Lee (Captain 2nd Destroyer Flotilla) had landed a small party at the pilot station at Tranøy near the head of the Vestfjord to glean what intelligence he could. The signs were that the Germans held Narvik in force; six large destroyers and a sub-marine had been seen entering the narrows. Warburton-Lee told London that he intended to attack 'at dawn high water'.[2] When the Military Co-ordination Committee met that evening to decide on the deployment of the expeditionary forces that were preparing for Norway, the illusion that Narvik was too remote to have fallen victim to a German assault was no longer tenable. Churchill admitted (on the basis of the crudest of estimates) that the Germans might have landed 3,000–4,000 men. Ironside reacted angrily. An opposed landing had never been part of the plan. The recap-ture of Narvik was now going to depend on 'the most careful preparation'; the expedition was 'doomed to failure if rushed'. He needed to concentrate all the available resources on this one objective and leave Bergen and Trondheim aside until Narvik had been retaken. Although when the meeting finally broke up there were still differences between the First Lord and the CIGS over how soon operations could begin, it was accepted that the coming military expedition should be directed against Narvik alone.[3]

The naval attack on Narvik had been proceeding meanwhile under the active encouragement of the Admiralty. Following the news from Tranøy,

Admiral Whitworth had considered strengthening the attacking force but he had held back at the last moment for fear of delaying the attack and causing confusion by a late change of plan. And he had been reluctant to interfere with a project that the Admiralty had initiated and which the C-in-C had accepted without comment. The Admiralty had continued to deal directly with Warburton-Lee throughout the evening. 'Attack at dawn', they had signalled at 2059, 'all good luck'. And in a valedictory message timed 0136 on the Wednesday morning (10 April) they had warned him that the coast defence ships *Norge* and *Eidsvold* might have fallen into enemy hands, adding: 'You alone can judge whether, in these circumstances [an] attack should be made. We shall support whatever decision you make.'[4]

Protected by darkness and driving snow, Warburton-Lee arrived off Narvik intact and undetected just as dawn was breaking. Leaving two ships off the harbour entrance to watch for enemies closing from the north and west, he took the *Hardy* into the Beisfjord, picked his way through a maze of anchored merchantmen and launched a salvo of torpedoes at a pair of German destroyers anchored off the eastern shore. He then turned hard for the harbour entrance engaging a third destroyer with guns and torpedoes as his ship gathered headway. As he withdrew, the *Hunter* followed him in and launched two full salvoes into the crowded anchorage; she withdrew ten minutes later leaving chaos and destruction in her wake. The *Havock*, next in line, found it difficult at first to identify any target through the pall of smoke that was now drifting across the anchorage but the flash of gunfire betrayed the position of one German destroyer and she turned her guns on that. She had then engaged a second destroyer with torpedoes. (The target had 'vanished'.) But the enemy was now showing signs of life. The *Havock* was straddled as she made for the harbour entrance and small-arms fire was coming from the shore.

This first attack was devastating in its effects. There had been five German destroyers in the inner harbour, two (*Künne* and *Lüdemann*) fuelling from the *Jan Wellem* and two more (*Schmitt* and *Heidkamp*) anchored to the southward awaiting their turn in the queue. A fifth, the *Roeder*, which had abandoned her patrol off the harbour entrance with the coming of daylight, had entered harbour only minutes before and anchored two or three cables north of the oiler. A weapon from the *Hardy*'s initial salvo struck the *Heidkamp* aft setting off a magazine and leaving the after end of the ship an inferno of blazing ammunition. The explosion caused fearful casualties, Commodore Bonte among them. The *Schmitt* had taken two torpedo hits in quick succession. She had broken in half and turned over leaving most of her ship's company swimming for their lives. The *Künne*, which had left the tanker when the attack began, parting wires and hoses in her haste, had ended up close to the *Schmitt* when the second torpedo hit; the explosion had shaken her from end to end and left her dead in the water. The *Lüdemann* had engaged in a brief gun duel with the attackers; one of her forward guns had been wrecked and fires aft had forced the flooding of a magazine. Only the *Roeder*, the latest arrival, had emerged unscathed.[5]

But with German gunners now fully alert, Warburton-Lee was forced to change his methods. Following the withdrawal of the *Havock*, he deployed the first three ships clear of the harbour entrance to engage with gunfire while the *Hotspur* and then the *Hostile* went forward (with due caution now) to use torpedoes. Progress was slow. The *Hostile* had searched in vain for a warship target though the pall of smoke and had attracted a volley of torpedoes in return. Impatient at the delay and, worried that the enemy's next torpedo salvo might spell disaster, Warburton-Lee pulled his ships out of harm's way while he took stock of the situation. Calculating that he had sufficient force to deal with any other German destroyers that he might meet, he led his flotilla in a final pass across the harbour entrance to engage targets of opportunity and to give the *Hostile* at the rear of the line a final chance to use torpedoes.

His luck now deserted him. As he withdrew westward on completion of his attack, he found himself caught between three ships of the 4th Flotilla, led by Commander Erich Bey in the *Zenker*, that had been anchored in the Herjangsfjord and which were now, belatedly, closing from the north-east, and the two that had been sent westward to Ballangen Bay. It was this second pair (the *Georg Thiele* and the *Berndt von Arnim*) that did the damage. They deployed across the head of the British line and with the range closing rapidly soon started to register hits. Warburton-Lee, who had been preoccupied with the enemy astern, turned to port to bring his after battery to bear on the new arrivals and made the signal 'Keep on engaging the enemy', but immediately afterwards a salvo of high-explosive shells wrecked his forward guns, reduced his bridge to a charnel house of dead and wounded and left the *Hardy* pilotless and heading for the southern shore.

The *Hunter* cleared the smoke from the ships ahead to find herself the next target for German guns. She replied as best she could but, moments later, an enemy salvo struck home amidships, starting a raging fire near the forward funnel and causing a catastrophic loss of power. She came to a stop so suddenly that some suspected a torpedo. Her next astern, the *Hotspur*, unable to manoeuvre because a hit below the bridge had jammed the engine-room telegraphs and cut the lines to the steering motors, ran on board her leaving the two ships locked together under a hail of enemy fire. The *Hotspur*'s captain, Commander H.F. Layman, dashed aft to man the emergency conning position in a desperate attempt to get his ship clear.

The *Havock* and the *Hostile*, still undamaged, had seen the catastrophe at the centre of the British line as they swept past. When it became clear that Layman had got his ship clear of the wreck they turned back to give him their support. They found the *Hunter* sinking and the *Hotspur* drawing the fire of four enemy destroyers. But by now the *Thiele* and *Arnim* were nursing injuries of their own and Bey, worried by this new onslaught, had broken off the pursuit and had turned his attention to the rescue of the *Hunter*'s survivors. The two British destroyers had then shepherded the damaged *Hotspur* towards the narrows.

The *Hardy* was beyond help. The stunned survivors of the German salvo had roused themselves to find the ship out of control and heading for the rocks. Paymaster Lieutenant Stanning, the Captain's Secretary, seriously wounded, had limped down to the shattered wheelhouse and taken the wheel himself until relieved by a seaman. He had returned to the bridge to find the ship blowing off steam, losing way and burning fiercely. He decided to beach the ship and get the wounded ashore rather than keep her afloat as a target for German guns. The last that her consorts had seen of her was the *Hardy* aground and on fire with men clambering over the side.[6]

The final episode in this first battle of Narvik occurred an hour later and was symptomatic of a more general problem affecting the progress of German plans. As the surviving ships of the 2nd Destroyer Flotilla approached the narrows, they met the *Rauenfels*, inbound for Narvik with the heavy weapons and ammunition for General Dietl's troops. The ship ignored their order to stop and they opened fire. Soon afterwards they saw the crew taking to the boats. The *Havock* sent a boarding party to investigate but the ship was now burning fiercely and they left in a hurry. The *Havock* then put two high-explosive rounds into the target, causing a violent explosion and sending a column of flame and debris to the height of the surrounding mountains.

The three ships now continued to the westward, making for a safe anchorage in the lee of the Lofotens where the full extent of the damage to the *Hotspur* could be assessed and emergency repairs initiated.

Churchill said little about this action when the War Cabinet met at 1100 that morning. He spoke about the air attacks on the Home Fleet and about a successful strike by Fleet Air Arm aircraft on the ships in Bergen earlier in the day. He had then presented his committee's conclusions from the night before and warned against spreading the available military effort too thinly. The immediate priorities were to stop Narvik being reinforced, 'seal up' Bergen and Trondheim with the German naval forces inside them and then deal with them one by one. The War Cabinet accepted that the 'first aim should be the recapture of Narvik' and noted that the First Lord would present proposals very soon.[7]

Preparations for what was now being called Operation 'Rupert' were moving forward with all speed. Orders being drawn up in the War Office reflected the cautious and deliberate approach that Ironside had demanded. The first step would be to establish an advanced base in Norway so that the expedition could be 'sorted out' prior to the landing at Narvik itself. Major General Mackesy, the land force commander, would sail at once for Harstad (a minor port on the Vågsfjord) with two regular battalions to make contact with Norwegian forces and 'obtain the information necessary to plan further operations'. He would be reinforced before the start of any larger move. The rest of his force (four more battalions from Operations 'Avonmouth' and 'Stratford') would begin to arrive on 16 April, and a demi-brigade of Chasseurs Alpins five days after that. He would not be expected to land in the face of opposition but the landing would have to be carried out (somewhere else if need be) once he had enough troops.[8]

The Military Co-ordination Committee examined this outline plan later in the day. The mood, quite different from the evening before, had been lifted by the news of the naval action at Narvik. The new naval commander of the expedition (Admiral of the Fleet the Earl of Cork and Orrery), an energetic veteran of sixty-seven who had attended the meeting at Churchill's invitation, had left with the impression that the Government wanted to 'turn the enemy out of Narvik at the earliest possible moment' and that he was to 'act with all promptitude' to attain that result.[9] Even the CIGS had found his confidence in the Navy restored. Late that night he added a pencilled note to Mackesy's orders suggesting that the Germans might have been 'knocked about by the naval action'. He (Mackesy) had enough troops to prepare the base and carry out a reconnaissance before the bulk of his forces arrived. He might get the chance to exploit the effects of the naval action and he was to do so if he could. The note ended: 'Boldness is required.'[10]

First fragmentary reports of the British attack on Narvik reached staffs in Berlin and Wilhelmshaven just after six o'clock, but few hard facts had been available when Admiral Raeder left the Tirpitzufer for a noon conference with the Führer. The Grand Admiral stuck firmly to the brief prepared the night before, emphasizing that the first phases of the operation had passed off 'on the whole successfully' and that losses had been 'in proportion to the risks run'. The third phase (the recovery of the German Fleet) was now beginning and would 'probably entail further losses'. The Führer expressed his full appreciation for the Navy's great achievements.[11]

Some of the dangers of this third phase had already manifested themselves. The first significant loss had been inflicted during the evening of

Weser-day itself when the *Karlsruhe*, homeward bound from Kristiansand, had been torpedoed by a British submarine. The weapon had wrecked rudders and screws and left the stern of the cruiser open to the sea. Desperate attempts had been made to save the ship but, in the end, the crew had been taken off and the waterlogged hulk despatched with a torpedo.

An attack by long-range bombers on the ships of the Bergen group during the evening of *Weser*-day had caused no significant damage. Its main effect had been to impress on German minds the dangers of delay and, soon after the raid, the *Köln* had left the anchorage off Bergen and concealed herself in the Hardangerfjord until the coast was clear. (She sailed for Germany twenty-four hours later and reached home safely.) But her sister ship, the *Königsberg*, damaged by shore fire during the assault phase, had been surprised at dawn next morning by Skua dive-bombers from the Royal Naval Air Station at Hatston in the Orkneys. She had barely had time to man her guns. The cruiser had taken three direct hits and, within minutes, had rolled over in her berth, the first cruiser ever to be lost to air attack.

The true extent of the Navy's difficulties in the far north had filtered through to Berlin during the course of the day. The staffs had taken what comfort they could from the miraculous survival of the *Jan Wellem* and from the thought that their ships might have thwarted a British landing, but the cost to the flotilla had been heavy. The *Schmitt* had gone to the bottom, the *Heidkamp* was a total loss and the *Roeder* permanently disabled. (Her transmitters and anti-aircraft weapons were being removed for use ashore and she was being left at the Post Pier to act as a floating battery.) Three other destroyers had sustained serious damage and, of the original ten, only four would be ready for an early return to Germany. Of these, just two would have finished fuelling by nightfall. That evening the staffs recalled all ships in Bergen, Trondheim and Narvik that were ready to move, leaving the rest to follow as best they could. They urged Erich Bey (Bonte's successor as Senior Officer Destroyers) to get out of Narvik as soon as possible and join the Fleet Commander 'somewhere west of the Lofotens'. And, in a belated attempt to bolster seaward defences, they ordered Admiral Dönitz to double the number of U-boats off the northern ports.[12]

The *Hipper* was the first to move. She sailed from Trondheim at dusk on 10 April taking the *Friedrich Eckholdt* with her and leaving by the hazardous Ramsøy Sound to avoid British patrols. She had then steered north-west at high speed to get clear of the Norwegian coast. (The *Eckholdt* had been unable to keep up with her in the heavy head sea and had been forced to turn back.) Thus it was that the Swordfish torpedo bombers that arrived over Trondheim at dawn on 11 April, expecting to find a heavy cruiser, found only two small ships that appeared to be destroyers. They attacked both and thought that they had hit one but a number of weapons had been seen to explode prematurely, apparently on a shoal.[13]

In the far north, the *Zenker* and the *Giese* left harbour as night was falling and looked cautiously into the Vestfjord. It was not as dark as they had hoped and the shadows of British ships were visible on the horizon. Bey pushed forward as close as he dared but found no way round them. He put down smoke to cover his retreat and returned to Narvik. That night, the staffs abandoned plans for the combined breakthrough that they had believed, from the first, to be the key to the survival of the surface fleet. The battleships were 300 miles west of the Lofotens steering for a rendezvous on the Norwegian coast. Relieved of his responsibilities for the safe recovery of the Narvik and Trondheim groups, Admiral Lütjens altered to seaward and started a dash for home giving the British fleet as wide a berth as possible.

Time had done nothing to relieve the anxieties of the German staffs. Submarine activity in the Skagerrak had remained intense. There had been three more merchant ship casualties in the approaches to Oslofjord and, in a stunning blow to the Navy's future plans, the *Lützow*, hurrying home from Oslo to prepare for her Atlantic sortie, had been crippled by a British submarine. The pocket battleship had spent an uncomfortable night drifting helplessly off the Skaw until a flotilla of minesweepers and a Danish tug had arrived to tow her in. The use of this valuable ship in *Weserübung* had been 'a definite strategic error'.[14] And it was becoming clear just how comprehensively the transport plan had failed. Of the five 'Export' units sent to Narvik, only the *Jan Wellem* had reached its destination. The second tanker, the *Kattegat*, and two freighters (*Rauenfels* and *Alster*) were missing, and a third had put in to Bergen. The export units sent to Trondheim were missing too. Crisis measures were being put in hand. OKW was urging General Dietl to press ahead with the construction of a runway near Narvik using civilian labour. Raeder was calling for the immediate despatch of supplies and reinforcements via the Swedish rail network and, at Hitler's behest, the Naval Staff was investigating the possibility of running supplies to the northern ports by submarine.[15]

An attempt by the Admiralty to organize a new attack on the German ships in Narvik foundered on the day following the battle when the light cruiser *Penelope*, diverted to investigate rumours of German reinforcements approaching via the Inner Leads, grounded in the approaches to the port of Bodø and sustained serious underwater damage. (That night she joined the crippled *Hotspur* in the Skjelfjord which had now become the forward repair and fuelling base for British ships.) Any further attempt on Narvik thus had to wait for the arrival of the C-in-C.

Admiral Forbes left Trondheim during the afternoon of 11 April and set course for the Lofotens, hoping that Narvik would provide his carrier aircraft with the targets that had so far eluded them. Best estimates suggested at least one cruiser in the inner fjords, five or six destroyers (some damaged) and the merchant shipping supporting the landing force. And it seemed possible that with so much at stake, the two battleships – missing since their engagement with the *Renown* two days before – might make a new appearance in the area.

During his passage northwards Forbes again attracted the attention of the Luftwaffe. Although his major units escaped damage the destroyer *Eclipse* was crippled and he was obliged to send her home with a second destroyer standing by. There was another flurry of excitement in the evening when signals intelligence pointed to a German rendezvous to the west of the Fleet and some 200 miles offshore. Forbes altered course to investigate but found nothing. Next morning it became apparent that the *Gneisenau*, the *Scharnhorst* and the *Hipper* were in fact some 600 miles to the south and within a few hours steaming of German bases. As he observed a little ruefully in his report to the Admiralty, the German squadron 'had been able to pass all the way from the Lofotens to the Skagerrak without being sighted by any of our air or surface vessels'.[16] Bomber and Coastal Commands put together the largest striking force yet launched against a naval target but visibility off the Danish coast was less than a mile and nothing was found.[17]

Forbes reached the Lofotens during the evening of 12 April. He sent the *Repulse* home to fuel and detached the *Valiant* to cover the passage of the troop convoy that was now getting ready to sail and, with the *Rodney*, *Warspite*, *Renown*, *Furious* and six destroyers, prepared to renew the assault on Narvik.

The air attacks launched that evening were no more effective than the earlier attack on Trondheim. Geography and weather were against them. Aircrew had no mountain flying experience and in the absence of proper maps, had been forced to rely on photographic copies of Admiralty charts that revealed almost nothing about the lie of the land. And, at the C-in-C's suggestion, they had been equipped for dive-bombing, a role for which the Swordfish was barely suitable and for which the aircrews were largely untrained. The leading squadron, which arrived over the target in early evening, pressed home its attack on the ships in Narvik and claimed four hits. In reality, the damage that they caused was trivial.[18] The second squadron, which left the *Furious* forty minutes later, ran into low cloud and driving snow. It was forced down to 100 feet in order to remain in touch with the surface and, wisely, turned about and returned to the carrier. It landed on, in darkness, at 2030. But Forbes was already preparing to renew

64

the attack on Narvik using the battleship *Warspite* and a force of nine destroyers.

The Admiralty's instruction to 'clean up' enemy naval forces in Narvik using a battleship betrayed the insecurities of a naval hierarchy sensitive to the charge that it had responded to the greatest crisis of the war with half measures.[19] The deployment of a capital ship into confined waters had no recent precedent and could hardly have taken place if flag officers had not, as a conscious decision, turned a blind eye to risks that had dominated naval thinking for a generation. Although the C-in-C may have been justified in assuming that the Germans could not, as yet, pose a significant air threat in the far north, the submarine threat was seriously, perhaps deliberately, down-played and it is hard to believe that, if U-boat numbers had been accurately assessed, the operation could have taken the form that it did. Yet Operation DW was to achieve the aim set for it in full and at comparatively modest cost. That it did not attract the penalties that twentieth-century orthodoxy prescribed was due to efficient scouting, to the ferocity of the British attack, to the legacy of the first battle, to the absence of a coherent defensive plan and perhaps also to the critical defects that were then affecting the fusing and depth mechanisms of German torpedoes.[20] Not long after these events, a frustrated BdU withdrew his U-boats from operations in Norway pending a resolution of the problem.

Vice Admiral Whitworth, who had appealed to the C-in-C for permission to lead the attack and who had transferred his flag to the *Warspite* during the dark hours, assembled his forces in the Vestfjord at 0730 on the morning of 13 April, and took them northwards towards the narrows under a gloomy overcast which brought occasional pulses of rain and wet snow. Cloud covered the tops of the mountains and snow lay thick down to the water's edge. Visibility was about 10 miles. Three destroyers with sweep gear streamed took station ahead of the *Warspite* to provide protection against mines, while six more (four of them ships of the celebrated Tribal class) formed an advanced screen. Aircraft from the *Furious* had orders to provide anti-submarine patrols, help suppress the defences in the narrows and shift their attack to warships and batteries in the inner fjords as the *Warspite* and her escorts closed their objective.[21] It was to be an essay in overwhelming force.

There was a submarine scare as the *Warspite* approached Tranøy but prompt action by the escort forced the U-boat down and no attack developed. The force entered the narrows towards noon passing the blackened bow of the *Rauenfels* on the starboard hand. There was no sign of the expected shore defences and the aircraft tasked to attack them were sent home. First contact with the enemy was established soon afterwards when the *Warspite*'s Swordfish aircraft, scouting ahead of the force, found a

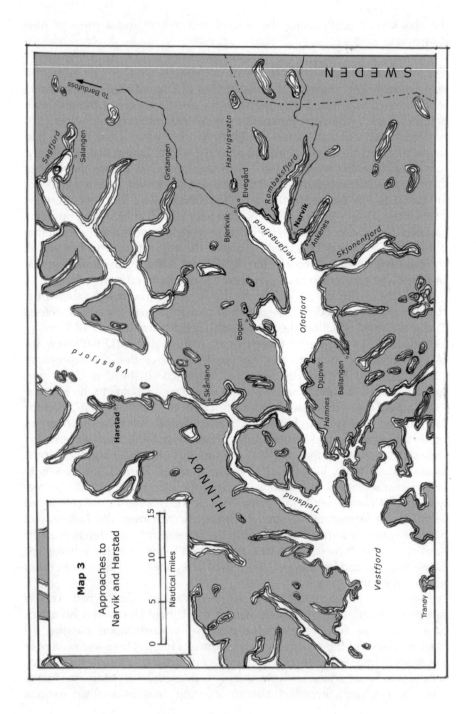

Map 3

Approaches to
Narvik and Harstad

Nautical miles

0 5 10 15

SWEDEN

To Bardufoss

Sagfjord

Salangen

Gratangen

Hartvigsvatn

Bjerkvik

Elvegård

Rombaksfjord

Narvik

Ankenes

Herjangsfjord

Skjonenfjord

Ofotfjord

Bogen

Djupvik

Ballangen

Skånland

Hamnes

Vågsfjord

Harstad

HINNØY

Tjeldsund

Vestfjord

Tranøy

German destroyer off Hamnes and, minutes later, a second enemy a little beyond the first. The aircraft continued eastward, looking into Ballangen Bay and Skjonenfjord without result before finding and reporting a third destroyer off the Narvik harbour entrance. It had then visited the Herjangsfjord and in the northern reaches found a U-boat riding at anchor. It had delivered a pair of anti-submarine bombs with perfect accuracy and, twenty minutes later, was back scouting ahead of the Fleet.[22]

By now the first of the contacts reported by the aircraft had been visible from the forward screen and the *Bedouin*, leading on the southern wing of the formation had opened fire. The enemy had turned away and withdrawn to the eastward, keeping at the margins of visibility and firing the occasional shot. But the aircraft had returned in time to report that the second destroyer was making for the small bay at Djupvik on the southern shore, a place where it would be hidden from view and which seemed tailor-made for an ambush. Warned of what lay ahead, the destroyers on the southern wing (*Bedouin*, *Punjabi* and *Eskimo*) trained their guns on the bearing and, as the target came into view round the headland, smothered it with fire. They then launched torpedoes and moved on, barely slackening their pace, leaving the ship a smoking wreck. The *Warspite* completed their work twenty minutes later with salvos from her 15-inch guns.[23]

The action in the van meanwhile had become more general. Hampered by poor visibility and by the smoke of the destroyers' guns, it had been hard for observers on the bridge of the *Warspite* to establish what was going on. They had counted at least four enemy ships. They seemed to be sweeping to and fro across the fjord bringing guns and torpedoes to bear and turning as they approached the limit of their run. At 1318, the aircraft had warned of a torpedo salvo approaching from ahead but the weapons had passed clear to port and exploded harmlessly on the northern shore. There had been few opportunities for the battleship to use her guns. The enemy's movements had been too unpredictable and the forward visibility too poor to offer much chance of success. The enemy's gunfire had posed little threat. The *Hero*, still sweeping ahead of the *Warspite* and restricted in her ability to manoeuvre, had felt uncomfortable during this phase of the battle but, after almost an hour under fire, only one small splinter had come on board.[24]

Any attempt to reconstruct what was in Erich Bey's mind at this critical time must include an element of speculation. But his general plan had been to distribute his flotilla round the bays and inlets of the Ofotfjord in the hope of confusing an attacker and reaping some of the benefits that a dispersed formation had shown in the earlier battle. It seems likely too that during this interlude he had identified a site where, as a last resort, he could scuttle his ships and get his men to safety. His ship's companies had done much in the three days since the first battle to restore the fighting capabilities of their ships. Three that had been seriously damaged on 10 April had been brought back to some semblance of operational readiness and their tubes and magazines had been replenished with weapons salvaged from the cripples. But there had been setbacks too: of the four destroyers that had emerged from the first battle unscathed, two had since been damaged in grounding incidents, one (the *Koellner*) so seriously that she was fit only for static defence. (Bey intended to conceal her in the outer fjord where her guns and torpedoes would cover the narrows.) In all, he would now dispose of six mobile units and two that were largely or, in the case of the *Roeder*, completely immobile. Like Bonte before him he seems to have relied on intelligence from Group West and on reports from the submarine force to provide warning of attack. He had ordered no patrols himself but he had demanded a meeting with the senior U-boat captain and, during the early hours of 11 April, the *U46* had berthed on the *Zenker* and a common channel of communication had been agreed.[25]

The Narvik force was to find itself woefully unprepared for what was to come. When Group West's urgent warning reached Bey just after ten o'clock on the morning of 13 April, his ships were still in harbour, some with their furnaces cold. He sailed the *Künne* and the *Koellner* at once, the latter much too late to reach the position planned for her and she soon fell victim to British fire. And when Bey left harbour a little after midday with *Zenker*, *Lüdemann* and *von Arnim* to join the *Künne* in the outer fjord, the *Thiele* and the *Giese* were still trying to raise steam; he therefore left them behind with orders to follow as soon as they could. Despite his best intentions, the submarine force received no warning at all. The *U64* had remained at anchor in the Herjangsfjord with fatal consequences. The *U51*, fuelling from the *Jan Wellem*, had assumed that the panic signalled another air attack; she had submerged and taken no further part in the proceedings.

Bey improvised a defence as best he could. When he first made contact with the enemy, he tried to attack through smoke but the screen provided little cover and he was forced back by the weight of enemy fire. He had settled for a long-range artillery duel until a better opportunity presented itself. By 1330, he had fallen back as far as Narvik itself. Here, the *Thiele* had finally joined him, and with the mountain walls closing in and scope for concerted action diminishing, he had decided on a final throw of the dice. At 1340, the *Zenker* launched the last of her torpedoes at a group of destroyers on the northern wing. (The *Warspite* recorded seeing one of them detonate on the shoreline 20° on her port bow.) Next, the *von Arnim* had lunged forward and launched two salvos in quick succession, the first at the same group of destroyers and the second at the *Warspite*, whose bulk was just visible beyond the screen. (One weapon had passed underneath the *Cossack* without exploding adding to a growing list of such incidents, and the battleship had been forced to take avoiding action although, in the event, no weapon had passed near enough to be seen.) The *von Arnim* had attracted a hail of fire during this manoeuvre but had retired eastwards to be harassed (though not damaged) by Swordfish from the *Furious* that had arrived over Narvik as the battle reached its climax.[26] The *Künne* and the *Thiele* had aimed their torpedoes at the destroyers on the southern wing and followed up with a barrage from their 5-inch guns. Their shells had fallen close. Near misses had peppered the *Bedouin* and the *Punjabi* and both had been forced to make a radical change of course to spoil the enemy's aim.

By 1350, gun crews in the *Zenker* and the *von Arnim* were loading star shell and practice ammunition. With further resistance impossible, Bey ordered a general retirement on the Rombaksfjord, a narrow cleft in the mountains to the north and east of Narvik, which he had chosen as the final resting place for his flotilla. Four ships started in that direction putting down smoke to cover their movements while the *Künne*, cut off from the rest and with the *Eskimo* and the *Forester* in hot pursuit, retired in the direction of the Herjangsfjord. There, just after two o'clock, her captain put her on the rocks. The two pursuers had closed to a range of 5,000 yards from which distance the ship looked untouched. They fired torpedoes and watched as a tall column of smoke rose above the wreck. The *Eskimo* had then turned for the Rombaksfjord with the signal 'enemy in sight' flying at her yardarm.

An action of a grimmer kind had meanwhile been developing on the southern flank where, on passing Ankenes, the *Bedouin* and the *Punjabi* had come under fire from the *Giese*, lying across the harbour entrance, and from the *Roeder* moored at the Post Pier. Immobilized by machinery breakdown, the *Giese* had fought to the bitter end and forced the *Punjabi* to retire from the battle to douse fires and repair a shattered steam pipe before she was herself reduced to a silent, smoking ruin by the combined firepower of the *Bedouin* and the *Warspite*. (She lost eighty-three men killed, more than the rest of the German flotilla combined and matching the numbers killed with Bonte in the *Heidkamp*, three days before.) The *Roeder* had seen the Post Pier reduced to rubble by torpedoes intended for the *Giese* and by the *Warspite*'s heavy shells, but her guns had survived intact to savage the *Cossack* which, shortly after two o'clock, had nosed into the harbour to eliminate this stubborn pocket of resistance. In the space of a few minutes, the *Cossack* had taken seven hits, lost power and drifted ashore near Ankenes on the opposite side of the harbour. (And there she had stayed, the target for a desultory fire from the shore, until the next high water when, after much plugging of leaks and shedding of topweight, her captain had finally succeeded in getting her free.) The *Roeder* had emptied her magazines in this final encounter. Her gun crews had gone ashore to join their shipmates in a railway tunnel overlooking the harbour leaving only a small demolition party behind.

On the other side of the Narvik peninsula, the surviving German destroyers had negotiated the Strømmen narrows and entered the inner part of the Rombaksfjord, a dark defile, less than half a mile wide with cliffs rising steeply on either hand. Bey had taken the *Zenker* and the *von Arnim* straight to the head of the fjord leaving the *Lüdemann* and the *Thiele* to delay the British advance. The *Eskimo* (leading the chase) had emerged from the narrows to be confronted by two German ships, covering her approach with guns and torpedoes. She had taken the offensive at once and, with the *Forester* and the *Hero* in support, had quickly silenced the *Lüdemann*'s guns. (The German had launched a final salvo of torpedoes towards the narrows and retired out of sight towards the head of the fjord.) Bold manoeuvres in that narrow space had been sufficient to keep the *Eskimo* clear of the pattern but not to evade a torpedo fired soon afterwards by the *Thiele*. This weapon had hit home under 'A' mounting destroying the hull structure beneath it and allowing the bow of the ship as far aft as 'B' gun deck to hinge downwards at an angle of 60°. But the fight had continued with barely a pause and at 1500, her magazines empty and her bridge reduced to a bloody shambles, the *Georg Thiele*, the ship that had turned the tables on Warburton-Lee three days earlier, had driven herself hard onto the southern shore. Her momentum had carried her bow several yards up the rocky beach and her ship's company had been able to step onto the rocks dry-shod. The *Eskimo* had backed out through the narrows dragging her collapsed forepart and her anchors and cables behind her.

With the crippling of the *Eskimo* the British attack stalled. The dilemma facing the ships assembling in the inner fjord was spelt out by Commander J.A. McCoy of the *Bedouin* who, at 1520, warned Whitworth that if the surviving Germans still had torpedoes they were in a position of great tactical advantage.[27] His worries found little sympathy in the flagship. 'The torpedo menace must be accepted,' Whitworth replied. 'Enemy must be destroyed without delay. Take *Kimberley*, *Forester*, *Hero* and *Punjabi* under your orders and organise attack sending most serviceable destroyer first. Ram or board if necessary.'[28]

But while McCoy and the Admiral had been conferring, the *Hero*, the *Icarus* and the *Kimberley* had made their way to the head of the fjord without mishap and, finding that the enemy did not return their fire, had sent a boarding party to investigate. As the boats were approaching, one of the ships capsized, revealing another, also scuttled, behind her. But a third seemed intact and they made their way on board. They found the ship deserted and resting on the bottom with the engine room flooded. The charred remains of secret books were still smouldering on the bridge.

The ship was the *Hans Lüdemann*. Some wanted to tow her off and salvage her but time was pressing and they finished her off with a torpedo.

That night in Berlin, gloom descended on the Tirpitzufer. The Naval Staff war diarist wrote this. 'This evening a serious and depressed mood marks the Naval Staff's impression of events. Ten of our most modern destroyers, half of our powerful and most urgently required destroyer arm, lie shot to pieces, damaged or sunk in Ofot and Rombaken Fjords. Narvik has proved a "mousetrap" for our forces.'[29]

With the final destruction of the German flotilla, latent worries about the *Warspite*'s safety began to reassert themselves. An officer rescued from the *Giese* had spoken of several U-boats being present and although he was suspected of exaggeration it had been impossible to dismiss his statement out of hand. A Dornier flying boat had put in an appearance during the afternoon and, by early evening, a formation of up to a dozen aircraft had been seen circling to the westward, although no air attack had yet developed. At 1830, Whitworth began a hasty withdrawal from Narvik with a screen of four destroyers leaving the *Kimberley* to guard the *Cossack* and the *Punjabi* to escort the damaged *Eskimo*.

But nervous tension had quickly given way to an emotion bordering on euphoria. A prompt attack on a submarine contact by the *Foxhound* soon after leaving Narvik, and reports from shore that the U-boat concerned had been seen leaving the fjord, encouraged Whitworth to conclude that the situation for U-boats in narrow waters with destroyers operating overhead was 'not very enviable'.[30] He had been getting reports about the plight of the wounded in the *Cossack* and the *Punjabi* and, emboldened by his new assessment of the U-boat threat and by his continued immunity from air attack, he turned back towards Narvik and established a rendezvous for the transfer of the wounded. More significant for the longer term, however, was the growing conviction that a unique opportunity was being missed.

There had been nothing in Whitworth's orders about putting a landing party ashore. (The operation had been conceived, once again, in narrowly naval terms.) But when, that afternoon, opposition in Narvik Bay had finally subsided, Whitworth had told the C-in-C that he was 'investigating the possibility of occupying the town'. There had been little to guide him bar the advice of the *Cossack* which had been pressing strongly for a landing, and the experience of the *Foxhound* which had attracted small-arms fire while approaching to board the *Roeder* and had quickly backed away.[31] In the event, Whitworth had abandoned the idea since his ability to defend even a small foothold in the harbour area against a force of 2,000 well-trained German troops, had seemed wholly dependent on the guns of his ships, including those of the *Warspite*. And these he had not been prepared to leave behind. He was becoming certain, on the other hand, that the *Warspite*'s cannonade and the destruction of the German flotilla had left the enemy confused and demoralized, and that a 'trained and organised military force, ready to land directly the naval engagement had ceased' would have been able to establish itself so strongly that the capture of Narvik would have become a foregone conclusion. As the hours passed, Whitworth became convinced that the expeditionary force that was on its way to Norway should proceed direct to Narvik. At 2210, he signalled the C-in-C as follows:

> My impression is that enemy forces in Narvik were thoroughly frightened as a result of today's action and that the presence of *Warspite* was the chief cause of this. I recommend that the town be occupied without delay by the main landing force.[32]

Next morning he expanded his views for the benefit of the Admiralty:

> I am convinced that Narvik can be taken by direct assault, without fear of meeting serious opposition on landing. I consider that the main landing force need only be small but that it must have the support of Force B or one of similar composition.[33]

After completing the transfer of wounded and after distributing the survivors from the *Hardy* and the British merchant ships among his destroyers, Whitworth sent the *Cossack* and the *Eskimo* under escort to Skjelfjord and withdrew westward, leaving the *Kimberley* and the *Ivanhoe* to watch developments in the inner fjords.

Chapter 6

The Dilemmas of High Command

Whitworth's recommendations reached London at a time when the 'Narvik first' consensus hammered out in the MCC was coming under increasing challenge. The Foreign Office, preoccupied with developments in southern Norway and with the susceptibility of Sweden to German pressure, had led the attack – the familiar fault line in the Chamberlain Cabinet was as marked as ever – but the case for concentration of effort on a single objective had been further weakened by romantic notions about the potential of amphibious operations on the Norwegian coast. Churchill had brought the two ideas together in a letter to the Prime Minister on 11 April. He had wanted to induce the Swedish Government to enter the war on the side of the Allies by declaring a 'common cause' and by advertising the fact that Allied troops would be active on the Scandinavian 'Peninsula'. The historical analogy had been unmistakeable.[1]

In the MCC that evening, Ironside came under pressure to consider operations against Trondheim. The city's strategic importance as the gateway to Sweden was self-evident but this, he explained, would be a complex operation and one that would have to be ruled out until the full extent of the 'Rupert' commitment was known. The Committee agreed that the planning staffs would examine the options in central Norway under the label 'Maurice' but that active preparations would have to wait. But the debate continued outside the meeting and, sometime after midnight, Churchill led a gaggle of admirals and air marshals across the road to the War Office in an attempt to persuade Ironside to send the second 'Rupert' brigade to Namsos, a small timber port 100 miles north-east of Trondheim, in order to 'stake a claim' to the larger objective. Ironside refused to concede. It came out during the course of discussion that Mackesy's departure for Narvik had been delayed and that the Navy was already planning to land a party at Namsos to make contact with the people ashore. There were angry words; but the CIGS must have seen clearly enough which way things were moving for, that night, he sent for that ancient storm petrel, Major General Adrian Carton de Wiart VC, a much decorated (and much mutilated) hero of the Somme who, after more than a decade managing a sporting estate in the Prypet Marshes, was now commanding the Midland Territorial Division from his headquarters in Oxford.[2]

Dealing with these matters in Cabinet next morning (12 April) Churchill said that he wanted to see Namsos occupied as soon as possible, though not at the expense of Narvik. The Prime Minister jumped at the idea since the Swedes had been stressing the importance of Trondheim, and since Namsos seemed a good place to start. The groundswell of opinion in favour of change increased as the day progressed. During a visit to the Prime Minister's office, Sir James Grigg (Permanent Secretary at the War Office) referred openly to the growing feeling among his peers that the Allies ought to be concentrating on Trondheim rather than Narvik. 'We must get the PM to take a hand in this,' he told Colville, 'before Winston and Tiny [Ironside] go and bugger up the whole war.' In a later meeting of the War Cabinet, Halifax drew attention to telegrams from Sir Cecil Dormer, the British Minister in Norway, calling for early military operations in the southern part of the country. These, he declared, would have far greater political impact than operations in the arctic north. The Germans were pushing north from Oslo and south from Trondheim; if they met, the whole of southern Norway would fall into German hands.[3]

In an attempt to stem the flood, Churchill warned that, without adequate preparation, an opposed landing at Trondheim could end in a 'bloody repulse'. Preparations for Narvik were well in hand and the prospects for success good. The staffs, he continued, were working on plans for minor landings in central Norway and he would be reporting on these shortly. That night he drafted a directive for the Joint Planning Staff setting out his vision for amphibious warfare on the Norwegian littoral. 'Rupert', he said, was settled; nothing would 'mar its integrity or delay its speed'. But it was of 'very high political importance to act upon the mid-Norwegian coast' in order to put heart into the Norwegian resistance and to influence Swedish decisions. 'The use of flexible amphibious power,' he concluded, 'may give remarkable rewards.'[4]

The rearguard action to keep 'Rupert' at the top of the Government's priorities continued at the next Cabinet meeting. The Foreign Secretary declared that the most important thing was to secure Trondheim and the Norwegian railways. The CIGS replied that this could only be done if further troops were withdrawn from France. (The Prime Minister was in two minds; he fully understood the importance of Narvik but was also 'profoundly impressed' with the arguments in favour of Trondheim.) In spite of the stance he had taken the night before, Churchill was 'very apprehensive' about proposals to weaken 'Rupert' in order to undertake 'a much more speculative affair' in central Norway. Halifax warned that without firm assurances of help the Swedes and Norwegians might collapse. In the end, Churchill conceded that Narvik could be put on hold for the moment and undertook to seek French agreement to the diversion of the Chasseurs to central Norway. Cadogan, who had supported Halifax at the meeting, recalled that Churchill had made 'interminable speeches' but that they had wrung concessions from him. He later congratulated himself on having purged the First Lord and the Cabinet of the 'Narvik obsession'; it would now be possible to focus all attention on Trondheim which, in Scandinavian eyes, was the only place that mattered.[5]

The annihilation of the German destroyers in Narvik and Admiral Whitworth's (speculative) remarks on the demoralization of the German landing force made the shift in priorities inevitable. Churchill was full of exuberance on the night of the 13th and things that had once seemed impossible were now referred to as if they were accomplished facts. Even Ironside seems to have conceded that Narvik might be little more than a mopping-up operation. It was agreed at the MCC that, if further information 'justified the assumption' that a landing at Narvik would be unopposed, the Admiralty and the War Office acting together could divert the second brigade of the Narvik force to Namsos without further reference to the Committee. The difficulties were acknowledged; the Brigade Commander would have no orders and the troops would have no maps. But none of this would matter if Carton de Wiart was flown to Namsos in time to meet the Brigade as it arrived. The CAS promised to have a flying boat standing by. [6]

But things had not stopped there. If Narvik could be taken by direct assault in the way that Whitworth had suggested, there was no reason why the Navy could not pull off a similar stunt elsewhere. It was further agreed that, in view of the urgent need to occupy Trondheim, the Joint Planning Staff would examine the possibility that part of 'Maurice' could be put ashore in the city itself. But these modest steps forward were not enough for Churchill. In a second late-night confrontation with the CIGS he insisted that the time for decision had come and, riding rough shod over Ironside's objections, demanded that the rear half of the Narvik convoy should now be diverted to Namsos. The CIGS claimed later that he had protested 'with some heat' but that he had been obliged to yield to the authority of the MCC Chairman. What seems certain is that this second midnight meeting marked the point at which Ironside, isolated and exhausted, felt that he could resist the political pressures no longer and resigned himself to the dismemberment of 'Rupert' and to the opening of a new front in central Norway.[7]

In Cabinet on the Sunday morning Churchill referred to unconfirmed reports that the Germans were retreating from Narvik and being rounded up by the Norwegians. He said that he could now take a more optimistic view of operations in the Trondheim area and that the staffs were examining the possibility of a direct attack on the city. He had spoken to Reynaud on the telephone and had been given a free hand on the employment of the Chasseurs. The forces available would now include the second brigade from 'Rupert', three battalions of Chasseurs Alpins with the possibility of more French troops later and Maurice force, a total of 23,000 men. Against this the German defenders could muster only 3,500 and some of these had already been drawn northward towards Namsos.[8]

The executive order came late that evening after further discussion by the Chiefs of Staff. Convoy NP1, five transports carrying 24th Guards Brigade, 146th Infantry Brigade and large numbers of specialist troops, had left Cape Wrath twenty-four hours earlier escorted by the ships of the 18th Cruiser Squadron. The *Valiant*, the *Vindictive* (fleet repair ship) and six more destroyers had joined off the Shetlands. At 1907 on the Sunday evening, the Admiralty ordered Admiral Layton to divide the convoy. Two big transports, the *Chobry* and the *Empress of Australia*, escorted by the *Manchester*, *Birmingham*, *Cairo* and three destroyers, altered course for Namsos while the rest continued as planned for the Lofotens. Narvik, it seemed, was as good as taken; London could safely turn its attention to the larger prize – Trondheim.

Pound and Ironside had selected the leaders of the 'Rupert' expedition with little thought as to the compatibility of the two men. Major General P.J. Mackesy DSO, a capable if rather stiff-necked soldier who had served with distinction in Russia during the civil war and later as a brigade commander in Palestine, had been close to the Norwegian problem since the days of 'Avonmouth' and had become familiar with every nuance of government policy. After weathering successive changes of plan he had finally sailed for Harstad in the cruiser *Southampton* with two companies of Scots Guards to make contact with Norwegian forces and to arrange for the reception of 'Rupert'. His orders at the time of sailing had told him to expect the rest of 24th Guards Brigade and the three battalions of 146th Infantry Brigade thirty hours behind him; two more British infantry battalions would follow within the week and the first elements of the Chasseurs a few days after that.

'Ginger' Boyle, Admiral of the Fleet the Earl of Cork and Orrery, had replaced Admiral Evans at the last minute. (Evans's special skills had been needed on an Allied military mission to Stockholm.) Cork had been present at the meeting of the MCC on the night of 10 April and after a second perfunctory meeting with the First Lord on the afternoon of the 11th had left for Rosyth on the overnight train, and hoisted his flag in the *Aurora* the following morning. The appointment of so senior an officer was highly unusual. Cork was sixty-seven years old and senior to the C-in-C. He had been unemployed at the start of the war and had left his last sea command more than five years before. He owed his appointment to his availability and to the patronage of the First Lord, for when recalled to the Admiralty to work on Plan 'Catherine' (a project close to Churchill's heart), he had quickly shown that he had lost none of the fire and energy on which he had built his reputation.[9]

Mackesy had arrived off Harstad early on the Sunday morning (14 April). He had been unsure of his reception and had kept his troops below decks. But his precautions had been unnecessary – he had been warmly received and the authorities ashore had soon provided him with a broad appreciation of the military situation. Harstad itself, situated on the island of Hinnøy at the head of the Lofoten chain, did not appear to be threatened but German forces had, it seemed, pushed northwards from Narvik in the direction of Bardufoss and Tromsø, and were being held by elements of the Norwegian 6th Division at Gratangen where the road touched the head of the fjord. Aware of the need to sustain Norwegian morale and recognizing the importance of holding Bardufoss, site of a regimental depot and a small airfield, Mackesy had at once crossed to the mainland and landed his half battalion of Scots Guards in the Sagfjord (a deep indentation some 10 miles north of Gratangen) where they would be in a position to act as a reserve. He had then returned to Harstad to prepare for the arrival of the convoy.

Cork had sailed for Harstad at noon on 12 April, expecting to arrive soon after the General, but while approaching the Lofotens he had received Whitworth's signal expressing the conviction that Narvik could be taken by direct assault. Determined to profit from the demoralization of the German landing force, he had altered course for the Skjelfjord and pressed the *Southampton* to meet him there with a view to making a landing at Narvik with Mackesy's troops and a force of 200 seamen and marines, drawn from the ships present in the area.[10] But his message had not arrived in time to prevent the landing of the Scots Guards; nor had his bold suggestion found unqualified support in London. That evening he had received a signal from the Admiralty stressing that the naval and military commanders should 'be together and act together' and that no attack should be made 'except in common'.[11] He had sailed once again for Harstad and had met the incoming convoy at the entrance to Andfjord on the Monday morning. He had made something of a grand entrance – as the convoy approached its destination, the destroyers *Brazen* and *Fearless* had gained contact with a U-boat and blown it to the surface with a well-placed depth-charge pattern. The destroyers had pulled most of the crew out of the water – some of them were reported to have been screaming horribly –

77

and they had also recovered a chart showing the U-boat dispositions for 'Weserübung'.

The two leaders of the expedition met that afternoon. There was no concealing at this first meeting the serious differences between them. Cork had been looking for an immediate assault on Narvik against what he assumed was a disorganized and demoralized defence. Instead, he had met a General who was by no means convinced that the morale and effectiveness of the German defenders had been critically damaged and whose effective fighting strength had just been halved by the diversion of 146th Infantry Brigade to Namsos. He had found, moreover, that the expedition had been loaded for the peaceful occupation of a friendly and organized port, that it would not be ready for operations for several days and that the General's orders, issued just prior to sailing, appeared to preclude any attempt at an opposed landing. As Cork remarked in his report to the Admiralty three months later, the two men had left the United Kingdom with 'diametrically opposite views as to what was required'.[12] There had been no alternative but to disembark 24th Guards Brigade and its impedimenta and to put it into some kind of fighting order.

Disembarkation had started that afternoon. Muddle and confusion, the product of sweeping decisions made in Whitehall, had soon become apparent. Stores and equipment belonging to 146th Infantry Brigade had turned up at Harstad. Captain L.E.H. Maund, the naval Chief of Staff, had been astonished to meet a brigadier whose brigade had gone to Namsos.[13] (The man had shown little interst in the progress of disembarkation; he had just wanted a destroyer to take him south.) The harbour had proved too small to accommodate the transports and they had been sent to the nearest suitable anchorage at Bygden Bay, 10 miles away across the fjord. It had thus been necessary to ferry men and material to Harstad in destroyers and in several dozen local fishing craft hired for the purpose, a laborious and time-consuming process. (The expedition was to become heavily dependent on Norwegian *skøyter* – or 'puffers' – despite their tendency to disappear during air raids and not to return afterwards.[14]) Ashore, troops had found off-road movement impossible and night temperatures that were unimaginably bitter. Accommodation in a town where newcomers soon outnumbered inhabitants by two to one had come under acute pressure. There had been a serious shortage of storage space and dockside areas had become heavily congested. But in spite of all difficulties and in spite of the best efforts of the Luftwaffe, which had put in an appearance during the first afternoon, the landing had progressed steadily until, by nightfall on 16 April the entire expedition was ashore.

While unloading was still in progress, Cork told London of his discussions with Mackesy and broke the news that an immediate assault on Narvik appeared out of the question. Churchill (who had looked on Narvik

78

as a fait accompli and whose ambitions had shifted to Trondheim) was scornful. The General, he told the MCC on the morning of 17 April, seemed content to take up a couple of unoccupied positions on the road to Narvik and wait there until the snow melted. His reply to the Admiral, approved by the Committee, referred to a 'damaging deadlock' at Narvik and to the 'neutralisation of one of our best brigades'. The matter was 'most urgent' he asserted; it was no use the General waiting for the Chasseurs – he was not going to get them – and the *Warspite* would soon be needed elsewhere. Cork was to give his 'full consideration' to an assault on Narvik covered by the guns of the Fleet and send his appreciation to London. The First Lord returned to his theme in a personal message to the Admiral later that night. If he thought that the situation was being 'mishandled' it was his duty to report the matter. In reply Cork explained that the General's actions were fully consistent with the orders he had received from the War Office and that the General and the Brigade Commander (William Fraser) were both opposed to an assault on military grounds, primarily because their men were unable to operate tactically in snow. He (Cork) had felt obliged to accept what had been the unanimous view of the experts.[15]

Next day Mackesy grudgingly agreed to embark in the *Aurora* and to examine the topography and defences of Narvik for himself. 'Very well', he told the War Office, 'we will do what we can.' But he took the opportunity to point out that the diversion of 146th Infantry Brigade made him inferior to the enemy and that he had got no artillery, no anti-aircraft weapons and virtually no mortar ammunition. Operations, he insisted, had to be based on an eastward advance on Narvik along the shores of the Ofotfjord while the Norwegians closed from the north. (He had already taken the decision to proceed on these lines by moving the 1st Battalion Irish Guards to the Bogen Inlet on the north shore.) Tactical movement had to be ruled out for several weeks and, without artillery, offensive operations would remain impossible.[16]

Mackesy made his 'personal reconnaissance' on 20 April. Far from persuading him that a direct attack was feasible, it confirmed him in his view that a landing under present conditions was unthinkable and that naval gunfire with its flat trajectories would be ineffective against the enemy's defences. The chances of a successful landing from destroyers, he told the War Office on his return to Harstad, were 'non-existent' while attempts to land from open boats would involve 'not the neutralisation but the destruction of 24th Guards Brigade'. The Admiral, he said, appeared to be relying on the demoralizing effect of naval gunfire. Those with direct experience of the matter knew that steady troops were not so easily demoralized and that machine-gun detachments soon reappeared once the bombardment had ceased. Furthermore, any bombardment would have to include the town of Navik itself and would involve its civilian inhabitants 'to the highest degree'. This would have grave implications for relations with Norway and, he suggested, should only be undertaken on the direct order of the Cabinet. He said, in conclusion, that the only circumstance that would permit a landing under existing conditions was a German surrender; that he hoped that no action would be taken to force his hand; and that unless he had that assurance he would feel unable to continue.[17] But Churchill had already persuaded his colleagues in the MCC (including Ironside) that progress could only be made if Lord Cork was placed in sole command of operations.

Cork had now become the buffer between an impetuous Churchill and a stubborn and resentful general. In a private letter to the First Lord on the day following this new appointment, he acknowledged that the Army's inertia had been difficult to overcome but he had described some of the genuine difficulties that the expedition was facing. The snow, particularly on northern slopes, was still many feet deep and continuing heavy falls were making matters worse. (He had landed with a party of Royal Marines and tested the conditions for himself.) The big mistake, he suggested, was to have assumed that the force would meet no resistance; the Army had no reserves of ammunition or water but 'tons of stuff and personnel that they do not want'. As for the defences at Narvik, he had flown over the town himself but to little obvious benefit. Everything had been covered in a blanket of snow and it had been impossible to determine the nature of the foreshore. His most pressing need was for fighters since he was 'overmatched' in the air. German reconnaissance was looking into Harstad daily and whenever a transport was in harbour the bombers followed. Sooner or later, a ship was bound to be hit.[18]

Cork's hopes now centred on a bombardment of Narvik to be followed by a reconnaissance in force to test the possibility of landing and, although this compromise attracted little enthusiasm in London, the operation was ordered for 23 April, or the first opportunity thereafter. He encountered bitter opposition from the Army. Mackesy responded to his order with a formal letter stating that there was not an officer or man under his command 'who would not feel shame for himself or his country if thousands of Norwegian men, women and children in Narvik [were] subject to the bombardment proposed'. Cork signalled the text to the Admiralty without comment and the response was savage.[19] 'If this officer appears to be spreading a bad spirit through the higher ranks of the land force,' Churchill replied, 'do not hesitate to relieve him or place him under arrest.' He went on to advise Cork that if he needed to go beyond the bombardment guidelines issued by the Cabinet he should take all necessary steps to alert the civil population and warn the German commander that, if he prevented civilians from leaving the town, he would be held responsible. Cork replied that the occasion for relief or arrest was unlikely to arise and that the town had already been warned in a broadcast from Tromsø that it might be subject to bombardment at any time.[20]

The blizzard conditions that Cork had alluded to in his letter to Churchill had continued without a break, and even on 24 April when the bombardment finally took place, the weather remained 'tempestuous'. The bombarding force assembled for the occasion included the *Warpite*, the cruisers *Effingham*, *Aurora* and *Enterprise*, and a total of ten destroyers. The *Vindictive* was ordered to Bogen Bay to embark the 1st Battalion Irish Guards to exploit the situation if the Germans surrendered. Operations began at dawn. It was the anniversary of the landings at Gallipoli. The *Aurora* and the *Zulu* fired on positions in the Rombaksfjord and later engaged targets in the Herjangsfjord, while the rest concentrated their attacks on the harbour and on 'fixed defence areas' around Narvik itself. Cork directed operations from the *Enterprise* with Mackesy and Fraser beside him. The Germans showed no inclination to surrender. After about three hours Cork called the proceedings to a halt and ordered the Irish Guards to suspend embarkation.

There was no attempt to repeat the experiment. After further heavy falls of snow on 25 April, Cork seems to have accepted that, for the moment, he had little choice but to support the General's plan for the patient invest-ment of Narvik. Late that evening he told the Admiralty that a direct assault appeared impossible and that the plan now was to work eastward from Bogen and Ballangen along both shores of the Ofotfjord. The Chasseurs, due within forty-eight hours, would be employed against German positions in the hills above Bjerkvik and work forward to isolate Narvik from the east. 'The stage,' he concluded, 'would then be set.'[21]

There is little sign that Eduard Dietl, tough infantry soldier and pioneer of mountain warfare, was intimidated by his enemy's preparations. In the days following the naval battles of Narvik he had rallied his men and taken decisive steps to make his beachhead as secure as his limited resources allowed. When he had consolidated his hold on the town, he had pushed forward on the road to Bardufoss; by the time of Mackesy's arrival he had taken Gratangen and occupied high ground at Lapphaugen, 12 miles north of Bjerkvik. Next day he had strengthened his hold on the land-ward approaches to Narvik by surprising a Norwegian company (part of the former Narvik garrison that had been holding a blocking position 15 miles east of the town) and occupying the line of the railway as far as the Swedish border.

He had remained seriously short of heavy weapons. The crisis measures initiated in Berlin had achieved partial success on 13 April when a squadron of Ju-52 transports bringing in a mountain battery had put down on the frozen lake at Hartvigsvatn near the head of the Herjangsfjord.

There had been no further attempts of this kind, however; a handful of obsolete Norwegian aircraft had succeeded in breaking up the surface of the lake and the transports had been unable to get off. Airdrops had continued but, while the weather remained foul and while the Værnes staging post at Trondheim remained isolated, quantities had remained too small to have a significant infuence on events.

The Norwegian depot at Elvegårdsmoen, on the other hand, had given Dietl a plentiful supply of uniforms, small arms and ammunition. The wrecks of the destroyers had provided yet more material and British merchant ships in the harbour had yielded a handful of naval guns. Dietl had thus been able to equip more than 2,000 survivors from the German destroyers and deploy them in defence of his seaward flank. One naval battalion had taken up positions along the eastern shore of the Herjangsfjord, and another had taken responsibility for the 10-mile stretch of railway along the southern shore of the Rombaksfjord. Other naval groups had fleshed out the defences of Narvik itself and of Ankenes, the village on the opposite side of the harbour. Dietl was not going to give up his prize until his defences had been put to the test.

A similar level of sang-froid was not to be found in Hitler's head-quarters. Here, news of the naval battle, growing evidence of Norwegian resistance and the inability of the men on the spot to find a solution to the political impasse in Norway had contributed to a mood of 'panicky excitement'.[22] On 14 April, General Jodl, Head of the OKW Operations Branch and a man more adept than most at handling Hitler's moods, recorded that the Führer had become 'terribly agitated' about the situation in the far north. 'We have had bad luck,' he was reported as saying and he had told von Brauchitsch, the Army C-in-C, that Narvik was lost. Jodl's deputy had later found the Führer, haggard from lack of sleep and hunched in a chair, 'the picture of brooding gloom'.[23] After further bad news during the night of 16 April, Hitler had demanded withdrawal southward or evacuation by air. Jodl had replied that a march south was physically impossible and that an airlift would lead to serious losses and critical damage to Group morale. Later in the day and on Hitler's orders, a professor from Munich (an expert on Norwegian conditions) had been brought in to advise on whether the highlands south of Narvik were passable for mountain troops.[24]

That afternoon, Hitler reached the conclusion that internment was preferable to defeat or surrender and signed an order directing Dietl to evacuate Narvik and cross the border into Sweden. Jodl held on to the signal pending a further attempt to dissuade Hitler from this feeble and unnecessary course, while Brauchitsch sent Dietl a message congratulating him on his promotion to Lieutenant General and expressing full confidence in his ability to hold Narvik come what may. Jodl's delaying action was finally successful; news of Luftwaffe successes in the south and continuing inactivity on the part of the British had made it possible to argue that the threat to Germany's toehold in arctic Norway was less critical than it had seemed. By evening, Jodl had got Hitler's signature on a new telegram instructing Dietl to hold Narvik as long as possible and then, if need be, to retire up the railway into the interior.[25] As a sop to Hitler's *amour propre*, the question of handpicked troops attempting a breakout to the south was left open for further study. Jodl had bought himself some time although with resistance continuing in many parts of the country and with the political question still unresolved, the command crisis was far from over.

While things at Narvik were inching forward at a snail's pace, the campaign in central Norway had been gathering momentum, driven on by Churchill's unbridled energies and by a generation of naval officers imbued with the idea that activity was the first of the military virtues. At dusk on 14 April (the day of Mackesy's arrival in Harstad) 350 seamen and marines from the cruisers *Glasgow* and *Sheffield* had been put ashore at Namsos to forestall a German landing and pave the way for 'Maurice'. The operation was codenamed 'Henry'.

The reports sent back by these early arrivals were less than encouraging. They told of deep snow, poor port facilities, and of a serious shortage of transport; any advance southward by a force larger than a battalion was likely to be slow and difficult to conceal from the air. Captain R.S.G. Nicholson of the destroyer *Somali*, left in Namsos to await the arrival of Carton de Wiart, reported that the facilities for landing and accommodating large numbers of troops were inadequate and warned of a grave risk to the town and to the troop transports arriving there unless command of the air could be assured.[26] The Chiefs of Staff took fright and ordered a delay in disembarkation while alternative sites were investigated.

Next day, Churchill alerted the War Cabinet to these new difficulties, and warned of the 'very hazardous nature' of operations at Namsos because of the terrain, the threat from the air and the state of training of the forces involved. (No one questioned the wisdom of going there.) Halifax expressed disappointment at the delay and stressed the 'great political importance' of an early landing in the Trondheim area. Chamberlain echoed his Foreign Secretary's disappointment but accepted that delay was better than risking a big reverse. That was to be avoided at all costs.[27] In the end, the transports were diverted to Lillesjona some 100 miles further up the coast in the hope of escaping the attention of the Luftwaffe and arrangements were made to lift the troops to Namsos in smaller ships. The landings were delayed until the night of 16 April.

A second minor operation, 'Primrose', had been launched meanwhile against positions to the south of Trondheim. (The original intention had been to create a diversion during the Namsos landings.) Interest had centred initially on Ålesund, an island in the southern approaches to the Romsdalsfjord, and, on 14 April, a landing force of 700 seamen and marines plucked from ships in refit had embarked in the AA sloops *Black Swan*, *Flamingo*, *Aukland* and *Bittern* with three field howitzers, two 4-inch naval guns and a battery of light AA weapons. But under pressure from Norwegian naval authorities, interest had quickly shifted to the Romsdalsfjord itself. The port of Molde on the northern shore held vital ammunition stocks, while Åndalsnes at the head of the fjord offered road and rail access to Trondheim and southwards via the Gudbrandsdal to Oslo. The 'Primrose' sloops, grossly overloaded, had sailed from Rosyth in atrocious weather and had been forced to run for shelter. They had been at anchor off Invergordon when, during the evening of 15 April, they got first intimations that they were being diverted to Åndalsnes to prepare the way for 1,000 men of Brigadier Morgan's 148th Infantry Brigade that would be following close behind them. They were then to put the naval guns ashore at Ålesund and hold that as well.

But Operation 'Hammer', the direct assault on Trondheim, had already begun to occupy centre stage. First hints that London was thinking along these lines had reached the C-in-C in the early hours of 14 April in the bright afterglow of Whitworth's victory. The Admiralty telegram referred to the advantages of a landing in the Trondheimsfjord and asked Admiral Forbes whether naval gunfire could dominate the coastal batteries sufficiently to allow troop transports to pass in safety. The Admiral replied that a battleship, suitably screened and protected, could do so in daylight if supplied with high-explosive ammunition. This, however, was a minor part of the task; the main difficulties would be: (1) to protect troop transports during their passage of the fjord: and (2) to conduct an opposed landing under the levels of air attack that would have to be reckoned with. He doubted whether the operation was feasible unless the Admiralty was prepared to accept heavy losses in troops and transports.[28]

In Cabinet next morning Churchill acknowledged the C-in-C's reservations but chose to stress the positive. The Chasseurs Alpins were 'probably the best troops in the world'. They would be ready in three or four days. By then, the situation in the far north would have been cleared up allowing further high-quality reinforcements to be sent from there.[29] That night he invited the C-in-C to think again. His telegram made it clear that the operation would not take place for seven days and that the interval would allow for 'careful preparation'. The RAF would attack the airfield at Stavanger and the heavy cruiser *Suffolk* would carry out a dawn bombardment to 'put it out of business'. Carrier aircraft would deal with the airfield at Værnes. The final sentence left few doubts as to the signal's authorship. It read, 'Pray, therefore, consider this important project further.'[30] Forbes's reply was conciliatory. His earlier signal, he said, had been misunderstood; he saw no insuperable difficulty from the naval side provided that the troops landed from warships. His main worry had been the defence of unarmed transports during the approach and landing phases. But he asked for an urgent meeting with the DCNS or an admiral of similar standing on his return to Scapa.[31]

But by now Churchill's initiatives were beginning to put Whitehall's decision-making machinery under unbearable strain. During a meeting of the Chiefs of Staff on 15 April, the Secretary of the Committee, General H.L. (Pug) Ismay, had cleared the room of Assistant Secretaries and begged the Chiefs to 'exercise the most rigid self-control ... and at all costs to keep their tempers'. He had later warned Sir Edward Bridges (Cabinet Secretary) that there was every chance of 'a first class row' if the MCC discussed the 'Hammer' question under Churchill's chairmanship.[32] Bridges alerted the Prime Minister and suggested that he might consider taking the chair himself. War Cabinet members, invited to approve hazardous operations without 'the customary written appreciations' by the Chiefs of Staff, were becoming uneasy too and on 16 April, the Prime Minister promised senior colleagues that he would take the chair at the MCC at least for the moment.

It is hard to believe that Churchill welcomed this attempt to clip his wings. But he stepped aside with apparent good grace, having first provided Chamberlain with a comprehensive summary of his views. The landings at Namsos and Åndalsnes, he told the Prime Minister, were diversionary operations designed to confuse the Germans and give heart to the Norwegians. The main attack would be mounted against Trondheim itself once the Navy had quelled the batteries and dealt with the airfields. Dates remained uncertain but 22nd to 23rd April 'might be worked to'. The assault would involve 7,000 to 8,000 of the best troops available. He still hoped that the Guards Brigade from Narvik could arrive in time to join the French. The *Suffolk* would bombard the Stavanger airfield at dawn on 17 April, and on the day of the attack the RAF would harass the place relentlessly.[33] When the meeting convened, Ironside refused to commit himself to a date or to make a statement on troop numbers; these matters were still being studied. Churchill urged that nothing should 'prejudice the effectiveness of the central thrust'. This would be a hazardous but, if successful, a 'brilliant' operation. He stressed the need for 'seasoned troops' and questioned the wisdom of sending the Chasseurs to Namsos. Admiral Pound promised two aircraft carriers and a total of eighty aircraft. The Germans would get two hours warning at the most, he advised, and aircraft from bases in Germany were unlikely to arrive in large numbers until the troops were ashore. The carriers would deal with aircraft based in Norway.[34]

By 17 April, the shape of the coming campaign was becoming clear to Whitehall decision-makers if not always to subordinate commanders. Operation 'Maurice' was already beginning. Two battalions of the 146th Infantry Brigade had reached Namsos during the night of the 16th and the third was expected within hours. Carton de Wiart had arrived to take command and Brigadier Phillips was on his way from Narvik. The General had had a 'rough time' getting in. German fighters had attacked his aircraft as it approached the Namsenfjord and his staff officer had been seriously wounded. But he would be ready to begin his advance on 21 April once the three Chasseur battalions had arrived. He was already in touch with Norwegian forces holding important positions on the rail line to Trondheim. Some Norwegian troops were said to be within 15 miles of the city itself.

The 'Primrose' landing party was expected at Åndalsnes late on 17 April and the two battalions of Morgan's 148th Infantry Brigade at dusk the following day. Under plans now codenamed 'Sickle', Morgan would advance south-east to occupy Dombås, the key rail junction at the head of the Gudbrandsdal, in order to block German reinforcements arriving from Oslo, and prepare for an attack northwards against Trondheim.

'Hammer', now the centrepiece of the campaign, would be a combined operation to force the entrance to Trondheim Fjord, make a landing east of the city and link up with 'Maurice' forces advancing from the north. Churchill had failed in his attempts to divert the Chasseurs to Trondheim (they had continued on course for Namsos) and he had been forced, reluctantly, to accept that the Guards Brigade from Narvik would not be available. The assault force would now include a regular brigade from France (15th Infantry Brigade) and two battalions of Canadian troops with the 147th Infantry Brigade in reserve. The date for the operation was set, provisionally, at 22 April. Orders given to Major General F.E. Hotblack, who was to command the landing force, emphasized the 'paramount need for speed'. Delay, it was said, might have the most serious impact on the course of operations in Scandinavia. A second demi-brigade of Chasseurs would reach Trondheim twenty-four hours after the assault and help consolidate the Allied position.[35]

Churchill's enthusiasm remained undimmed. He had been taken aback, he told the C-in-C, by Mackesy's decision to 'sit down in front of Narvik'. But he remained certain that Hitler's invasion of Norway had been a 'grave strategic blunder'. There were already 25,000 men for a campaign in central Norway and he hoped to get 50,000, regardless of what might happen in Flanders. Everything now centred on the 'assault and capture of Trondheim'; here was an opportunity for a 'deed of fame'.[36]

But opposition to 'Hammer' had been gathering headway. A paper by the Joint Planning Staff taken by the Chiefs of Staff on 15 April had been openly critical. When questioned, Air Commodore Slessor (the senior planner) had acknowledged that Trondheim could be taken by assault but he had gone on to suggest that the Luftwaffe would quickly make the place a liability.[37] He was forcefully reminded by the CIGS that the Cabinet had decided on Trondheim as the only way of saving Norway and that they were there to consider *how* to attack the city, not *whether* to do so.[38] Planning had continued. But the weight of German air power in central Norway was already making itself felt. That same day the *Somali*, acting as Carton de Wiart's communications link with London, had counted eighty-one bombs aimed at her in the space of two hours, although none had fallen close. The *Suffolk* had been less fortunate; the bombardment of Stavanger had continued as planned but the Luftwaffe had made a determined effort to sink her and, thanks to a mix-up over her RAF fighter escort, had nearly succeeded. The C-in-C, had ordered every Skua at Hatston to her relief and had detached the battlecruisers *Renown* and *Repulse* to give her support. In the end, the heavy cruiser had limped into Scapa, steering by main engines and with her quarterdeck awash. She had been beached for essential repairs.

The Fates had been conspiring against 'Hammer' too. Rear Admiral L.E. Holland had duly arrived at Scapa on 18 April to brief the C-in-C on London's latest thinking; but not General Hotblack. The General had been found unconscious the night before at the bottom of the Duke of York's steps and was now in hospital. (A stroke was suspected.) Next day Hotblack's successor, Brigadier H.P. Berney-Ficklin, rushed north to fill the gap, had been seriously injured in a crash landing at Hatston. Two members of his staff had been injured too.

Despite these setbacks, planning had continued in London and Scapa and, by the evening of 19 April, the essentials of the naval plan had been settled. But at noon on the 20th, the order went out cancelling 'Hammer'. It remains hard to pinpoint the exact moment when the Chiefs of Staff shifted their position from one of qualified support to one of uncompromising opposition. What is clear is that on the morning of 19 April they presented the MCC with a new paper giving a dour assessment of the risks and offering a more palatable alternative. Their paper pointed to the extreme complexity of this and similar combined operations, and stressed the need for intelligence gathering, planning and rehearsal. (There had been little time for any of these important preliminaries.) It invited the committee to recognize the serious implications of concentrating virtually the entire Home Fleet in an area where it would face heavy air attack, complained of open speculation in the press and pointed to signs that the Germans had been reinforcing their positions.[39] The strategic aim (the capture of Trondheim) remained unchanged but the unexpected success of the landings at Namsos and Åndalsnes presented the Government with an alternative and less hazardous approach. The Chiefs had proposed abandoning 'Hammer', reinforcing 'Maurice' and 'Sickle' and then enveloping Trondheim in a classic pincer movement.

This claim to independent judgement on the part of the Chiefs of Staff was long overdue. Churchill saw it as a volte-face.[40] But with the Prime Minister chairing the MCC his ability to browbeat and cajole had been severely curtailed, and since the paper had represented the collective view of the Government's principal military advisers and had been endorsed by each of their deputies, there was little that could be done anyway without risking a constitutional crisis of some magnitude. Churchill had offered a rival paper to the MCC seeking to preserve the fiction of a direct attack, but by evening of 19 April he had fallen in with the Chiefs of Staff proposals. Next morning he had defended the new concept in Cabinet. 'All Trondheim plans unset,' Cadogan recorded afterwards. 'Frontal attack given up and we can't expect anything for a month! This was the recommendation of the Chiefs of Staff, approved by PM and Winston. But it seems to me awful!'[41] Reactions in Paris were equally adverse; visiting staff officers found French military leaders openly critical and calling for the decision to be reversed.

Chapter 7

'Maurice' – a Step too Far

Namsos was an unpretentious town at the head of the Namsenfjord specializing in the export of timber. It boasted a single stone quay and two wooden wharves capable of accommodating ships of moderate size. It was connected to Trondheim by road and rail (an advantage quickly noted by the staffs in London), although as long as winter persisted both needed frequent ploughing.

The direct road to the provincial capital followed the southern arm of the Namsenfjord past Bangsund and crossed a range of barren hills before touching the head of the Beitstadfjord at Hjelle (a distance of some 40 miles). The railway (and an alternative road) followed a longer and gentler route striking eastward along the Namsen valley towards Grong. Here, road and rail swung gradually to the south and west following the line of the Snåsavatn until they rejoined the first road at Steinkjer, a point of self-evident military importance, occupying the narrow neck of land between the eastern extremity of the Beitstadfjord and the lake. Road and rail crossed the rocky peninsula south of the town before touching the Trondheimsfjord at Verdalsøra. Both then followed the trend of the fjord westward until they reached the city. The road distance between Namsos and Trondheim was 130 miles, the rail distance some 40 miles longer.

Early British arrivals found the Norwegian 5th Division, responsible for the defence of this area, in a state of disarray. Caught totally off guard by the speed and ruthlessness of the German attack, Major General Jacob Laurantzon had abandoned Trondheim and attempted to regroup at Steinkjer while he mobilized the 5th Field Brigade. His difficulties were formidable. His main mobilization centre had been overrun, he had lost his divisional artillery, and attempts to cobble together a force to defend the airfield at Værnes had failed. (He had been forced to surrender it to the Germans the day after the invasion.) His single ready battalion (II/13th Infantry) had been due to relieve a sister unit on the Finnish border and had expected to inherit much of its material. The battalion, 750 strong, was critically short of ammunition and there was nothing to spare for new

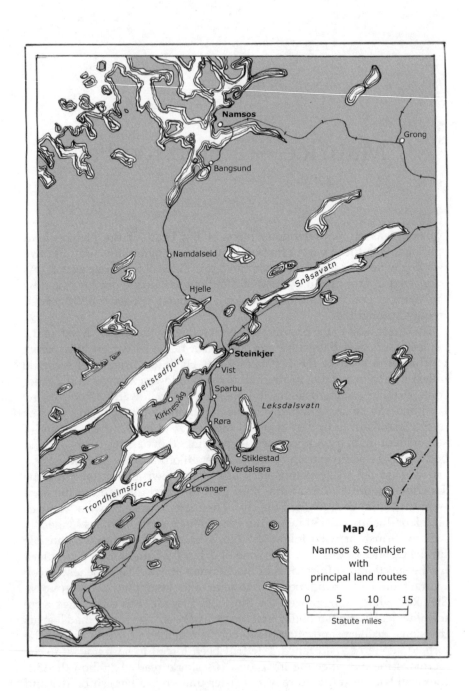

Map 4

Namsos & Steinkjer
with
principal land routes

0   5   10   15

Statute miles

details coming forward to join the colours. There was little more, even for an enterprising commander to play with – a training company hastily withdrawn from Værnes and a mixed force of light infantry and Dragoons that had just been mustered for the neutrality watch. British staff officers visiting Laurantzon's headquarters on 16 April found 'low spirits and leadership lacking'.[1] And indeed his responsibilities had quickly overwhelmed him for a day later the General handed his burden to someone better able to bear it, Colonel O.B. Getz, the commander of 5th Field Brigade. But his dispositions were still in place when British forces landed. The II/13th Infantry were holding defensive positions around Steinkjer with mobile units (3rd Dragoons) stretching eastward along the Snåsavatn and watching the eastern flank. The newly raised III/13th Infantry Battalion ('inexperienced militia' according to Getz) was held in reserve while, 20 miles south of Steinkjer, a Dragoon detachment held the river crossing at Verdalsøra to give warning of a German advance.

Laurantzon's dispositions around Steinkjer had not, so far, been tested. The two mountain battalions put ashore during '*Weserübung*' had lacked the strength to extend into the hinterland and further moves to secure the Trondheim beachhead had depended on rapid reinforcement from the south. The near disaster at Oslo and the failure to seize immediate control of the Norwegian railways had upset Group XXI's calculations and left the landing force dangerously exposed. In Berlin, the situation had looked critical. After rumours of British landings at Åndalsnes, OKW had ordered Falkenhorst to make the relief of Trondheim his top priority and Hitler, already in a lather of anxiety following the naval attacks on Narvik, had demanded immediate reinforcement by air.[2] Falkenhorst had detailed the 181st Infantry Division then disembarking in Oslo, but bad weather had intervened and more than a week had elapsed before the divisional commander (Major General Kurt Woytasch) had been ready to begin operations.

Admiral Layton anchored his convoy off Lillesjona early on 16 April. He had welcomed the late change of plan since, following the *Somali*'s reports from Namsos, he had doubted his ability to defend two large and unwieldy transports while they unloaded in the Namsenfjord. After conferring with Carton de Wiart who came up to Lillesjona to meet him, he agreed to transfer his troops to destroyers and to land them at Namsos over two successive nights. That afternoon, five destroyers left Lillesjona with the 1st/4th Royal Lincolnshire Regiment and the 1st/4th (Hallamshire battalion) of the York and Lancaster Regiment, and set course for the Namsenfjord. The landings went accoding to plan and, towards midnight, Carton de Wiart reported to London that he had brought 1,000 men into Namsos without loss; he expected to get his third battalion (1st/4th King's

Own Yorkshire Light Infantry) next day. He intended, he said, to occupy Bangsund and Grong, and take up positions astride the Beitstadfjord. He had no fresh information about the enemy but German aircraft, he warned, were 'still bombing at leisure'.[3]

The landing of the Brigade's stores, divided as they were between the two transports, the *Chobry* and the *Empress of Australia*, proved much more difficult. The original plan had been to shift everything to the *Chobry* (the handier ship of the two) and to send her into Namsos with the second wave. But, all through that first day, the ships off Lillesjona had been harassed by German aircraft, and Layton had become worried about the effect of continuous air attack on the morale of young and untried soldiers. A visit to the troopships confirmed his fears and he decided to clear the anchorage before dawn and stand to seaward until the destroyers returned. Work continued throughout the hours of darkness but, when dawn came, there were still 170 tons of stores awaiting transfer. Layton sailed his ships regardless – he felt that there was no alternative. He sent the *Empress of Australia* home hoping that the contents of her holds could be reloaded and returned to Namsos in smaller ships. He closed the entrance to the Namsenfjord at sunset and sent the *Chobry* into Namsos with the five destroyers and the AA cruiser *Curlew* as escort. The third battalion landed without mishap but the unloading of stores continued late into the night. Carton de Wiart was eventually forced to suspend the operation so that he could clear the harbour area before the arrival of the Luftwaffe. The *Chobry* sailed with the job half done and was forced to return to Namsos the following night to discharge the rest.[4]

There was something quixotic (and peculiarly English) about the force that came ashore in the Namsenfjord on 16 and 17 April. Equipped (under Plan 'R4') for what amounted to garrison duties in the Norwegian ports, 146th Infantry Brigade landed at Namsos without transport, without artillery and without AA weapons. One battalion (1st/4th KOYLI) had lost its 3-inch mortars and most of its signalling equipment, and the failure to complete the unloading of the *Empress of Australia* had reduced reserves of food and ammunition from a planned two weeks to a matter of days. It was, however, well prepared for winter. When ordered to Narvik, battalions had received copious quantities of winter clothing, far more than a man could carry. Observing his men struggling through eighteen inches of snow in unfamiliar fleece-lined coats and arctic boots, the General thought that they looked like 'paralysed bears'.[5]

Like most Territorial units in the early months of war, the Brigade had progressed little beyond the essentials of military training. (Carton de Wiart suspected that the officers had little experience in handling men and that troops had little real appreciation of the capabilities of their weapons.[6]) Yet he had taken to Brigadier Phillips and he had been impressed with the speed and efficiency with which the Brigade had expunged all signs of its arrival. German aircraft flying over Namsos on 18 April had, he believed, detected nothing. And the purpose of this force was, at least in part, symbolic – it was being rushed in quickly to provide a rallying point for Norwegian forces and to establish a base for future operations. The advance against Trondheim, timed to coincide with the direct attack on the city, would depend on reinforcements arriving during the next few days. Ironside had promised the 148th Infantry Brigade by 17 April, two battalions of Chasseurs on the 18th, with a third following close behind, and artillery on the 20th and 21st.[7] Carton de Wiart had given the War Office an outline of his thinking when he returned from Lillesjona on the night of the 16th. He had stressed the need for early forward movement despite the risk of detection from the air. (There was little natural cover and still a lot of snow.) He would time his move against Trondheim to exploit the success of the naval attack, using the French battalions as the best-trained troops at his disposal and the ones best adapted to winter conditions. In the meantime he would push forward as far as he could to shore up the Norwegian hold on Steinkjer and to seize advanced positions that would provide a springboard for the coming attack.

Carton de Wiart began his advance as soon as his third battalion was ashore. He used every railway wagon, bus and lorry that he could lay his hands on. It was a triumph of improvization, put together by two enter-prising Intelligence officers whom he had co-opted as his staff: Peter Fleming (brother of the novelist and well known as a travel writer) and Martin Lindsay, arctic explorer and adventurer. 'A better pair never existed,' the General wrote later; they were 'perfect staff officers, dispensing entirely with paper'.[8] One detachment moved eastward up the railway towards Grong. Another moved south in requisitioned transport and secured the northern shores of the Beitstadfjord. A third occupied Steinkjer, the key to road and rail communications in the northern Trøndelag, and by the evening of 17 April, Brigade Headquarters was established in the northern outskirts of the town. By 19 April, when the first of the Chasseurs came ashore at Namsos, the Lincolns were holding Vist in the southern approaches to Steinkjer and 1st/4th KOYLI were established at Røra on the Trondheimsfjord, with one company further forward still at Stiklestad, watching the minor routes leading northward along the banks of the Leksdalsvatn. An Engineer field section had joined the Dragoons at Verdalsøra, and was pondering how to repair the rail bridge, blown prematurely by the retreating Norwegians.

The contrast between these bold moves and the excessive caution in the far north had not gone unnoticed; even Churchill had been surprised and impressed. The position of the Namsos force must be regarded as 'somewhat hazardous', he told the MCC on 19 April, 'but its commander is used to taking risks'.[9] But, with the brigade spread thinly over more than 50 miles of rough terrain and with units coming under increasing scrutiny from German reconnaissance aircraft, battalion commanders were becoming restless.[10]

Since Carton de Wiart's arrival at Namsos, Whitehall's plans had been mutating at bewildering speed. On 16 April, 148th Infantry Brigade, already loading in the Forth, had been taken away from 'Maurice' and ordered to Åndalsnes instead. (The opportunity to seize key positions on the Oslo–Trondheim railway had seemed too good to miss.) Churchill had wanted to take the Chasseurs as well but the MCC, meeting under the Prime Minister's chairmanship, had endorsed the original plan and the French convoy had remained on course for Namsos. By the evening of 19 April (with Carton de Wiart's Territorials occupying their forward positions in front of Steinkjer) London was preparing to abandon 'Hammer', the centrepiece of the campaign, in favour of an enveloping movement based on the two minor ports. Next morning, the Cabinet had approved the division of 'Hammer' forces between the two. The second demi-brigade of Chasseurs would now join their countrymen on the Namsen-fjord, increasing the French contingent to a full light division, while 15th Infantry Brigade (a British regular brigade recently withdrawn from France) would land at Åndalsnes and become the cutting edge of 'Sickle'.

It is hard in retrospect to understand how these changes could have passed the scrutiny of the Whitehall committees at a time when every commander on the Norwegian coast (naval as well as military) was warning about the danger from the air. It was partly that the full impact of German airpower had yet to be appreciated. Ironside's verdict after the initial landings at Namsos was that bombing had been persistent but ineffective.[11] And thanks to the careful precautions of Layton and others, losses had been avoided. But there were deeper reasons for the failure to anticipate what was to come. The Joint Planners and the Chiefs of Staff had seen 'Maurice' and 'Sickle' as operations of limited liability. Feeding extra battalions into minor ports under cover of darkness had been an easier pill to swallow than a daylight assault on Trondheim involving the main strength of the Home Fleet, and they had seized on this new scheme as the lesser of two evils. If they did so without giving full weight to the likely consequences, it should perhaps be remembered that the Chiefs of Staff were driven men and that the staff structures that might have provided a modicum of critical scrutiny were not yet in place. But the defects of Whitehall's command arrangements were becoming clear. The Prime Minister had recognized the plight of the Chiefs of Staff and had authorized the appointment of Vice Chiefs whose collective advice would carry equal weight, and who could now share in the burden of committee work that was occupying their seniors' every waking hour. Ironside, meanwhile, was hurriedly forming a Corps Staff under the leadership of Lieutenant General H.R.S. Massy, to take over the day-to-day management of the central Norway campaign.

The French convoy arrived in the approaches to the Namsenfjord on 19 April, bringing with it the leading battalions of Brigadier General Béthouart's 5th demi-brigade and a Corps Headquarters under Major General Maurice Audet. Most of the ships that had covered the British landings had left for home, some to prepare for 'Hammer', some (like the *Somali*) to replenish AA ammunition, others escorting the returning transports. Of Layton's original force, only the anti-aircraft cruiser *Cairo* had remained on the Norwegian coast to lead the four French auxiliaries and their escort into the Namsenfjord. Rear Admiral Derrien, flying his flag in the *Emile Bertin*, made his approach in daylight and came under heavy air attack. The auxiliaries carrying the troops reached Namsos unscathed but the French flagship was severely damaged. Derrien left at once for British waters and took the *Cairo* with him. Disembarkation had then gone smartly and by dawn nearly 3,000 men had landed and dispersed to bivouacs in wooded areas around the town. Béthouart and Audet could now prepare for the arrival of the third battalion and the heavy equipment for the whole brigade (motor transport, artillery and anti-aircraft weapons) following forty-eight hours behind them.[12]

Next morning the Luftwaffe hit Namsos in force. When, by late afternoon, the weight of attack had finally eased, a large part of this compact wooden town, including the railhead and the dockside area, was ablaze. The *Nubian* approaching the town that night found the place 'a mass of flames from end to end'. Carton de Wiart, who had picked his way through cratered roads to reach the ship, spoke openly of his concerns. Covered space close to the wharves had been flattened and all transport had disappeared; any further stores that came ashore would be destroyed before they could be dispersed. Soon after midnight, he informed the War Office that he could accept no more men or material through Namsos. (He suggested the port of Mosjøen 150 miles to the north-east as an alternative.) He added that there was an acute shortage of transport and of petrol and that he could see 'little chance of decisive operations, or indeed any operations, unless enemy air activity [was] considerably restricted'.[13] The plan to replace 'Hammer' with a new offensive mounted through the minor ports (a plan which was bound to put more strain on those ports and which had received the Prime Minister's final approval only that morning) was already in serious jeopardy.

The Luftwaffe returned next day to complete the work that it had begun. The *Nubian* found herself the target for repeated attacks, a development not lost on those watching from the shore. A strike on Audet's head-quarters had killed two NCOs and injured the General himself. (Béthouart reports him as having 'bled profusely' although his injuries were not serious.[14]) He had sent a liaison officer to the *Nubian* to press for the return of the French destroyers to help relieve the pressure on the land forces. For the moment there was no better source of protection. The Army's anti-aircraft weapons were still at sea and Bomber Command's raids on Værnes and Stavanger had done nothing to blunt the German air offensive. (Most of the German bombers came from further afield.) And the Navy's carriers, rushed home from the Mediterranean to take part in 'Hammer', were only now embarking their fighter squadrons and preparing to sail for the Norwegian coast. It would thus fall to a dwindling number of hard-pressed AA ships, a few of them cruisers but most of them sloops, to provide for the air defence of the base areas for what remained of the central Norway campaign.[15]

With little sign of a lull in the enemy's air offensive, Carton de Wiart refused to accept the French auxiliary *Ville d'Alger* when she arrived off Namsos on 21 April to land the third Chasseur battalion and Béthouart's heavy equipment. The ship finally entered the Namsenfjord during the evening of the 22nd escorted by the AA cruiser *Calcutta*. When she sailed again with the coming of daylight, the Chasseurs were ashore and so was a consignment of skis – minus their essential bindings. But the transport, artillery and AA weapons were still on board and did not reach their destination for another week. By then, they were largely redundant.

When Brigadier Phillips visited 5th Field Brigade headquarters on 18 April, Getz had warned him that the Steinkjer–Verdalsøra road would become vulnerable to attack from the sea when the ice in the Beidstad and Trond-heimsfjords began to melt – a development that was already imminent and which had contributed to Laurantzon's reluctance to advance beyond the Steinkjer bottleneck.[16] But this warning and the later protests of battalion commanders had seemed of little account when weighed against the pressing need to occupy forward positions in anticipation of 'Hammer'. Phillips had thus pushed south from Steinkjer and despite signs that small vessels were beginning to enter the Beitstadfjord, his forward units were still holding Røra, Verdalsøra and Sticklestad when the German attack began.

First hints that something was afoot reached Brigade Headquarters at 0400 on 21 April when a German destroyer and a small merchant vessel were reported entering the Beitstadfjord.[17] At 0600, it was reported that the Norwegian Dragoons watching the bridge at Verdalsøra were in action with German troops advancing northwards along the railway. A company

96

from 1st/4th KOYLI was rushed south from Røra, some in ramshackle buses and some on foot, to stiffen the defence. But, as the battle for the river crossing developed, forward units found their line of retreat threatened by a German landing on the road behind them; after three hours of confused fighting they retreated inland to Sticklestad and joined the company stationed there. The whole group had then started a long and arduous retreat over snow-covered roads leading northwards along the banks of the Leksdalsvatn. Wheeled transport had quickly become a liability; the Dragoons had taken to horse-drawn sledges.

But Woytasch had not been content simply to lever the Allied covering force out of its forward positions. Soon after 0600 a battalion of mountain infantry had landed at the sawmill jetty at Kirknesvåg on the southern shore of the Beitstadfjord and pushed north-east towards the Lincolns at Vist and south-east towards KOYLI positions at Røra. The southern thrust was held at the Strømmen bridge but, despite rough country and narrow roads, the northern thrust made good progress. By 0930 German troops were probing for weak spots in the Lincolns' defences, bringing up mortars in motorcycle sidecars and attempting to drag light mountain guns up to higher ground.

At noon the Luftwaffe struck at Steinkjer and burnt it to its foundations. Water supplies were cut, the road bridge set on fire and rail traffic brought to a standstill. By evening, the situation was judged precarious. The Lincolns were still holding at Vist although heavy shelling from the fjord had forced one company to pull back. That night Phillips withdrew the two KOYLI companies from their forward position at Røra to strengthen the defences at Vist. And, fearing further attacks on his seaward flank, he sought Carton de Wiart's approval for a general withdrawal along the northern shores of the Snåsavatn towards Grong. Signalling to London that night, Carton de Wiart reported that his men were under pressure and that his attempts to get French troops forward were being frustrated by a lack of transport. The position, he feared, was becoming 'untenable'. He gave provisional approval to Phillips's plans but changed the direction of the proposed retreat north-westwards towards Hjelle and Namdalseid to avoid interference with Norwegian forces withdrawing astride the Snåsavatn. That night, he dropped the first hint to Whitehall that evacuation might soon become necessary.[18]

Morning found the Lincolns still holding at Vist with the KOYLI in their new positions astride the road and rail a little to the southward. Towards 0800, a German aircraft marked the KOYLI position with flares and mountain troops with mortars and machine guns attacked through the gap between the two battalions, threatening the line of retreat and forcing the KOYLI companies to retire eastward through difficult and heavily wooded country towards the Leksdalsvatn. The Lincolns, shelled from the sea and

97

machine-gunned from the air, held their positions throughout the morning but, finding their left flank exposed, retired north-eastward towards Steinkjer in an attempt to maintain contact with the KOYLI. (One company was cut off and this too was forced to make a difficult night march across country to reach safety.) An attempt to organize a final stand in front of the town failed and with another German landing apparently imminent, the Lincolns continued up the railway towards the lower reaches of the Snåsavatn. That night, the Germans occupied the neck of land between Steinkjer and the lake and, having secured their immediate objective, pressed their pursuit no further.

This first and very brief contact with German ground forces cost 146th Infantry Brigade nineteen killed, forty-two wounded and ninety-six missing.[19] That the figures were not worse was attributable to firm discipline and cool heads at unit level, and to the morale and physical endurance of young, untried soldiers many of whom had covered almost 60 miles over snow-covered terrain to reach safety.[20] There was no concealing the fact, however, that 'Maurice' was now on the defensive. On 23 April, Carton de Wiart told the War Office that Phillips's Brigade had been 'very roughly handled' and that, without air superiority, there was no choice but evacuation.[21]

While the last of the Lincolns were retreating through the ruins of Steinkjer, the members of the Supreme War Council were meeting in the Grande Salle at the Quai d'Orsay. Churchill, quick to appreciate that the bombing of Namsos had destroyed any prospect of mounting an offensive through that port, argued (successfully) that the 27th Chasseurs, embarked at Scapa as the reserve for 'Maurice', could no longer be absorbed there and should be switched to Narvik. (They were the only winter-trained force available to 'round up the retreating Germans'.) And, in a less-than-candid assessment of the situation in central Norway, he argued that the move could be made without prejudice to operations further south.[22] Others were finding it more difficult to adjust to the bewildering pace of events. Ironside, fresh from a meeting with French commanders at Vincennes, was astonished at the shift in the First Lord's position. 'He is so like a child in many ways,' he recorded in his diary. 'He tires of a thing and then wants to hear no more of it. He was mad to divert the Brigade from Narvik ... and would hear of no reason. Now he is bored with the Namsos operation and is all for Narvik again. It is most extraordinary how mercurial he is.'[23]

Back in London, Ironside found the Secretary of State for War 'very glum' and describing the situation in Namsos as 'desperate'. Yet there were more Allied troops ashore in Namsos than there were Germans in

98

Trondheim, and talk of evacuation was, surely, premature. 'Too many damned strategists,' he confided to his diary, 'all amateurs who change from minute to minute and are either very optimistic or very pessimistic ... We must get back to allowing soldiers to make decisions.'[24]

In the absence of clear direction from above, General Massy, the newly appointed C-in-C North Western Expeditionary Force, simply told Carton de Wiart to hold on.

Chapter 8

'Sickle' – Hard Lessons in the Norwegian Highlands

Although the JPS and the Chiefs of Staff had presented 'Sickle' as the counterpart to 'Maurice', and as the right-hand component of the enveloping movement directed against Trondheim, the forces that landed at Åndalsnes between 19 and 23 of April quickly found themselves absorbed in a new and quite different battle that was developing some 200 miles to the southward – the battle to control the two great axes of communication between Trondheim and the capital.

Some brief description of the geography of the region is unavoidable. On leaving Åndalsnes, a minor port offering no better facilities than Namsos and developed to serve the tourist trade, road and rail began what seemed an interminable climb through bleak mountain scenery towards Dombås, a junction of considerable strategic importance and the high point on the long mountain route between the Trøndelag and the populous lowlands of south-east Norway. To the north of Dombås, road and rail dropped down via the Driva valley to Oppdal and thence to Støren and the Trondheimsfjord; to the south-east they followed the line of the Gudbrandsdal (the great cleft in the mountains carrying the Lågen river) to Lillehammer, and thence along the shores of Lake Mjøsa (a huge stretch of inland water still frozen in mid-April) to Lillestrøm and finally to Oslo. The importance of Dombås had been recognized by strategists on both sides. There was, however, a second avenue of communication between Trondheim and the national capital; this skirted eastward round the mountains of the Dovrefjell to Røros and from there followed the Østerdal and the valley of the Glomma river south-east to Elverum and Kongsvinger. The battle for control of these two routes would now become the focus of the central Norway campaign.

Otto Ruge, hero of the moment and his Government's best hope for saving Norway, reached Army Headquarters in the Glomma valley at noon on

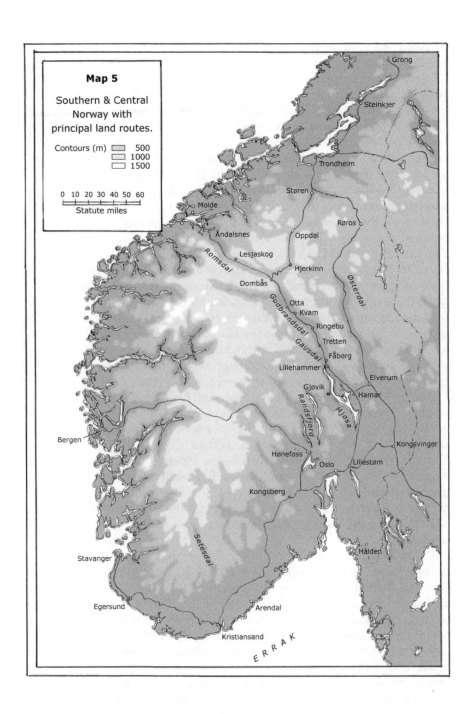

Map 5

Southern & Central
Norway with
principal land routes.

Contours (m) 500
1000
1500

0 10 20 30 40 50 60
Statute miles

Grong

Steinkjer

Trondheim

Molde

Støren

Røros

Åndalsnes

Oppdal

Lesjaskog

Hjerkinn

Dombås

Otta

Kvam

Ringebu

Tretten

Fåberg

Lillehammer

Elverum

Gjøvik

Hamar

Bergen

Hønefoss

Oslo

Lillestøm

Kongsvinger

Kongsberg

Stavanger

Hålden

Egersund

Arendal

Kristiansand

ERRAK

Romsdal

Gudbrandsdal

Gausdal

Østerdal

Randsfjord

Mjøsa

Setesdal

11 April and tried at once to conjure a coherent defence from the badly fragmented Norwegian Army. He had hoped to contain the German attack while his forces mobilized and his few ready units had soon been watching the roads in the northern outskirts of Oslo. But he had been clear from the first that, without help from outside, his army would quickly succumb. Contact with the external world was difficult but on 13 April Francis Foley, lately First Secretary of the British Legation in Oslo, reached Ruge's headquarters with a stenographer and a codebook for use with London. Over the next few days, and with Foley's help, Ruge addressed a succession of telegrams to the authorities in Whitehall describing the pressures that he was facing and calling for immediate assistance. On the evening of the 13th he stressed the importance of Allied operations against Trondheim and outlined the military contribution that his own forces could make. Next day, in a telegram addressed to the Prime Minister, he identified the critical factor in the coming campaign as the area north of Oslo where he was attempting to rally his forces. Without help from outside, he stated, resistance would become impossible. He called for the bombing of Fornebu and for action against Trondheim while his own hard-pressed forces were still capable of influencing the outcome. His strategy, meanwhile, was to play for time. In a directive issued to his army commanders on 15 April, he spoke of defence in depth, of holding actions, of demolitions and of swift night retreats when enemy pressure became too great.

It seems clear beyond doubt that Ruge and his willing accomplices came to exert a wholly disproportionate influence on Allied strategy. He had moved his headquarters to Øyer, just north of Lillehammer, on 12 April and had been joined there by Lieutenant Colonel E.J.C. King-Salter, formerly the British Military Attaché in Helsinki, and by the French Attaché, Commandant Bertrand-Vigne. But while these new converts to the Norwegian cause may have viewed developments from a somewhat narrow perspective, they did not exaggerate the gravity of the situation already facing the Norwegian Army in the lowland areas surrounding the capital.

The loss of men and material in the *Blücher* and the even more critical losses inflicted by British submarines on the ships of the 1st Sea Transport Unit had forced Falkenhorst to abandon plans for an immediate movement on Bergen and Trondheim, and to restructure and re-equip his follow-on divisions. But, early on 12 April, a revamped 196th Infantry Division, operating in three columns, struck southwards down the eastern side of Oslofjord towards Fredrikstad and Halden, south-east towards Askim and Mysen and north-east towards Lillestrøm and Kongsvinger. The advance caught the Norwegian 1st Division half-mobilized. Nearly 1,000 men were taken prisoner and 3,000 more were driven across the border into Sweden. In a matter of forty-eight hours, the whole area south and east of the capital was in German hands and the 1st Division had been eliminated as a fighting force.[1]

A simultaneous offensive to the north and west of the capital made equally rapid progress. By 14 April a reorganized 163rd Infantry Division had taken Hønefoss and opened the routes to Bergen. Another column had moved westward towards Kongsberg, the mobilization centre for the Telemark Regiment and, on the 13th, had forced the surrender of 1,500 men reporting for duty. This local disaster had signalled a more general collapse in the 3rd Command District. The I/3rd Infantry Battalion, already mobilized for neutrality watch, had been deployed close north of Kristiansand to cover the mobilization centres in the valley of the Setesdal. Harrassed by German spearheads, it had retreated northwards along routes crowded with refugees, and after being prized out of a series of defensive positions had accepted the offer of a truce. At 0900 on 14 April, the Divisional Commander telephoned Ruge to report that the battalion was unfit for further operations and that his newly raised formations were in no better shape. Ruge insisted that a capitulation would shatter the morale of the entire Army and that, if defence was impossible, commanders should arm volunteers and send them eastward.[2] But nothing effective was done. The truce turned into a capitulation, men who refused to surrender retreated into the mountains and organized resistance in the 3rd Command District ceased.

As the German offensive turned northwards for the relief of Trondheim, forward units began to encounter elements of Major General Jacob Hvinden-Haug's 2nd Field Brigade, deployed to contest the parallel routes northward up the Glomma valley and along the shores of the Mjøsa lake. In the 196th Division's (eastern) sector, the 340th Infantry Regiment (Group Fischer) took Kongsvinger on the 16th and advanced up the Glomma valley towards Elverum. The 345th Infantry Regiment (Group Laendle) overran Norwegian outposts at the southern tip of Mjøsa and advanced up the eastern shoreline until it met a well-prepared defensive strongpoint at Strandlykka. There Laendle's battalions paused until an improvised column advancing up the western side of the lake pushed the Norwegians back to Totenvik and allowed a new battalion fresh from Oslo to cross the ice and turn the Strandlykka position. This move precipitated a general retreat. Hvinden-Haug, who had just detached an infantry battalion (II/5th) to strengthen his hold on the Glomma valley, pulled back beyond Hamar to prepared positions covering the lakeside road in the southern approaches to Lillehammer. (He was confident that he could hold these positions for several days unless he came under heavy attack from the air.[3]) But his retreat had uncovered the road to Elverum and on entering Hamar the Germans sent a battalion eastward across the hills to engineer a similar retreat in the Glomma valley. Elverum fell on 20 April and the reinforced infantry regiment operating on the German right continued its advance northwards until delayed by strong defences at the Rena river crossing nearly 30 miles to the northward.

In the western sector meanwhile, the 163rd Infantry Division had halted its advance up the railway towards Bergen and, with a panzer company in support, had pushed northward on parallel routes astride the Randsfjord. Colonel Dahl, commanding the mixed bag of Norwegian units hastily assembled to hold the area, had found no way to halt the German advance and, on 16 April, Ruge had called on the 4th District (Bergen) to send reinforcements across the mountains in the hope that he could stabilize the situation. But the relentless advance to the west of Lake Mjøsa continued. By late on 19 April, German columns were pressing hard on Gjøvik, site of the last munitions factory in Norwegian hands, and threatening to turn Dahl's western flank. Ruge was now defending his last toeholds in the Norwegian lowlands. Immediately behind him lay the mountains of Norway's central spine and the two great glens of the Gudbrandsdal and the Østerdal which channelled road and rail communications northwards towards Trondheim.

The men of the 148th Infantry Brigade, 1st/5th Leicesters and 8th Sherwood Foresters, had suffered more than most from Whitehall's inability to adopt any settled plan. They were part of the brigade that had been dumped unceremoniously on the jetty at Rosyth when the Norwegian affair had first begun and had since been living under canvas at Dunfermline, uncertain what the future might hold. But on 13 April they had received orders to move and, next day, Brigadier H. de R. Morgan and an advance party of Sherwood Foresters had embarked in the cruisers *Galatea* and *Arethusa* while the rest of the force, six rifle companies, the brigade signal section, an AA troop, an Engineer section and ancillary troops had been ferried out to the Great Orient liner *Orion*, anchored below the Forth Bridge. Orders from the War Office, delivered by hand that morning, showed that the Brigade's destination was Namsos.

That evening, Morgan got word that sailing was postponed. The Brigade spent the next twenty-four hours trying to put some semblance of order into its stores which in the haste of embarkation had been struck down into the liner's holds as and when they had arrived. But the threat to large liners on the Norwegian coast was now beginning to influence Admiralty thinking and, during the afternoon of 16 April, new orders from London prescribed the use of warships only. And, for good measure, they switched the destination to Åndalsnes.[4] The *Galatea* (flag of Vice Admiral Edward-Collins) arrived alongside the liner at dusk and the *Arethusa*, *Carlisle*, *Curacoa* and two destroyers followed quickly behind her and filled themselves to capacity, leaving just two companies of Leicesters to follow as soon as other ships could be found. But the liner's holds had become what Lieutenant Colonel Dudley Clarke (a Whitehall staff officer who had attached himself to the expedition) later described as a 'storeman's inferno' as bulk stores were broken open to be distributed among the various ships and as each unit searched in the semi-darkness of the liner's holds for that essential item of equipment that was inevitably at the bottom of the pile.[5] The Brigade was already aware that its transport would be following behind it in a separate ship (the *Cedarbank*) and that it would depend for the first forty-eight hours on what it could garner from local sources. It did not become aware, until too late, that its 40mm AA guns had no predictors, that its wireless equipment was incomplete and that it would go into action critically short of mortar ammunition.

The force sailed for its new destination the following morning. A flurry of helpful advice from the Admiralty followed it, stressing the importance of landing troops quickly and advising Edward-Collins to time his arrival for dusk. Since port facilities at Åndalsnes appeared minimal and since the cruisers might well have to lie off while discharging, the Admiralty pointed to the port of Molde (25 miles by water, nearly 40 by road and ferry) as a suitable alternative since here cruisers could berth alongside. Morgan's instructions told him simply to 'secure Dombås then operate northward and take the offensive against the Germans in the Trondheim area'.[6] Later information told him that he would encounter little opposition between Åndalsnes and Dombås, and urged him to push small units forward 'really rapidly'. When he had secured Dombås, the starting point for his offensive northwards, he was to prevent the Germans using the railway to reinforce Trondheim and make contact with Norwegian forces believed to be operating in the Lillehammer area.[7]

The force entered the Romsdalsfjord during the late evening of 18 April and, to complete the landings during the short hours of darkness, divided itself between the ports of Åndalsnes and Molde. Morgan, who had been uncertain whether his reception would be friendly or hostile, was surprised to be welcomed ashore at Åndalsnes by a Colonel of Marines (Lieutenant Colonel H.W. Simpson, Commanding Operation 'Primrose') who informed him that the port had been under British occupation for twenty-four hours, that all steps had been taken to secure the approaches and that a train was at two hours' notice to leave for Dombås. Edwards-Collins was delighted by what he found. He told the Admiralty that Åndalsnes had excellent facilities for a small expedition but warned that further air defence measures appeared essential since a few well-aimed bombs could destroy the jetty and the railway station, the main assets of the place.[8]

A conference on the military situation followed. The Norwegian C-in-C was said to be at Lillehammer with his army astride the Mjøsa. The garrison at Trondheim was isolated and Dombås safe although the remnants of a German parachute company, dropped some days before, was still preventing road and rail movement to the southward. Soon after midnight Morgan set off by train for Dombås with two companies of Sherwood Foresters. He arrived soon after dawn and, while the Foresters were digging in went on, down the line, to witness operations against the German paratroops holding out in a farmhouse overlooking the valley. He found Norwegian skiers preparing for an attack while a 3.7-inch howitzer, mounted on a sand-bagged railway wagon and manned by a party of British sailors, pounded German positions. (The Germans surrendered soon afterwards.) At noon, Morgan returned to Åndalsnes so that he could remain in touch with London but he was soon summoned back to Dombås for an urgent meeting with the British Military Attaché on the deteriorating situation around the Mjøsa lake.

The meeting at Dombås during the late afternoon of 19 April was far reaching in its effects. King-Salter and his French colleague presented a 'grim disturbing narrative'. The Norwegian Cabinet, they said, was near to capitulation; the only thing holding it back was the hope of British help. This was the tenth day since the German invasion and the Norwegian Army was 'nearly spent'. Unless British troops appeared in Lillehammer within the next day or so, resistance would cease.[9] It was also argued, albeit on a very partial interpretation of a message from London, that the War Office had acknowledged a moral duty to help the Norwegian C-in-C. Recognizing that he could not ignore this desperate appeal, Morgan asked the War Office for further instructions. Then, having ordered the Foresters to prepare for an immediate move, he set out with Dudley Clarke in tow to visit Ruge at the mouth of the Gudbrandsdal.

They met the Norwegian C-in-C late that night in his austere and carefully concealed headquarters on the outskirts of Øyer. There was no ceremony. Ruge had clearly been hoping for something more than a lightly armed Territorial brigade and (despite his recent pleas to London) he was distinctly cool about British plans for an attack on Trondheim. That, he now said, could wait. His overriding priority was to concentrate every available man on the decisive front south of Lillehammer and keep a foothold in the lowlands until help from outside had restored the numerical balance. (After that, perhaps, an offensive.)[10] And he left Morgan in no doubt that as the duly appointed Commander-in-Chief he expected all forces operating on Norwegian soil to conform to his strategy. Recognizing the force of Ruge's arguments, Morgan promised all the help he could give and ordered the rest of the Brigade forward. The party (Ruge included, despite his obvious lack of sleep) then went off to the railway station at Lillehammer to witness the arrival of the Foresters.

106

A further and more formal conference convened at Ruge's headquarters next day. Morgan faced pressures that he was ill-prepared for and which amounted to moral blackmail. Ruge claimed that his hard-pressed soldiers needed to see visible evidence of the British presence and wanted to distribute Morgan's men across the whole front, a scheme that prevented the Brigade from fighting as a coherent unit and which placed its component parts under Norwegian officers. Morgan protested but Ruge remained adamant and backed his demands with the threat of resignation. (In an attempt to keep matters on an even keel King-Salter found it best to withhold a message from the War Office telling Ruge that Morgan would not come under his orders.) In the end, Morgan agreed that raising the flagging spirits of the Norwegian Army was the paramount consideration and set out that afternoon on a guided tour of the forward positions.[11]

There is little sign in Dudley Clarke's record of this reconnaissance that either man gained any clear idea of what had been happening on this southern front. They noted that the lakeside road leading to Dahl's positions west of Mjøsa was vulnerable to German fire. They were worried about reports of German armour and wondered how their men would react to panzers, armed as they were only with the obsolete 'Boyes rifle'. But their overall impression was of a 'queer, casual sort of war'. The Germans did not seem to be pushing strongly on either side of the lake. And there was little sign of the collapse in Norwegian morale that they had been led to expect. The units in front of Lillehammer were clearly tired after ten days of retreat but the German pursuit had apparently been leisurely and they had suffered few casualties.[12] As they completed their tour of inspection and turned back towards Ruge's headquarters, two companies of Foresters were moving forward to positions west of Gjøvik to counter the threat to the Dahl's right flank while, on the eastern side of the lake, the rest of the Foresters and the two companies of Leicesters (the last to arrive) were taking up reserve positions behind Lundehøgda, a ridge covering the main (lakeside) road to Lillehammer, and Åsmarka, a scattered hamlet a little to the eastward, where the 2nd Dragoons were covering the minor roads leading northward through the hills. They were due to relieve Norwegian units in the front line the following afternoon.

The 345th Infantry Regiment, reinforced as it passed through Hamar by a motor machine-gun battalion and now numbering some 4,000 men, launched its attack on the Norwegian defences during the morning of 21 April. Outnumbered and outgunned, the Torkildsen battalion holding the Lundehøgda ridge was soon under severe pressure and by afternoon Norwegian commanders were making hurried preparations for retreat. (The Foresters were told not to take up their position in the front line but to occupy a covering position in front of Lillehammer instead.) At Åsmarka, the situation was hardly better. The Leicester companies, strafed by German aircraft as they moved forward to relieve the Dragoons, arrived to find the Norwegians defending a stretch of bleak and snow-covered hillside with no definable boundaries. With the Germans pressing forward on the flanks, the Norwegian colonel declared the position untenable and the Leicesters, confined to the roads because of the deep snow, retired to a covering position where the front was narrower and where dense woodland offered a measure of flank protection.

At about 1800 that evening Hvinden-Haug ordered a general withdrawal to prepared positions at the Balbergkamp (the mountain marking the entrance to the Gudbrandsdal) some 20 miles to the northward. It was a desperate decision – one which made an orderly retreat all but impossible and which forced units on both sides of the lake to pull back north of Lillehammer before the Germans seized the town. The British units found themselves covering this withdrawal. At dusk, the 2nd Dragoons (still in good order) passed through the Leicesters' lines bound for new holding areas and promising to send their transport back when they reached their destination. The Leicesters waited in vain and at midnight abandoned what they could not carry and set out over steep and icy roads to march the 14 miles to Lillehammmer. To their right, the two Forester companies covered the retreat of the Torkildsen battalion before they in turn got orders to retire beyond Lillehammer. The Leicesters were the last through the town. As dawn approached they met the Norwegian transport coming to collect them but the margin was fine. They were forced to abandon the stores stockpiled at the railway station and a party of thirty men including six officers was surprised and captured by the German vanguard.

It now fell to the two half-battalions to hold the Germans at the Balbergkamp while Ruge's bruised forces withdrew into the Gudbrandsdal. After a brief reconnaissance of the position during the small hours of 22 April, Morgan gave broad directions to his battalion commanders and set off on a desperate (and unsuccessful) quest to get help, first from 2nd Division Headquarters and then from Ruge. In his absence, parties of tired men who had covered the retreat from Lundehøgda and Åsmarka, who had escaped through Lillehammer by the skin of their teeth and who, for want of transport, had abandoned much of their equipment, took up pre-prepared positions at the mouth of the Gudbrandsdal to give Hvinden-Haug's troops a respite, and to hold open the first of the crossing points that would allow a junction with forces west of the river.

The position was, on the face of it, a strong one. Looking south from the village of Fåberg, the dark mass of the Balberkamp, densely wooded, rose steeply from the valley floor squeezing road and railway onto a narrowing neck of land between mountain and river. With half the Foresters still missing (their whereabouts remained unknown) Brigade Headquarters could muster four rifle companies only.[13] Two were deployed on level ground astride the road with a good field of fire to the southward, and a third on rising ground to the left to guard against a flanking move along the lower slopes of the mountain. The fourth was some 2 miles back holding the bridge.

The Germans made contact in late morning bringing howitzer and mortar fire to bear on forward positions and searching for areas of weakness on the lower slopes of the mountain. German reconnaissance aircraft were much in evidence. But no major attack developed along the road. Instead, using their small contingent of mountain troops, the Germans began a wide flanking movement until by 1400 they had gained a position above and behind the British lines. And in mid-afternoon they caused something of a panic by mounting a machine-gun attack on Brigade Headquarters 4 miles back behind the village.[14] With pressure on the forward positions increasing and with the line of retreat seemingly threatened, battalion commanders called for withdrawal, and Morgan and King-Salter hurried northwards to identify a suitable covering position (Hvinden-Haug had made no evident attempt to do so) and find the troops to man it.[15]

Breaking contact with the enemy, difficult enough in daylight, was made worse by the lack of signals equipment. Much of it had been abandoned earlier in the retreat and few men in the forward positions got the order to retire. And transport was critically short. To get the men away it became necessary to empty a supply convoy that had been moving forward to the front, and rations, ammunition and equipment in large quantities were dumped beside the road. The retreat continued through the evening along the narrow congested road, harassed by German aircraft. By the time the German advance was brought to a halt by a fresh company of Leicesters (landed at Åndalsnes the day before and rushed forward by train and bus) the Brigade had lost a good part of its two forward companies and all cohesion as a fighting force.

Morning saw a desperate attempt to prepare and man a defensive position in front of Tretten, the last reliable crossing point for the companies still isolated to the west of the river. Morgan found Ruge in the small hours and told him plainly that he could not guarantee to hold the position through the coming day. Ruge, however, insisted that the attempt should be made; he restored the British contingent to Morgan's command and assigned him a squadron of Dragoons to help secure his mountain flank.[16]

At Tretten the Gudbrandsdal narrowed to a gorge and the road skirted the foot of a mountain saddle, the Vardekamp, densely wooded on its lower slopes, a mile or two below the town. As the survivors of the recent action straggled back during the early hours of 23 April, they were rallied at the Vardekamp, organized into composite companies, one of Leicesters and one of Foresters, and assigned to half-reconnoitred and ill-prepared positions on the lower slopes. Behind the line chaos reigned. Dudley Clarke, who had been returning to London with a new and desperate appeal for help, saw Norwegian troops still retiring through the village unaware of the threat behind them. A new company of Leicesters, the last of the contingent that had left Scotland late for want of space in the cruisers, marched smartly through the village towards the front, still cocky enough to care what people thought of them.[17] (They were no better equipped than their predecessors – the *Cedarbank* which had sailed in convoy with them and which had been carrying the Brigade's transport and much of its heavy impedimenta had been torpedoed by a German submarine.) Finally, towards 0530 on the morning of the 23rd, the two companies of Foresters that had covered Dahl's withdrawal crossed into the village from the far side of the river. The men, most without greatcoats, had spent the last eight hours in open lorries negotiating mountain roads with no opportunity for food or rest. They were given a hot meal and a cup of tea before taking up their positions. One company stayed to cover the western approaches to the bridge. The other, at King-Salter's behest, set off down the road to help shore up the forward positions at the foot of the Vardekamp. When the action opened two companies of Foresters were overlooking the road, hastily blocked with logs and fallen trees, while the Leicesters with the Dragoons in support held the saddle above and to the left of them to prevent the kind of move that had opened up the British position the day before.[18]

At about 0830 the sound of firing to the southward showed that the Leicester company that had held the Germans overnight was already in action. (It was overrun while attempting to withdraw and few made it back to British lines.) The German column approached the Vardekamp defile soon after midday, with three tanks in the lead and with infantry and light artillery close behind. There was no flanking move. While the German infantry inched forward covered by mortar and artillery fire, making full use of the natural cover on the lower slopes, the tanks advanced along the road, barged the road blocks aside and, impervious to the Boyes rifle, forced their way past British lines, preventing all possibility of reinforcement and blocking the line of retreat. King-Salter, who in mid-afternoon went forward to visit the front line, was dismayed to meet exhausted stragglers, all reporting that the Germans had broken through. He summoned help from the village and continued towards the fighting. He was then forced to plunge into the trees as tanks and infantry approached. (He spent the next three days behind enemy lines before being shot and captured by a German patrol.)[19] The village was held throughout the afternoon in the hope that men in the forward positions might get back.

The Dragoons with their own transport did so using a farm track that ran parallel to the road; but few others did so. When Tretten was finally abandoned in early evening, muffled sounds of firing from the direction of the Vardekamp could still be heard.

There is little more to tell. An improvised rearguard held a position a mile north of Tretten until dusk. It was then overrun. When Morgan's brigade retired through Norwegian positions during the night of 23/24 April, it had an effective strength of nine officers and 300 men.[20]

The success of this offensive had done little so far to cool the febrile atmosphere that had prevailed in the Reichs Chancery since the breakdown of negotiations with the Norwegian Government. Quisling had shown himself a broken reed; far from bringing the political stability that the situation so clearly demanded, his attempts to form a cabinet had produced little but anger and derision, and on 14th April Ambassador Bräuer had tried to reopen negotiations with the Nygaardsvold Government on the basis of an alternative candidate. His approaches had been rebuffed. But Bräuer and Falkenhorst had found in Paal Berg, President of the Norwegian Supreme Court, someone who appeared to recognize the need for a return to normality and, on 15 April, Berg had agreed to form an 'Administrative Council' of seven prominent citizens to 'exercise civil administration in areas of the country occupied by Germany'. The scheme had soon run into difficulties. A spokesman for the Nygaardsvold Government, broadcasting on 17 April, had given Quisling's demotion a guarded welcome (he had been made Commissioner for Demobilization) but he had made it clear that the new body had no basis in law and that it would have to give way to the established government as areas of the country were brought back under government control.[21] When told of this development Hitler took matters into his own hands. Bräuer (charged by Raeder and Göring with failing to take decisive action in the early stages of the invasion and then with failing to give Quisling adequate support) was recalled and sent to a job on the Western Front.[22] And on 19 April, Hitler appointed Josef Terboven as Reich Commissioner for Norway, a man with few qualities to recommend him bar total loyalty to the Nazi cause and total absence of humanity.

But the dangerous isolation of the Trondheim garrison had continued to prey on Hitler's mind. Early reports of British destroyers off Åndalsnes had given a new edge to his anxieties and on 14 April he had attempted to shortcut what he saw as the Army's cautious and pedestrian plans by ordering a parachute drop in the central highlands near Dombås to seize control of this pivotal point on the Oslo–Trondheim railway. (Göring had flatly refused to commit further resources to this adventure and Morgan had witnessed the last stand of the exhausted survivors on first arriving in

111

Norway.) The British landings at Namsos and Åndalsnes had prompted a new surge of anxiety. Hitler had ordered the immediate destruction of the two ports and had followed the progress of the bombing campaign with total absorption. On 21 April (the day of the Woytasch gambit at Steinkjer and of 196th Division's equally successful assault on Lundehøgda) Hitler had stopped the move of the 11th Motor Rifle Brigade to Norway and demanded a complete motorized division in its place. And despairing of the Army's ability to open the overland routes in time to save the garrison, he had called on the Navy to cover the move of a full division to Trondheim in the ocean liners *Europa* and *Bremen*, only backing down when told bluntly by Raeder that the operation 'would entail the certain loss of the transports and of the whole fleet'.[23] 'Tension has risen yet another notch,' wrote Jodl on 23 April, 'as the northward progress ... is very slow and new destructions of bridges are being reported.'[24] But relief was at hand. News of events at Tretten and of the isolation of a substantial part of the Norwegian 2nd Division to the west of the river showed that the end was in sight. On 24 April, Falkenhorst abandoned plans for a concentration south of Trondheim and ordered his forces in the Gudbrandsdal (known from now on as Group Pellengahr) to press on to Åndalsnes and complete the destruction of the British. It would now fall to Colonel Fischer and his weaker column in the Østerdal to open the way to Trondheim.[25] By 25 April the mood in Hitler's Chancery was, in Jodl's words, 'definitely optimistic'.

Group XXI was now poised to complete its conquest of southern and central Norway. In the centre, Pellengahr, reinforced on passing Lillehammer by the regiment on his left, and now with seven infantry battalions and a motor machine-gun battalion under command together with two artillery batteries, a platoon of tanks and two companies of mountain troops, pushed forward against weakening resistance in the Gudbrandsdal. On the right, Fischer's smaller but more mobile force bypassed Norwegian demolitions at the Rena river crossing and pushed flying columns northwards up the Glomma and Rena valleys to reach Rendal on 24 April, and Røros and Kvikne on the 25th, the latter less than 80 miles from Trondheim and less than 50 from the garrison's southern outpost at Støren. And, on the left, a reduced 163rd Division, diverted westward into the mountains on reaching the head of Lake Mjøsa, had advanced on the Sognefjord on two parallel axes to block the approach of General Steffen's 4th Field Brigade coming east to join the battle.

Relief in Berlin had been matched by deepening gloom in London. Ironside had returned from Paris to find the Secretary of State for War 'very down at heart' and with his mind fixed firmly on evacuation. The Prime Minister had been more concerned with reactions in the House of Commons than with issues of military strategy and had called a special meeting to consider the 'rather unsatisfactory position' in Norway. He had concluded that everything had been done with the best of intentions; evacuation might represent a 'psychological reverse and a blow to our prestige', but his Government would emerge with its honour unsullied.[26] Churchill's reaction to the deteriorating situation had been to call firstly for an immediate advance on Trondheim by 15th Infantry Brigade, a proposal which colleagues had found 'maddening' and 'wholly unrealistic',[27] and then for the revival of 'Hammer' since, without the use of Trondheim and its port, it was hard to see how the southern front could be sustained. General Massy's V Corps headquarters had injected a hint of sanity into this conceptual turmoil. Orders for Major General Bernard Paget,[28] commander of the expanded 'Sickleforce', made no mention of an offensive against Trondheim and concentrated simply on 'preventing the northward advance of the German army' and – a new and necessary preoccupation in view of the German advance in the Østerdal – on securing the northern and eastern approaches to the bridgehead. In a paper for the Chiefs of Staff on 25 April, Massy advised that, given adequate air support, there was no reason why present positions could not be held and the offensive against Trondheim resumed. Without air support, on the other hand, evacuation would become inevitable.[29] His assessments were not too wide of the mark. Although it would be the lack of air support that decided matters in the end, the ground operations of the next few days would reveal standards of tactical competence and qualities of generalship far beyond anything seen so far and which offered a refreshing alternative to the careless adventurism of Namsos and sullen inactivity of Narvik.

15th Infantry Brigade was the natural choice for the expanded 'Sickleforce'. The Brigade's three regular battalions (1st Battalion King's Own Yorkshire Light Infantry, 1st Battalion York and Lancaster Regiment and 1st Battalion Green Howards) had been pulled out of the line in France to take part in 'Hammer' and had been waiting near Rosyth, ready for embarkation. In equipment terms, the Brigade differed little from the territorial units that had gone before it, although its nine 25mm Hotchkiss anti-tank guns gave it a capability against armour that the others had lacked. In general, however, it shared the handicaps of its predecessors. The decision to transport the Brigade in warships, made largely inevitable by the lack of specialist shipping, meant that it arrived piecemeal and without supporting arms. (As usual, transport and artillery were to follow later.) The first wave (1 KOYLI and 1 Y & L) landed at Åndalsnes and Molde on the evening of 23 April; the third battalion (1 Green Howards) together with General Paget and the advanced Corps Headquarters that was to organize and defend the base areas arrived forty-eight hours later.

While Morgan's brigade was retreating from Tretten, the leading elements of 15th Infantry Brigade (1 KOYLI less two companies) were moving cautiously towards the front. They passed through the smoking ruins of Dombås in the early hours of the 24th and started the long descent southwards, stopping at each station to check with the railway authorities that the line ahead was clear. They finally detrained at Otta, a small town at the confluence of the Otta and Lågen rivers, and hid themselves from prying eyes while waiting for orders from the Brigade Commander (Brigadier W.E.F. Smyth) who had gone ahead to make contact with Morgan and the Norwegian command. Smyth found Hvinden-Haug at Ringebu, 30 miles further on, and agreed a joint plan. The remnants of the Torkildsen battalion and a fresh battalion sent forward from the Romsdal (I/2nd Infantry) were taking up positions south of Ringebu where, it was hoped, they would hold until nightfall on the 25th. Smyth, in the meantime, would bring his leading battalion forward to Kvam, so that the hard-pressed Norwegians could retire through his lines to rest and reorganize at Dombås.

The men of the KOYLI waited in Otta during the hours of daylight, planning to move forward at nightfall and expecting ample time to prepare their new positions. They were harassed for much of the day by German aircraft but they were well dispersed and suffered few casualties. But during the afternoon, Norwegian troops began to stream northward through Otta, bringing with them large numbers of wounded. By evening it was clear that the line at Ringebu had broken and that the Norwegians were clinging to a last position on the road northward. The battalion moved forward as planned but it would now have to face the enemy sooner than expected.[30]

Kvam presented many of the features of the earlier Gudbrandsdal battlefields. The village, a few dozen wooden buildings scattered along the road and a handful of farms climbing the slopes behind them, occupied a narrow stretch of level ground on the left bank of the river. Just in front of the village, the river bent sharply to the right, ran straight for a mile or so and then curved left behind a mountain shoulder clothed in birch and pine. The Battalion Commander put his forward companies at the river bend with a good field of fire over the enemy's approach, one guarding the sloping ground to the left of the road and the other occupying a flat lozenge-shaped island to the right that seemed to offer good protection against infantry attack. The three remaining companies were deployed behind these positions, one in the village itself and one on either flank. First signs of spring were beginning to show. In the valley, snow had receded from the middle of the fields although it still lay thick along walls and hedges. On the mountain slopes it remained as deep as ever.

114

Soon after dawn on 25 April, Battalion Headquarters got word that the Norwegians were retiring and at 0730 the troops that had been holding the line at Vinstra, 5 miles down the road, withdrew through British lines in apparent good order. The Germans were slow to put in an appearance but towards noon they arrived in force. The column, almost a mile long, approached along the road with tanks and infantry in the lead, and with an endless file of motorcyclists, motorized infantry and guns following behind. (The lack of a few field guns on the British side was keenly felt.) As the head of the column reached 150 yards, the forward rifle companies opened fire. The German infantry went to ground and the tanks made for a dip in the road where they disappeared from view. The Germans then deployed their artillery and treated the defenders to a 'masterly display of gunnery'.[31] Every house and every piece of cover received attention, the gunners shifting quickly and accurately from one target to the next. The light infantrymen could do little but squat in their holes and wait for the storm to pass. Casualties began to mount. Brigadier Smyth was among the wounded and the command passed to Lieutenant Colonel Kent-Lemon of the Y & L.

The Germans then mounted a deliberate attack on the British right, bringing concentrated mortar and machine-gun fire onto A Company, holding the forward edge of the island. The position was an exposed one and the troops suffered terribly. Towards 1400 the Battalion Adjutant found men retreating along the riverbank and recognized at once that the line had to be restored if B Company on the left was not to be outflanked. He moved a reserve company forward and re-established the line in a new and less hazardous position. The Germans then switched their attention to the left, launching attack after attack on B Company, dug in on the lower slopes. Each attempt was driven back and it was a 'jubilant and pugnacious' group of men that, at nightfall, fell back to new positions abreast the village.[32] But as the day ended, it was clear that A Company could no longer keep its place in the line and a fresh company (C Company 1 Y & L) was sent forward to relieve the strain during the coming day.

The German artillery resumed its bombardment at 0530 on the morning of the 26th. The Germans then launched two infantry attacks against the British left in quick succession. Both were driven back, but by mid-morning German infantrymen had worked through a gap between company positions and heavy fighting had developed on the level ground close to the village. The day brought moments of comedy as well as examples of great personal gallantry and sang-froid. There was a momentary scare when clouds of evil-smelling yellow smoke drifted across the lines. Gas masks were put on until it was established that the cause of the problem was pollen from the scrub on the river banks. Soon afterwards, a tank had waddled forward from the hollow where it had been hiding to support the infantry attack on the village. The anti-tank gunner was un-sighted and a volunteer crawled forward to dismantle a roadblock that was obstructing his view. Then, with a succession of carefully timed shots, the gunner stopped two tanks and an armoured car and left their smoking wrecks blocking the road.

Bitter fighting continued around the village throughout the afternoon, one attack on the right flank almost breaking through before being driven back. But casualties were mounting and there was relief in Battalion Head-quarters when, in early evening, news came in that the 1 Y & L were in position behind them and that the Battalion was to retire at nightfall. The Battalion had held the Kvam position for two long days and had administered the first substantial check to the German advance since it had begun in Oslo fourteen days before.

The first day of the battle at Kvam, 25 April, saw the failure of a brave but ill-fated plan to establish a fighter squadron in central Norway. First attempts to counter German air supremacy had, of course, started much earlier. On 11 April, Bomber Command had moved two squadrons to the Moray Firth and, from then on, had launched near-daily attacks on the airfield at Sola (Stavanger), keeping it in a constant state of alarm. Squadrons based in East Anglia had raided Ålborg and occasionally Fornebu, but Germany's northern airfields (the real basis for the Luft-waffe's ascendancy) had remained immune, protected by the government interdict that still forbade attacks on German soil. The practical difficulties facing Bomber Command had been formidable. Problems of weather, of navigation, of finding and identifying targets at extreme range had made operations over Norway unproductive, while the strength of German defences had tended to make them costly.[33] If the Air Staff seemed half-hearted in its support of the campaign – and this was a widespread impression, particularly among soldiers in the front line – it had its own reasons. It made little sense to men steeped in the doctrines of Trenchard and Douhet to risk their slowly maturing strategic weapon in a theatre of war that everyone knew was peripheral.

There had been fewer inhibitions about risking fighter squadrons and the Air Staff had started looking for an airfield in central Norway as soon as the prospect of operations in the Trondheim area had become clear. They had settled on the lake at Lesjaskog, a long strip of frozen water halfway between Åndalsnes and Dombås, and well served by road and rail. The pressure to get the airstrip into operation had then become intense. No. 263 Squadron had embarked its eighteen Gladiator fighters in the carrier *Glorious* and a hastily formed advance party had been sent to Åndalsnes with the essentials needed to support the squadron in the field. This party had landed on 23 April, moved to Lesjaskog in requisitioned

116

The business of Admiralty. The First Lord with Admiral Sir Dudley Pound, Whitehall 1939. (Taylor Library [T/L])

Sir Edmund Ironside (right) photographed on taking up duties as CIGS in September 1939. With him is Lord Gort who was leaving the War Office to take command of the BEF. (IWM H2)

Erich Raeder, disciple of Tirpitz and architect of the German Navy's revival in the inter-war years. He was the first to alert Hitler to the dangers on his nothern flank. (T/L)

A driven personality with a hatred of Bolshevism. The Norwegian neo-fascist Vidkun Quisling in an election poster for his party of National Unity. (T/L)

Below: Wilhelmshaven, 6 April 1940. Troops of the German 3rd Mountain Division prepare to embark for Norway in the heavy cruiser *Hipper.* (Bundesarchiv)

Oslofjord, 9 April 1940. The heavy cruiser *Blücher* in trouble off the Oscarsborg fortress. (T/L)

Oslo after the German invasion. German transport aircraft massed at Fornebu. (Bundesarchiv)

Retribution. The battleship *Warspite* in action off Narvik on 13 April 1940. She is photographed from her Swordfish aircraft. (IWM A38)

Driven ashore in the Rombaksfjord. The German destroyer *Georg Thiele* after the second battle of Narvik. Her ship's company stepped on to the rocks dry-shod. (T/L)

Ships' graveyard. The Narvik ore terminal after the naval battles of 10 and 13 April. The ship on the left is the German tanker *Jan Wellem* which survived intact. (Bundesarchiv)

Nowhere to go. German Ju 52 transports on the Hartvigsvatn April 1940. They had flown in a mountain battery but were unable to get off. (T/L)

'Ginger' Boyle, Admiral of the Fleet Lord Cork. He was 'very professional, alert, businesslike and official; sometimes a little intolerant of easygoing things and people'. (T/L)

Below: 'The dullest campaign ever.' Carton de Wiart with unidentified staff officer (sartorially challenged) outside his Namsos headquarters, April 1940. (IWM N68)

Harsh critic of improvised campaigns. Paget, one of the few British commanders to emerge from Norway with credit. (National Portrait Gallery, charcoal portrait by Henry Lamb)

'Live wire'. Brigadier General Antoine Béthouart, alpine specialist and commander of the French Light Division. He was the main architect of the successful assault on Narvik and later became one of de Gaulle's principal lieutenants. (T/L)

'The Auk'; Claude Auchinleck (GOC-in-C designate, Narvik) with his air component commander (Group Captain Moore) while en route to Harstad in the Polish liner *Chobry*, May 1940. (IWM N135)

Above: Mountain warfare pioneer. Eduard Dietl, who defended the Narvik enclave against the Allies. He was an associate of Hitler from Munich days. (T/L)

Right: Plain man with no frills. Otto Ruge, Norwegian C-in-C and his Government's best hope for saving Norway. (T/L)

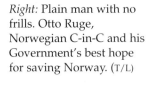

The victors. Generals von Falkenhorst (XXI Corps) and Dietl photographed in Trondheim, July 1940. (T/L)

Monarch on the run. Haakon VII with Crown Prince Olav photographed near Molde, April 1940. (T/L)

'Real soldiers...' Brest, April 1940. Béthouart's Chasseurs prepare to embark for Norway. (T/L)

Storeman's nightmare. 146th Infantry Brigade, Namsos, April 1940. (T/L)

It's a matter of hygiene! Harstad, April 1940, a reluctant South Wales Borderer reaches the head of the queue. (IWM N241)

The decisive factor? Stuka squadron at Trondheim (Værnes) in April 1940. The inspecting officer is General Milch, State Secretary for Aviation and a powerful advocate of the tactical bomber. (Bundesarchiv)

Winter warfare. Troops of the 3rd Mountain Division in action near Trondheim in April 1940. (Bundesarchiv)

Irresistible force. German mortar battery in action in central Norway, late April 1940. (Bundesarchiv)

Their 'thoroughness and foresight ... were extraordinary.' Mountain troops using collapsible boats during their advance northwards. (T/L)

Vigilance. A British 40mm AA gun defends the Fleet anchorage at Skånland. (IWM N180)

'Sooner or later they must get hit.' Trawlers attend a stricken ship off Harstad, May 1940. The cruiser in the middle distance is the *Aurora*. (T/L)

Safe and timely arrival. RAF ground staff arriving in the Vågsfjord, May 1940. (T/L)

Something new to look at. British troops admire a French light tank at Skånland, May 1940. (IWM N229)

Reprisal. Narvik under air attack in early June 1940, after the Allied capture of the town. (T/L)

transport and, using local labour to clear a runway, had been ready to receive the first arrivals on the 24th. But closer inspection of the support package that they had brought with them had revealed the kind of errors and omissions that had bedevilled the Army's operations on first arrival in Norway. Stores were neither listed nor labelled; there were only two refuelling troughs to be shared among eighteen aircraft; and the batteries of starting trolleys were uncharged. And, in a startling lapse of foresight, only one trained armourer had been provided to service the seventy-two Browning machine guns that the Squadron brought with it.

The two carriers (*Ark Royal* and *Glorious*) arrived off the coast of Norway on 24 April and, after waiting some hours for a clearance in the weather, sent the Gladiators inshore with a Skua leading the way. (The carriers then made off to prepare for a raid on Trondheim.) The aircraft landed safely and a start was made on preparing them for a launch at dawn. But night temperatures in the Norwegian highlands were still bitter. When the time came for the first launch, carburettors and control surfaces were frozen solid and it took almost two hours to get the first aircraft off the ground. Others followed during the course of the morning (by the end of the day the Squadron had flown a total of forty sorties and had achieved six 'kills') but the green and increasingly edgy support party was unable to keep more than a handful of aircraft in the air. Turnaround times became extended and the Luftwaffe caught most of the Gladiators on the ground. At noon, only eight survived. By nightfall there were only four and there were signs that the ice was breaking up under the impact of German bombs. Next morning, what remained of the Squadron withdrew to Setnesmoen, an airstrip on the outskirts of Åndalsnes. It mounted a few sorties from there on the 26th but, in less than forty-eight hours, this gallant but misconceived attempt to redress the imbalance in the air had come to nought. Although pressed on the matter, the Air Staff refused to repeat the experiment and it was left to the carriers and the hard-pressed AA ships to do what they could to blunt the edge of the German air offensive.

During the final week of April the two carriers held their position off the Norwegian coast for five successive days. (By then, aircrew, most of them recent products of the training machine, were showing 'definite signs of strain'.[34]) Working from a position some 120 miles offshore they endeavoured to maintain fighter patrols over Namsos and Åndalsness, as well as to make some impression on the fighting in the Gudbrandsdal. By the end of the month they had claimed twenty enemy shot down in air-to-air combat and a further twenty damaged, for a loss of fifteen of their own, mostly through accident.[35] They had also mounted attacks on shipping and installations at Trondheim, causing extensive damage at Værnes and destroying several aircraft on the ground. Yet despite General Massy's fulsome tribute to their work, the influence of the Fleet Air Arm on the

117

course of the campaign was to remain marginal. In the days immediately following the debacle at Lesjaskog, German bombers raided Åndalsnes setting fire to the wooden quay, destroying a large quantity of stores and rations stockpiled nearby and igniting an ammunition dump on the edge of the town. They also raided Molde, sank a Norwegian torpedo boat and several AS trawlers (used as maids of all work in the harbour approaches) and drove off the local craft that plied between the two ports. Captain M.M. Denny, the naval officer in charge, warned the Admiralty that it was only a matter of time before the line of communication through Molde and Åndalsnes failed altogether. Moulton's conclusion that the British air effort (land based as well as sea based) was 'belated, unorganised and dispersed' can hardly be faulted.[36] What is beyond dispute is that reinforcements arriving at Åndalsnes during these days and moving forward to the front line found towns burning, railway tracks pitted with craters and roads littered with burnt and abandoned vehicles.

The battle at Kvam was already raging when Paget reached Åndalsnes. After a brief meeting with Sir Cecil Dormer who had kept in loose touch with the Nygaardsvold Government during its wanderings in the Gud-brandsdal, and whose faith in Ruge's abilities had remained undimmed, he set out for the Norwegian GHQ at Brennhaug, some 10 miles south of Dombås. He found Ruge critical of the modest scale of the British contribution and frustrated at London's reluctance to disclose its plans, but he established an immediate rapport with the Norwegian C-in-C and the two men had settled down amicably enough to review the military situation. Hvinden-Haug's exhausted battalions were withdrawing into the Romsdal; there was little prospect that they could make another stand until they had been thoroughly rested and re-equipped. Colonel Dahl, still isolated on the west bank of the Lågen, was making a lunge towards Fåberg and Lillehammer in a last-ditch attempt to relieve pressure on the southern front. (If he was to escape from his precarious position, the bridge at Otta remained a last and rather desperate option.) To the north and east of Dombås, an area of growing interest in the light of V Corp's latest instructions, small detachments of Norwegian troops at Hjerkinn and Folldal were all that stood between the two Allies and the German advance in the Østerdal.

Paget entertained few illusions about the dangers of his situation. His base and his lines of communication were at the mercy of the Luftwaffe and would remain so until adequate air support could be provided. Morgan's brigade was a spent force and 15th Infantry Brigade, as lightly equipped as any of its predecessors, was already locked in battle with an enemy that could call on a complete spectrum of modern weapons. Paget nevertheless accepted full responsibility for the defence of the

Gudbrandsdal and of the mountain area north of Dombås, asking only for ski detachments to guard his flanks. He recognized that infantry units would be hard pressed to hold any single position for more than forty-eight hours, but he was certain that, with a series of delaying actions, he could give London the time it needed to restore the balance.

He laid his plans accordingly. The KOYLI, which had been holding the line unaided for the last twenty-four hours, would withdraw overnight and make their way to Dombås. The Y & L would hold the line at Kjørem (just north of Kvam) for the next twenty-four hours, while the Green Howards prepared a third defensive position at Otta. Morgan's brigade, meanwhile, critically short of officers and men but with a company of Green Howards attached, would take up a position on the Hjerkinn road as a first step to securing the northern and eastern approaches to the bridge-head.

The defence of Dombås beyond the short term would need a third infantry brigade, air parity, artillery support and anti-aircraft weapons. Without these things, his force would find itself in jeopardy 'within a period of from four to five days'.[37]

1 KOYLI retired through the Kjørem position at midnight on 26 April leaving it to the 1 Y & L and B Company 1 Green Howards to hold the line in the Gudbrandsdal. The next day was the third successive day of desperate fighting. German infantry made contact early, pushing forward on both sides of the narrowing valley and making repeated attempts to pass small parties of men round the flanks of the British positions. They gained an early advantage when, in a tactic first adopted the evening before, they used incendiary shells to set the pine woods ablaze and ejected D Company 1 Y & L from its position on the left flank. They followed up quickly with tanks and heavy weapons, and repelled the counter-attack which followed. The line was re-established further back but from now on the Germans were able to harass British positions across the valley with enfilading fire.

Paget, meanwhile, found himself pulled in two directions. The French Military Attaché had arrived at his headquarters that morning with alarming news of German advances in the Østerdal. The want of reconnaissance aircraft to confirm or deny these reports was keenly felt and the General had left by car on a personal reconnaissance of the area north of Dombås, but was frustrated by deep snow on the Hjerkinn road. (Norwegian patrols later reported no sign of Germans in the area.) His attention, however, was being drawn towards Otta where the Green Howards were preparing their positions. Dahl's feint towards Lillehammer had been blocked by German forces and his left flank was now being threatened by Pellengahr's reserve. Ruge had made a strong appeal on Dahl's behalf and Paget had undertaken to hold Otta for as long as he could in order to keep an escape route open.[38] The position was a strong one but, with avenues of approach on both sides of the river, the place needed two battalions to defend it – much would now depend on whether the 1 Y & L could make a clean withdrawal from Kjørem overnight and be ready to support the Green Howards at Otta in the morning.

This condition was not fulfilled for the efficient withdrawal of the night before was not repeated. When towards midnight on 27 April lorries carrying the battalion stores left Kjørem heading northward, they ran into a German roadblock that had been established behind the lines. A battle patrol cleared the road but was unable to dislodge the Germans altogether and the two companies that had been defending the left bank of the river became involved in desperate platoon and section actions in the darkness. The companies on the right meanwhile had been blundering along the river, making for the suspension bridge at Sjoa and attracting spasmodic fire from German patrols. One company missed the bridge altogether and eventually rejoined at Dombås after an adventurous crossing of the snowfields. The others, including B Company 1 Green Howards, reached Otta at seven o'clock in the morning and went straight to their positions. The small rearguard left to cover their withdrawal was, however, overrun by German armoured cars. On the morning of 28 April there were just twelve officers and 300 men of 1 Y & L to help man the Otta position.[39]

Paget took immediate steps to revise his plans. In the final hours before the usual start time for German air reconnaissance, he moved A Company 1 Green Howards from its position on the Hjerkinn road to a concealment area south of Dombås with the transport needed to take it further forward if need be. And he put 1 KOYLI at one hour's notice to move. It was while he was making these precautionary moves that he received a telegram from V Corps telling him that evacuation had been decided on and inviting him either to accept the embarkation schedule proposed or to suggest an alternative.

Chapter 9

Painful Decisions and a Parliamentary Occasion

The Chiefs of Staff met to consider Churchill's call for the revival of 'Hammer' during the evening of 25 April. It was a 'damnable' meeting according to Ironside at which Churchill tried (quite improperly) to push the Chiefs towards an affirmative answer. With the southern front in disarray and disturbing news of German progress in the Østerdal, a *coup de main* against Trondheim had seemed the only alternative to a humiliating retreat, but the arguments that had turned staff opinion against 'Hammer' six days earlier remained as valid as ever. In their report to the MCC the Chiefs of Staff advised that the operation would take ten days to mount and that it would be impossible to make Trondheim safe against the scale of air attack that the Germans would bring against it. Once these propositions were accepted, the way ahead became clear. Troop withdrawals from France could be stopped, central Norway could be evacuated, and the capture of Narvik (the primary object all along) could be pursued 'with all the speed and energy possible'. The Prime Minister (still chairing the MCC) was worried about the effect of withdrawal on neutral opinion and on the Government's standing at home, and had wanted to present the evacuation as part of a deliberate plan to concentrate effort in the far north. It was agreed that no date would be set for the operation and that evacuation would be postponed as long as possible – preferably until after the capture of Narvik.[1]

Cabinet members were uneasy when presented with these proposals but Chamberlain had taken care in recent days to keep his colleagues abreast of the situation and criticism was muted. Anthony Eden, Secretary of State for the Colonies, wanted to hold Namsos as an 'outpost for Narvik' and Sir John Simon, the Chancellor, argued that the abandonment of central Norway was inconsistent with undertakings given at the SWC only four days previously. There was logic in his arguments for the French were furious at this new example of British backsliding. Alerted (by Ironside)

121

that big decisions were in the offing, General Maurice Gamelin (the French military Supremo) flew to London at the behest of the Comité de Guerre to argue the case that Trondheim should be taken *'coûte que coûte'*. That evening (26 April) he attended a special session of the War Cabinet. Churchill explained the Government's dilemma, stressing in particular the effects of German air action and the strain on naval resources. The situation, he said, had profoundly altered since the meeting of the SWC and was now 'very grave'. HMG had reviewed the case for a direct attack on Trondheim but had rejected the idea after very careful consideration. Plans for Narvik remained unaffected and this had always been the 'primary strategic objective'. In reply, Gamelin argued the case for maintaining a bridgehead in the mountains near Åndalsnes (a job tailor-made for his Alpine troops) and pointed out that the defence of Narvik began in central Norway. It was agreed that the planning staffs would study his proposals and that an answer would be given at an emergency meeting of the SWC to be held next day.[2]

Gamelin returned to his theme in a meeting with the Chiefs of Staff the following morning, stressing once again the need to keep a bridgehead in central Norway and offering a second light division to carry out the task. And he suggested that, if Namsos could not be held, his Chasseurs could conduct a fighting retreat northwards along the Norwegian coast. (Ironside, he thought, was sympathetic to his views although Pound and Newall[3] seemed *'beaucoup plus réticents'*.) The meeting of the SWC followed with Reynaud and Daladier in attendance. There was little meeting of minds. The British delegation continued to insist that the capture of Trondheim would place an excessive strain on Allied resources and that a decision on Åndalsnes would soon become urgent. The only points of agreement were that the capture of Narvik remained a vital strategic objective and that the staffs would give further thought to French proposals for a fighting retreat along the Norwegian coast. After the meeting Gamelin waited at the French Embassy for the British Government's decision. He received Ironside's message shortly before midnight. The Cabinet had decided that the evacuation of central Norway was inevitable and had instructed General Massy to submit plans.

Massy brought his ideas to the MCC during the evening of 27 April. He had considered the option of holding on for an interim period but he had been unable to recommend it since it would mean landing transport, artillery and AA weapons, and possibly additional infantry brigades. Instead, he favoured an immediate evacuation that minimized losses in men and materiel. A decision made now, he asserted, would allow 'Maurice' and 'Sickle' to be pulled out during 1 and 2 May. If the current supply and reinforcement schedule was allowed to continue, evacuation might take thirty days or more.[4] That evening the MCC approved a set of instructions for General Massy, stating that the policy of HMG was to evacuate central Norway. There were, inevitably, face-saving clauses: the Government did not wish to impose any delay that might jeopardize military security but they hoped that it would be possible to postpone evacuation until after the capture of Narvik. The timing, however, would rest with Massy and with the responsible naval and air commanders. He was to include Norwegian forces in his evacuation plans if the Norwegian C-in-C so wished and, in the interests of secrecy, he was to restrict knowledge of the plan to those who would be directly responsible for carrying it out.[5] An addendum to these instructions warned him that a number of 'independent companies' were being formed to operate on the Norwegian coast and told him to arrange for the French detachment at Namsos to withdraw northwards along the road to Mosjøen to obstruct any German advance against Narvik.

The exchanges between Churchill and Admiral of the Fleet Sir Roger Keyes, hero of Zeebrugge and, before that, passionate defender of the attempt on the Dardanelles, make a curious footnote to these events.[6] Keyes had been lobbying for re-employment since the start of the war and had seen, in central Norway, an opportunity tailor-made for his talents. He had approached the Admiralty with his own plans for storming Trondheim and, after some days of bullying and string pulling, had gained access to Churchill's office to present his case in detail, and to advertise his unique qualifications to command the attack in person. Sent away unsatisfied, he had then bombarded the First Lord with letters claiming that the heroes of old had often returned from periods of unemployment to strike resounding blows against the nation's enemies. He had utter confidence in the feasibility of his plan. 'It can't fail and it won't fail,' he told Churchill on 24 April, 'if you let me do it and be responsible for it.' But the moment had passed. 'It astonishes me,' wrote Churchill in reply:

> that you should think that all this has not been examined by people who know exactly what resources are available and what the dangers would be ... You will I hope appreciate the fact that I have to be guided by my responsible Naval advisers, and that it is not open to me to make the kind of appointments you and Eva have in mind on the ground of friendship.[7]

Churchill refused him another interview and Keyes had then started lobbying the Prime Minister and other members of the War Cabinet. Frustrated enthusiasm was now turning to rancour. In a parting shot at Churchill on 28 April, he referred to the Navy's 'shocking inaction' at Trondheim 'for which you and your pusillanimous, self-satisfied, short-sighted Naval advisors must bear the responsibility'. He now had bigger targets in his sights. 'If the scuttle is persisted in,' he continued, referring to rumours of evacuation, 'the Government will have to go and I shall do my damnedest to speed them.' He was as good as his word. It was far too late to shift the staff consensus (the battle for central Norway was lost and all eyes were now turned on Narvik) but his was to be one of the more memorable interventions in the Commons debate on Norway that took place a week later.

With the destruction of Namsos and the retreat from Steinkjer, Carton de Wiart had remained on the defensive, his forward battalion, the Hallam-shires, holding the neck of land between the Beitstadfjord and the Snåsavatn, and sending out patrols to watch for signs of movement on the part of the Germans. He was certain now that the campaign could serve no useful purpose, that an advance on Trondheim was out of the question and that there was little point in his men remaining where they were 'sitting out like rabbits in the snow'. Peter Fleming (still acting as his principal staff officer) had returned from a mission to the War Office with tales of confusion and uncertainty, and the General had formed the impression that he could do more or less what he liked. His choice was studied inactivity, although he was content to allow Audet to start preliminary discussions with Getz on possible Franco-Norwegian counter-moves. For Carton de Wiart, this had become the dullest campaign ever.[8]

There had been a lull in the enemy's air activity following the Luft-waffe's blitz on the port of Namsos and London's attempts to reinforce and resupply the expedition had continued. Naval fighters had appeared over the town on 25 April and had lifted the spirits of men on the ground. But with unloading now confined to the single stone quay, the landing of stores and equipment had become more difficult than ever. A ship arriving on 27 April with a Royal Marine howitzer battery, a field ambulance and a large consignment of rifles and ammunition for the Norwegian Army had found the berth occupied by a French supply ship that was unloading transport for the Chasseurs and had sailed with most of its cargo still on board. A few guns had been put ashore (but no ammunition) and the General had, at long last, got part of his headquarters staff – but nothing of any real value.

Carton de Wiart had thus responded to Massy's telegram announcing evacuation with some alacrity. At a hastily summoned conference with Audet, Phillips and Rear Admiral J.G.P. Vivian, who commanded the AA cruisers, he decided to make full use of the French supply ships that were already in port and to evacuate a battalion of Chasseurs there and then. During 28 April, therefore, 850 men of the 53rd Battalion were withdrawn from positions along the railway and embarked in the waiting ships. This early initiative was to have a significant influence on later events.

The original plan, drawn up by the Admiralty and V Corps Headquarters envisaged an evacuation spread over two nights using the three French transports that had delivered the Chasseurs to Namsos, followed on the second night by the cruisers *Devonshire* (flag of Vice Admiral J.H.D. Cunningham), *York* and *Montcalm*. On 29 April, therefore, Carton de Wiart withdrew the 13th Chasseurs from positions overlooking the Beitstadfjord and started to concentrate what remained of the French contingent close to Namsos, ready to embark as soon as the transports arrived. His reasons for evacuating the Frenchmen first were largely prosaic. Admiral Cadart's ships would be the first to arrive and half the Chasseurs were in Namsos already. (The story that Audet had 'begged him' not to leave the Chasseurs until last, called him '*un vrai gentleman*' and made as if to embrace him is vintage Carton de Wiart, and at best an embellishment of the truth.) After this initial move he started a phased withdrawal, taking care to conceal his movements from the Germans and aiming to have withdrawn his whole force through a final rearguard position at the Bangsund river crossing by the start of the second night.

Secure in his reputation and convinced of the ineptitude of the higher headquarters, he simply ignored instructions to organize a rearguard at Grong and to conduct the kind of fighting retreat towards Mosjøen that Gamelin had advocated. He regarded the route as impassable during the spring thaw, an opinion reinforced by the experience of his two minions, Peter Fleming and Martin Lindsay, who had attempted to get along it by car. He had even opposed the suggestion that a small party of Chasseurs should withdraw along it and he had done nothing to interest Colonel Getz in the project for fear of alerting the Norwegians to the forthcoming evacuation. In the end, 100 Chasseurs had left by sea for Mosjøen but the land route was left to look after itself. A few days later – and to Massy's intense irritation – the Germans used the road without apparent difficulty and seized Mosjøen before the Allies had consolidated their positions. While history suggests that Carton de Wiart was right in his instincts, he did not escape censure at the time. 'The importance of this operation,' wrote General Massy of the projected fighting retreat, 'was strongly stressed in several telegrams from these headquarters [but] its feasibility could only be left to the judgement of the man on the spot. In this case an error of judgement was made.'[9]

As Carton de Wiart began his withdrawal towards Namos, the Luftwaffe returned in force, underlining the need for a full complement of AA ships during the critical phase of the evacuation. Vivian left at once for the Skejlfjord to fuel the *Carlisle*, aiming to return by nightfall of 30 April and leaving the sloop *Bittern* to guard the fjord in his absence. That day the Stukas mounted attack after attack on the *Bittern* and on the (largely defenceless) AS trawlers present in the Namsenfjord. The *Bittern* fought them off until her gun crews were red-eyed with fatigue, but towards evening a direct hit crippled the ship, ignited the depth charges stowed on the quarterdeck and set fire to the small-arms magazine. The ship was abandoned, her crew being taken off by the destroyer *Janus*. At nightfall only five of the eight trawlers survived. When Vivian returned from fuelling he decided to keep his ships clear of the fjord during the hours of daylight in order to preserve them for the evacuation. He sailed at dawn on 1 May with the *Carlisle* and three of the remaining trawlers, planning to return with the French auxiliaries later in the day.

At dusk, the Chasseur battalions began to muster on the quayside to await embarkation. The prompt arrival of the transports was essential if they were to clear the fjord before daybreak for it was becoming almost impossible to believe that the Germans had not come to appreciate what was going on. But at 2130 on 1 May, Force Headquarters heard that Admiral Cunningham had run into dense fog in the approaches to the Namsenfjord and had ordered a 24-hour postponement. The situation was worrying. There had been no sign so far that the German Army was aware of Allied intentions but it could only be a matter of time and delay might ultimately mean embarkation under the pressure of German guns. It was also becoming increasingly difficult to find plausible stories to tell the Norwegians. (Getz had been told that the French were pulling out to mount an attack on the forts in the Trondheimsfjord.) The Chasseurs were quickly dispersed to concealment areas on the outskirts of the town.

Next morning, Vivian returned from seaward with plans for evacuation in a single night. Cunningham had floated this idea some thirty-six hours earlier when he had first heard that a battalion of Chasseurs had left already, but Carton de Wiart had turned it down on the grounds that he would be unable to withdraw his forward troops in time. Audet and Vivian had also expressed reservations. But in the new circumstances, the plan seemed more appealing. It would mean bringing sufficient ships into the fjord to evacuate the rest of 'Maurice' in a single lift – the three French transports, a cruiser and three or four destroyers. It would put pressure on the quay space available (already strictly limited) and might leave men or ships (or both) at the mercy of the Germans if it extended into the hours of daylight. It would almost certainly mean leaving guns and stores behind. Yet with risk of German interference increasing by the hour and with operations subject to the vagaries of the weather it had seemed essential to make full use of every opportunity that presented itself. The two generals had therefore accepted the idea.

For the men ashore the day seemed endless. Four ships of the 5th Destroyer Flotilla (Captain Lord Louis Mountbatten) had nosed into the fjord at daybreak but had been driven back by the ferocity of the German air attack, and the troops had had to wait for nightfall. But, at the appointed hour, the evacuation force appeared off the town. The French auxiliaries *El d' Jezair* and *El Kantara* berthed at the stone quay – a feat of seamanship that earned their captains much credit – and a shuttle service of destroyers and trawlers ferried men from the damaged wooden pier (previously ruled out as an embarkation point) to the *York* and the *El Mansour*, lying off the town. Ships sailed independently as they finished loading. And as the first hint of dawn began to show, the last of the transports left. The *Afridi* (Captain Phillip Vian) waited behind to pick up the British rearguard which, after blowing the bridge at Bangsund, faced a lonely 15-mile journey into Namsos. Then, after shelling the French motor transport abandoned on the quayside, the destroyer left at high speed to overtake the rest of the force. Relief was palpable. Most attributed their deliverance to the work of the Navy, a view reflected in General Massy's later observations on the 'tireless devotion' and the 'complete disregard of personal safety' shown by the men of the sister service.[10] Some credit seems due to Carton de Wiart and Audet for their skill and judgement in withdrawing their forward units without alerting the enemy. Yet something was wanting in their generalship. They kept their Norwegian ally in the dark about their intentions until the late evening of 2 May when the ships were already loading. As Moulton observes, this was 'scurvy treatment'. Colonel Getz, abandoned to his fate, was forced to open negotiations with the Germans the following day.[11]

The ships that cleared the fjord early (*York*, *El Mansour* and their escorts) reached Scapa on 4 May after an uneventful passage. (It was Carton de Wiart's sixtieth birthday; he had been away just eighteen days.) The rest of Cunningham's force was less fortunate. The fog cleared as they left the Norwegian coast to bring 'perfect bombing weather' and shadowing aircraft soon made contact. Wave after wave of bombers followed, concentrating their attacks on the warships. The *Devonshire* and the *Montcalm* escaped serious injury but, towards noon, the French destroyer *Bison* was critically damaged. Three other destroyers (*Grenade*, *Imperial* and *Afridi*) closed the burning wreck and succeeded in recovering most of her ship's company. But while steaming to rejoin the convoy the *Afridi* too fell victim to German dive-bombers and sank in twenty minutes with heavy loss of life. Among the casualties were thirteen men of the 1st/8th York and Lancaster Regiment who had formed part of the British rearguard. They were the only casualties suffered by the Allied armies during the evacuation of central Norway.

Many of the difficulties encountered at Namsos were mirrored at Åndalsnes and Molde. The two ports became unworkable in daylight and the unloading of stores and equipment during the brief hours of darkness was frustrated by damage to wooden quays and the wholesale destruction of AS trawlers and harbour craft. In the absence of the carriers (*Ark Royal* was resting her air group and the *Glorious* was embarking new aircraft in Scapa) air defence was left to the AA sloops. A succession of these ships left for home between 26 and 30 April with their magazines empty and their 4-inch guns showing advanced symptoms of wear. One of them, the *Black Swan*, sailed for Scapa with a 3-foot hole in her bottom where a German bomb had passed through the hull without exploding. In the previous forty-eight hours she had fired 2,000 rounds of 4-inch ammunition and double that number of smaller rounds. Her successor, the *Fleetwood*, left during the early hours of 30 April in a similar state and there had been no AA ship available to replace her.

Plans for the evacuation of Åndalsnes were complicated by a breakdown in communications between the base areas and the front line. 'Communications with Sickle Force have all gone to hell,' was Ironside's verdict when Dudley Clarke called on him in the War Office to deliver a letter from Ruge and to receive instructions for the coming evacuation. Clarke returned to Åndasnes on 28 April to find the town in ruins, men on half-rations and those responsible for the functioning and defence of the base areas in a state of dejection and uncertainty. He met a few old friends at a planning conference on the morning of the 29th, including a 'tired and haggard' Morgan who was trying to cobble together a force to secure the road from Dombås, left unguarded by the retreat of the Norwegian Army. The meeting was a gloomy one. Brigadier Hogg, the base commander and Massy's QMG, believed it quite possible that 'Sickle' had been overrun and that the Germans could break through at any moment.[12] The plans that Clarke had brought from London already seemed impracticable. They had assumed embarkation on the nights of 30 April and 1 May, and the large-scale use of Molde, dates that took little account of the urgency of the situation and a port that was largely inaccessible following the sinking of the trawlers and disruption of the ferry service. The authorities in Åndalsnes urged London to bring the evacuation forward by twenty-four hours. They took the opportunity of the *Fleetwood*'s departure to send 340 men home with her, most of them wounded, 'a prodigious number' for a ship of that size. Hogg and Denny had hoped to evacuate more but the ships that arrived at dusk on 29 April were bent on a different purpose.

In Cabinet that morning, Churchill had read out a message from Sir Cecil Dormer warning that the withdrawal could lead to the total collapse of Norwegian resistance. He had urged all possible steps to retain the confidence of the Norwegian Government and recommended that, if evacuation was unavoidable, King Haakon and his ministers should be moved to a place of safety.[13] That night the cruiser *Glasgow* arrived off Molde with an escort of two destroyers. An air attack was in progress for the Luftwaffe was now continuing its attacks into the night hours. The scene was one of

Wagnerian intensity. The ship approached the pier with 'fire hoses playing, the whole scene being brilliantly lit by the flames of the burning town'.[14] She sailed for an unknown destination with 280 passengers and a quantity of gold bullion, and, two days later, transferred King Haakon, Crown Prince Olav and members of the Government to a Norwegian destroyer in the approaches to the arctic port of Tromsø.

Paget received Massy's evacuation order on the morning of 28 April just as the defence of the Otta position was beginning. He felt unable to comply without first discussing the matter with Ruge whose co-operation he considered essential. Showing a sensitivity to the broader issues that was wholly lacking in his counterpart at Namsos he went straight to the Norwegian GHQ to explain the position fully. He was, he later wrote, 'perfectly frank'. Ruge 'took the news quietly' but he despatched a bitter note of protest to Ironside, referring to recent undertakings by the British Government and to the sacrifices made by his Army during three weeks of war.[15] Yet, both men recognized that they were dependent on each other. 'He [Ruge] told me he would not let me down,' Paget later reported, 'provided that I would cover the withdrawal of the Norwegian forces in my area, and this I agreed to do.'[16] Paget undertook to hold Dombås until Ruge could withdraw his detachments from Folldal and Hjerkinn, and until Hvinden-Haug could disband what remained of his Division in the Romsdal.

The difficulties facing Paget in extracting his force from the Gudbrandsdal appeared formidable. The Germans were pressing hard on both flanks of the Otta position and the defenders were heavily engaged. Evacuation meant breaking contact with an aggressive and highly mobile enemy and pulling back nearly 100 miles along a single line of retreat that, in daylight, would be dominated by the enemy's air force. The movement of men in any appreciable numbers would be limited to the hours of darkness. The rate of his withdrawal would be determined by the availability of rail and road transport (neither under his direct control) and which would have to be 'wheedled out of the Norwegians'. And his freedom of action would be further limited by his obligations to the Norwegian Army. This was going to be a difficult operation ('precarious' was the term that he used in his despatches) in which success or failure would rest on a knife-edge.[17]

That evening, Paget established a new defensive position in the approaches to Dombås and sent 1 KOYLI to man it. He withdrew a section of 55 Field Company Royal Engineers from the forward area to prepare demolitions in the Røsti Gorge a few miles behind the fighting front and sent A Company 1 Green Howards (previously occupying positions on the Hjerkinn road) to cover them. He needed breathing space, calculating that if the road and rail bridges could be blown successfully the Germans would be unable to get tanks, transport and guns forward for some forty-eight hours. As darkness approached he sent a train and what transport he could muster to positions close behind the front line.

As the tempo of the action at Otta wound down, HQ 15th Infantry Brigade withdrew the forward companies on both sides of the valley and assigned them to assembly areas at the railway station. The road and rail bridges into Otta were blown and in the early hours of 29 April the Green Howards and the Y & L companies that had supported them set off up the valley by train (sleeping carriages reserved for officers), leaving their rear parties to follow by lorry. As they passed through the Røsti Gorge the bridges were blown behind them. They passed through the KOYLI position between five and six o'clock in the morning and soon afterwards dispersed into concealment areas around Dombås. The break was a clean one, testimony to the bitterness of the struggle the day before. Only C Company, 1 Green Howards, had encountered difficulties. This Company, heavily engaged on the left flank of the Otta position, had escaped over the bare rock of the mountain slopes to find the village already in German hands. But it had broken into small parties and rejoined the battalion at Dombås later in the day. The critical first step in this complex operation was over; if he had gauged the effects of his demolitions correctly, Paget had two clear nights in which to get his men the remaining 60 miles to Åndalsnes. But there were no grounds for complacency. Ruge had been unable to extract his detachments from Folldal and Hjerkinn until the night of the 29th, making the night of the 30th the earliest point at which Paget could relinquish Dombås. This cut safety margins to the bone and made another battle virtually inevitable. But the KOYLI were well established on the Dombås position and Ruge had provided a half-battery of field guns to support them. They were the first that British forces had seen since they arrived in Norway.

The 29th of April passed quietly for the men of 15th Infantry Brigade. They were well hidden in the woods around Dombås and were untroubled by German aircraft passing overhead to complete the destruction of Åndalsnes and Molde. Of the German Army there was no sign. That night Paget released 1 Y & L, severely mauled in its retreat from Kjørem, keeping the other two battalions to hold the Dombås position until the Norwegian column on the Hjerkinn road had passed through. (1 Y & L reached Åndalsnes the following morning having completed the final stage of the journey on foot – a worrying development that underlined the fragility of the rail link with the Romsdalsfjord.) In a more hopeful sign, the Norwegian column had moved through Dombås on schedule, its rear-guard clearing the town and beginning the long descent towards

Åndalsnes during the morning of 30 April. The two remaining battalions were warned to be ready to entrain at 2200.

The morning of 30 April passed quietly too. The men of the KOYLI kept their positions in the broken ground astride the Lågen but towards noon a company commander on the right flank became alarmed by the break-up of the ice and by a sudden rise in water levels. Fearing that the river was becoming unfordable and that he would be cut off, he moved his men a mile down the valley to cross by the nearest bridge. It was while he was completing this precautionary move that the German Army made its first appearance. Demolitions in the Røsti Gorge had done little to curb the enterprise of the German infantry. They had marched up the valley in force, bringing mortars and ammunition in handcarts, and relying on supplies from the air. Their arrival at this critical moment with some ten hours of daylight remaining destroyed any illusion that the final withdrawal of 'Sickleforce' could be trouble-free.

The action at Dombås was as bitter as any in the campaign. Although caught unawares by the British presence (the German infantry were marching in column when the first volley hit them) they recovered themselves quickly. With the road ahead heavily defended they made their customary flanking moves, but the battalion was deployed in depth and the intruders were forced back. A reconnaissance plane attempting to probe British positions was brought down by small-arms fire and the Norwegian battery continued its work unmolested. An attempt by the Germans to cross the swollen river in collapsible boats ended in failure. C Company sank the boats and drowned the crews. At 1800 Brigadier Kent-Lemon reported that he was confident that he could hold the position and that he was 'adopting an aggressive attitude'.[18]

But preparations for the withdrawal were now well advanced. The Green Howards had occupied a rearguard position in the outskirts of Dombås, transport was assembling to evacuate Brigade Headquarters and the rear parties of both battalions, and a train was raising steam in a tunnel outside the town. The number of men to evacuate was estimated at 1775. In early evening, the line to Åndalsnes was reported clear and the withdrawal began, companies pulling back through the rearguard position one by one and assembling at the ruined railway station. The train departed at 2230 followed a few minutes later by the transport of the rear parties. Sporadic action continued until the very last and the train pulled out of the station to the rattle of German rifle fire.

The regimental history of the KOYLI describes the next few hours as 'trial by rail'.[19] The train set out through the bitter Norwegian night with men huddled together for warmth in the open trucks. They stopped at Lesja, a few miles west of Dombås, to pick up the Norwegian flank guard and the brigade anti-tank company (sent back earlier to cover against a

131

German advance across the fells), and set off once again on the long, slow descent towards the Romsdalsfjord. An hour after midnight as the train was approaching Lesjaskog, men were jolted from their fitful slumbers by a rending crash. The train had run into a bomb crater, the two engines had overturned and the front coach had telescoped killing eight men and injuring thirty more. Fire had taken hold and rescue work had continued in the glare of blazing ammunition. To wait for rescue on this high and almost treeless plateau would be fatal. The troops fell in on the frozen potholed road and marched off north-westward carrying their rifles, Brens and anti-tank guns towards the nearest cover, a railway tunnel in the Verma Gorge some 18 miles ahead. There was a real danger that the Germans could overtake the retreating column. A Green Howard platoon was left at the crash site and a staff officer was sent ahead to Åndalsnes to arrange for a force of Royal Marines to form a rearguard and to cover a series of demolitions in the Verma Gorge.

The column of men, some 1,500 strong, reached Verma after an eight-hour march. They were harassed by German aircraft as they approached their destination but suffered few casualties and the tunnel provided complete protection. It offered few comforts on the other hand – it contained two trains, a Norwegian ammunition train and a long line of empty trucks. It was dark, bitterly cold and its walls were covered with oily soot. (There is a story, possibly apocryphal but illuminating nonetheless, of General Paget, a stickler for the military formalities, meeting a junior officer at the entrance to the tunnel and telling him to do something about his appearance.) Men slept as best they could, packed like sardines into the narrow space and disturbed occasionally by German attempts to block the tunnel entrances; many nursed frostbitten feet. By afternoon, however, they had started to recover their spirits.

Arrangements had been made, meanwhile, to continue the withdrawal at nightfall. A train would leave at 2230 and the rear parties would follow in motor transport half an hour later. In late afternoon the engine began to raise steam. The tunnel filled with acrid fumes and the men were forced out, to conceal themselves as best they could on the slopes of the gorge. There followed almost immediately confused reports that the Royal Marine detachment at the head of the gorge had given way and that the Germans were about to break through. Both battalions sent companies back to reinforce the rearguard. (They found little to do and the Royal Marine Lewis-gun detachment had later retired in good order.) The Norwegian stationmaster was told to advance the time of departure and an armed guard was posted on the engine footplate to encourage compliance. After a difficult manoeuvre to back the heavy train into the station (a manoeuvre that seems to have been forced on the reluctant driver), the

132

troops boarded the train at 2030. Three hours later they were mustering on the quay in Åndalsnes.

The final evacuation of Åndalsnes, Molde and Ålesund relied heavily on improvization and, in the end, on luck. At dusk on 30 April, as Paget's men were leaving their positions at Dombås to begin their epic journey to the sea, Sir George Edward-Collins arrived in the Romsdalsfjord with four cruisers, six destroyers and two Irish Sea packets (*Ulster Monarch* and *Ulster Prince*) to evacuate as many men from 'Sickle' and 'Primrose' as he could. Ignoring the warnings of the Base Commander, he put his smaller cruisers (*Galatea* and *Arethusa*) on the concrete quay at Åndalsnes and used his destroyers to ferry troops to the larger ships and to round up parties of men from outlying areas. By dawn he had embarked 2,200 men including most of the survivors of Morgan's Brigade and of 1 Y & L. The men were 'deadbeat and ravenously hungry'. Many had lost their rifles but they seemed steady enough and there was no sign of a breakdown in discipline.[20] No one seemed to know how many men were still to come. Edward-Collins told Admiral Layton who was to continue the operation the following night that there was little news from the front, but that he thought there were still some 1,500 troops to come plus a few Norwegians and refugees.

Edward-Collins's luck held. His force met no opposition until the arrival of the Luftwaffe in the early morning of 1 May, and even then the scale of attack was light. 'Once again,' he reported, 'and contrary to all expectation, the Romsdals Fjord was entered, the operation completed and forces withdrawn without loss or damage through enemy action.'[21]

A minor drama, meanwhile, had been taking place at Molde, where the remnants of the Norwegian 2nd Division were now dispersing. Ruge had resisted offers of evacuation until he had consulted the Norwegian Government and satisfied himself that the British ally genuinely intended to continue the fight at Narvik. The ubiquitous Dudley Clarke found him in Molde on 30 April after following in the wake of the Norwegian Army as it wound its painful way from Dombås to the sea. Ruge had delegated the 'melancholy task of surrender' to Hvinden-Haug and was now asking for a British ship to take him northward. The two men joined the throng of people waiting for evacuation at the burning quay – Captain Denny and his naval party, a group of airmen from Lesjaskog, the Norwegian Admiral and his staff, and a number of Swedish volunteers who were thought to be at particular risk. Towards midnight the *Ulster Prince*, arrived in Molde accompanied by the destroyer *Tartar*. Everyone embarked including Ruge's staff but, on being informed that the ship was going to Scapa rather than to a Norwegian port, the General declined to do so. The Captain demanded a decision; Ruge remained adamant. His staff trooped off and the ship sailed without them.

The Admiralty's attempts to ease the pressure on Åndalsnes and Molde during the period of the evacuation met with little success. An ambitious plan to draw off the Luftwaffe by simulating a landing in the approaches to the Trondheimsfjord was abandoned. Admiral Forbes had been willing to provide the battleship that London had asked for but not the transports since he had no escorts to protect them. 'Every destroyer fit to fight,' he told the Admiralty, 'is being used.'[22] The carrier group, heavily escorted, had provided fighter cover over Åndalsnes during 1 May and had later moved north to do the same at Namsos. But it had done little to relieve the pressure on the base areas. The carriers had come under heavy attack themselves and German bombs had fallen 'uncomfortably close'. That night Admiral Wells, Flag Officer (Air), withdrew to seaward reporting that he was unable to hold a position from which he could support operations ashore.[23] Luftwaffe ascendancy over the coastal waters of central Norway was now unchallenged.

Layton entered the Romsdalsfjord during the late evening of 1 May. (His last entry had been just six days before when his ships had landed General Paget and the Green Howards. Now he was coming to take them off.) He detached the *Somali* to recover the 'Primrose' party from Ålesund and on passing Molde (hidden under a pall of smoke) sent the *Diana* inshore for Ruge and his staff. He arrived off Åndalsnes at 2300 with the heavy cruisers *Manchester* and *Birmingham*, the two AA ships and a force of five destroyers. An hour later, the cruisers had taken on 1,300 men, leaving the rearguard (reported as 200 strong) still to come. Although the Luftwaffe had bombed the town earlier in the evening, the evacuation passed unmolested. Layton sailed at once since fog was threatening, leaving the *Calcutta* and the *Aukland* to collect the rest. The *Aukland* found the rearguard and embarked them in seven minutes. The *Calcutta*, however, found 700 more (mostly men from the 1 KOYLI) who, in the general confusion, had been left out of the reckoning. She got alongside the concrete quay at the third attempt and put down ten gangways. The men embarked in a matter of minutes and by two o'clock on the morning of 2 May, the town was deserted. Layton's force arrived at Scapa on 3 May after an uneventful passage. On board were General Paget and a total of 2,450 men.

During the afternoon of 2 May the Prime Minister announced the evacuation of Åndalsnes in the House of Commons.[24] He provided few details but promised a full statement in the week to follow. But the crisis in central Norway had been common knowledge in Westminster and Whitehall for several days and unrest had been growing. Those close to the Government tended to blame the Chiefs of Staff. Sir James Grigg, master of the calculated indiscretion, let it be known that he regarded Ironside as 'the worst and most incompetent of men'; R.A. (Rab) Butler (rising star in the Conservative firmament and now a youthful Under-Secretary of State for Foreign Affairs) accused the Chiefs of Staff of 'an appalling lack of foresight'.[25] The welling tide of criticism had soon threatened to engulf the Government itself. On 28 April the Sunday papers accused ministers of complacency and reignited the simmering debate about the Government's decision-making structures and about the composition of the War Cabinet. The House was soon fizzing with intrigue and Chamberlain men were beginning to see plots on every side. When the Commons met on 7 May to consider the recent happenings in Norway powerful emotions lay not far beneath the surface.

The two-day debate on the conduct of the war left a Government with a seemingly unassailable majority (213 seats) rocking on its foundations. It was a discursive affair which ranged far beyond the narrow question of Norway and which shone a cruel spotlight on the Government's pre-war record, and on the competence of the Prime Minister. Although speaker after speaker called on the Government to account for its failure to attack Trondheim and for its premature decision to disband the Finnish expeditionary force it was on the broader issues that ministers found themselves most vulnerable.

The Prime Minister opened the debate with a feeble, defensive speech, pointing to the modest scale of operations in Norway (this was 'not comparable to the withdrawal from Gallipoli') and suggesting that the implications of the setback had been 'seriously exaggerated'. Even Chips Channon, one of his most ardent supporters found him 'tired and embarrassed'.[26] He was aware of calls for changes in the structure of Government but he was not convinced of their merits; he had, however, strengthened Churchill's role in the development of strategy by authorizing him 'to give guidance and direction' to the Chiefs of Staff who would, from now on, 'prepare plans to meet the objectives set out by him'. He ended with a plea for support from both sides of the House.[27]

The opposition leaders were less concerned with the decision to evacuate (this they accepted had become inevitable) than with the decisions that had given rise to the debacle. After posing a series of detailed questions that still awaited answers from ministers, Clement Attlee, Leader of the Opposition, gave a voice to the growing public concern about the competence of the Chamberlain administration. He was not satisfied, he told the House, that the War Cabinet was 'an efficient instrument for conducting the war'. (As for the Prime Minister's latest proposal, it was 'against all rules of good organisation' that a man responsible for general strategy should also be in charge of a particular department.) Norway was the 'culmination of many discontents'. It was the work of men who, in the field of defence and foreign policy, had enjoyed 'an almost uninterrupted career of failure'.[28] The Leader of the Liberal Party, Sir Archibald Sinclair, followed with a 'venomous' speech comparing the Prime Minister to the eighteenth-century general who, according to Macaulay, had 'thought it much more honourable to fail according to rule than to succeed by innovation'.[29]

The Government might have fended off these brickbats had not some of its most influential allies sided with the opposition. Two speeches made a particular impact. Just after seven o'clock, Sir Roger Keyes had risen to his feet, dressed in the uniform of an Admiral of the Fleet (a gesture in 'questionable taste' according to some) and claiming to speak for the men of the 'fighting, seagoing Navy'. (It was clear that the First Lord's 'pusillanimous' naval advisors would be high on his target list.) It was not the Navy's fault, he assured the House, that the enemy had been left in undisputed possession of valuable ports and airfields and been allowed to reinforce them at will. The capture of Trondheim had been 'essential, imperative and vital'; he (Keyes) had begged the Admiralty and the War Cabinet to let him organize and lead the attack, but in vain. The result had been the Steinkjer fiasco, 'a shocking piece of ineptitude' which should never have been allowed to happen. He had watched as the Gallipoli tragedy was repeated step by step. That brilliant strategic concept had been defeated by the First Lord's then Principal Naval Advisor,[30] by those who could see no further than the barbed wire on the Western Front and finally by the dead hand of Whitehall. He had great admiration for his friend the First Lord of the Admiralty and 'longed to see proper use made of his great abilities'. He now challenged him to put the bitter experience of Gallipoli behind him and see to it that the Navy was more vigorously employed.[31]

The salvos fired by the veteran Tory, L.S. Amery, were just as memorable and a good deal more accurate. He did not feel, he told the House, that there was a single sentence in the Prime Minister's speech 'which suggested that the Government either foresaw what the Germans meant to do, or came to a clear decision when it knew what the Germans had done or acted swiftly and consistently throughout the whole of this lamentable affair'. Norway was a 'bad story, a story of lack of prevision, of preparation, a story of indecision, slowness and fear of taking risks'. But it was 'of a piece' with the rest of the Government's record. Peacetime conditions tended to breed peacetime statesmen. 'Facility in debate, ability to state a case, caution in advancing an unpopular view, compromise and procrastination' were the natural qualities of a political leader in time of peace. But they were fatal in war. 'Surely,' he went on, responding now to the upwelling of emotion in the House:

for the Government of the last ten years to have bred a band of warrior statesmen would have been little short of a miracle. We have waited eight months and the miracle has not come to pass ... Somehow or another we must get into the Government men who can match our enemies in fighting spirit, in daring, in resolution and in thirst for victory. Some 300 years ago, when this House found that its troops were being beaten again and again by the dash and daring of the Cavaliers ... Oliver Cromwell spoke to John Hampden. In one of his speeches he recounted what he said. It was this. 'I said to him, "Your troops are most of them old, decayed serving men and tapsters and such kind of fellows ... you must get men of spirit that are likely to go as far as they will go or you will be beaten still."'

He concluded with one of the most merciless dismissals of a Government in Parliamentary history. 'I have quoted certain words of Oliver Cromwell,' he told a breathless House:

> I will quote certain other words. I do it with great reluctance because I am speaking of those who are old friends and associates of mine, but they are words which, I think, are applicable to the present situation. This is what Cromwell said to the Long Parliament when he thought it was no longer fit to conduct the affairs of the nation. 'You have sat too long here for any good that you have been doing. Depart, I say, and let us have done with you. In the name of God, go.'[32]

There were still loyalists in the House who were prepared to argue that the charges levelled against the Government lacked substance, that the blame for the debacle lay primarily with the Norwegians and that attacks on the Prime Minister could only give comfort to the enemy. But the tenor of the debate remained overwhelmingly hostile and the hapless Oliver Stanley, left to defend the breach in the Government's defences, showed nothing of the pugnacity and conviction that might have produced a change of mood. The House adjourned at 11.30pm on 7 May with the Government wounded and its critics scenting blood.

Yet the change of tactics announced by the Labour opposition when the debate resumed seems to have taken ministers by surprise. Herbert Morrison, the Member for Hackney South, opened the attack. His speech ranged too widely to be wholly effective but he landed one or two telling blows. He had returned to the topic of government complacency and had unearthed a notably purple passage in which the Secretary of State for Air was quoted as saying, 'Today our wings are spread over the Arctic. They are sheathed in ice. Tomorrow the sun of victory will touch them with its golden light.' (The House had erupted in scornful laughter.) He had gone on to question the Prime Minister's decision to extend the First Lord's responsibilities and to accuse the Government of putting Churchill 'into the shop window' in the hope of silencing public criticism. He had kept his principal bombshell until last. He announced that, in view of the gravity of the situation, the Opposition would divide the House at the end of the evening and turn what had started as a routine adjournment debate (the House was about to rise for Whitsun) into a Vote of Censure.[33] The Prime Minister intervened at once and in words that struck many as introducing a narrow and partisan note into the proceedings called on his friends to support him. 'I accept the challenge,' he said, 'I welcome it indeed. At least we shall see who is with us and who is against us.' He was soon to pay for his outburst. Lloyd George, dismissed by many as a spent force in recent years, had pounced on Chamberlain's words and with the searing irony of his prime had declared:

> It is not a question of who are the Prime Minister's friends. It is a far bigger issue. The Prime Minister must remember that he has met this formidable foe of ours in peace and in war. He has always been worsted. He is not in a position to appeal on the grounds of friendship. He has appealed for sacrifice ... I say solemnly that the Prime Minister should give an example of sacrifice, because there is nothing which can contribute more to victory in this war than that he should sacrifice the seals of office.[34]

Churchill had for the most part escaped the scathing criticism meted out to his colleagues. When he had intervened to claim full responsibility for the Admiralty's part in the campaign, Lloyd George had urged him 'not to allow himself to be converted into an air-raid shelter to keep the splinters from hitting his colleagues' and Alfred Duff Cooper (Westminster, St George's) had spoken for many when he warned the House that they would soon have to listen to a powerful speech from the First Lord in which, with his usual eloquence, he would defend those who had previously ignored his counsel and treated his warnings with contempt. 'He will no doubt be as successful as he always has been,' he remarked, 'and those who so often trembled before his sword will be only too glad to shrink behind his buckler.'

Churchill wound up for the Government with a 'slashing, vigorous speech, a magnificent piece of oratory' in which he deftly dissociated himself from the Government's pre-war record and carried the fight to the Opposition.[35] Many of the country's present problems, he told the House, stemmed from the loss of air parity with Germany and the subsequent failure to regain it. When, five years before, he and a few friends had warned of the consequences, it had been the Opposition parties as well as the Government which had objected. His tone was far from apologetic; he defended the Admiralty's role in the Norway campaign with considerable verve and 'amused and dazzled everyone with his virtuosity'; he chided Keyes (and others) for failing to appreciate how the development of airpower had revolutionized the conduct of naval operations since 1918, and expressed full confidence in his current naval advisors (Pound and Phillips), whose massive good sense and professional knowledge were 'kept constantly up to date by contacts with modern conditions'. In the end, his taunting of the Government's critics reduced the House to disorder. But he struck a final blow at those who had turned the adjournment debate into a vote of censure, and at those who might be thinking of deserting the Government's cause. 'It seems to me that the House will be absolutely wrong,' he said, 'to take such a grave decision in such a precipitate manner and after such little notice.' Exception had been taken to the Prime Minister's appeal to his friends: 'He thought he had some friends and I hope he has some friends. He certainly had a good many when things were going well.'

'At no time in the last war,' he concluded, 'were we in greater peril than we are now, and I urge the House strongly to deal with these matters not in a precipitate vote, ill debated and on a widely discursive field, but in grave time and due time in accordance with the dignity of Parliament.'[36]

When the vote was taken the Government's majority of 213 had been cut to 81. Chamberlain appeared 'bowled over by the ominous figures, and was the first to rise ... He looked grave thoughtful and sad ... a solitary little man, who had done his best for England.'[37]

The final hours of the Chamberlain Government have been fully described elsewhere.[38] Suffice it to say here that, by mid-morning on Thursday, 9 May, it was clear, at least to his closest colleagues, that the Prime Minister was looking for a National Government and that, if need be, he would give way to someone who could command the necessary cross-party support. Who that candidate would be was determined that afternoon in a meeting between Chamberlain, Halifax, Churchill and the Tory Chief Whip, David Margesson. It is generally accepted that Chamberlain's preference lay with Lord Halifax but that, despite repeated attempts, it proved impossible to persuade the Foreign Secretary that the obstacle of his peerage could be overcome. Churchill had remained obstinately (and uncharacteristically) silent when the matter was discussed.

It remained to test the opinions of the Labour Opposition. When, early that evening, Clement Attlee and Arthur Greenwood were asked whether the Labour Party would serve in a Government of National Unity, they proved reluctant to commit themselves without first consulting their National Executive Committee that was gathering in Bournemouth for the forthcoming party conference. It was agreed that the two men would travel to Bournemouth the following day and provide answers to the following questions: would they join a coalition (a) under Chamberlain's leadership or (b) under someone else? The matter was therefore still undecided when the great crisis of the war erupted.

The early days of May had brought rumours of an imminent invasion of Holland and the War Cabinet had finally steeled itself to adjust its bombing policies in the event of such an attack. But scares such as this had been commonplace in recent months and there was little hard evidence to show that this one was different from the rest. In his diary for 5 May, a gloomy Ironside had foreseen 'the crisis of our existence', but he had expected the storm to break in mid-summer or later, and he had spent the next forty-eight hours in Scotland meeting the troops who had just returned from Norway.[39] Back in the War Office he had found new warnings of an attack on the Low Countries, though experts had later dismissed them as cover for an offensive against the Balkans. Rumour and refutation had followed in quick succession; on 9 May, the US Ambassador had reported an apparent ultimatum to the Dutch Government, a story quickly dismissed by the Foreign Office as unfounded. (Naval Intelligence thought the story had been planted and reported that the Dutch General Staff 'were not unduly apprehensive'.[40]) But on the Friday morning (10 May), ministers had arrived at their desks to find that Belgium and Holland had been invaded, that bombs were falling on Brussels and that parachutists were landing near The Hague.

The process of King-making had thus continued in the brief interlude between emergency sessions of the War Cabinet. Chamberlain had been inclined at first to see this new crisis through but his closest confidants had warned against it and he had found little support in Cabinet. The news from Bournemouth proved decisive. Sometime after 4.00pm that Friday afternoon, Attlee rang through to Downing Street to say that his party would be willing to join a coalition but not under Chamberlain's leadership. After a brief pause, Chamberlain went to the Palace to tender his resignation. And, since his preferred candidate had continued to rule himself out of the running, he advised the King to send for Churchill. By six o'clock the latter was busy forming his Government. Many members of the Whitehall establishment were aghast. They consoled themselves as best they could with the thought that if Chamberlain and Halifax were included in the new Cabinet, they might at least succeed in moderating some of Churchill's worst excesses. That evening Jock Colville, Alec Dunglass (the future Lord Home) and Chips Channon, Chamberlain supporters to a man, met in Rab Butler's room in the Foreign Office to share their deepest concerns. Rab came up with the most memorable phrase of the evening. In his view, 'the great tradition of English politics [had] been sold to the greatest adventurer in modern political history.'[41]

Chapter 10

'Rupert' – Breaking the Deadlock

A telegram from Churchill to Cork, sent from the Admiralty during the afternoon of 28 April, provides a glimpse of London's new priorities now that the final decision to abandon central Norway had been taken. 'It is upon Narvik and the German ore-fields,' the message read, 'that all efforts must now be centred ... Here it is that we must fight and persevere on the largest scale possible ... Plan out your scheme for establishing a strongly defended base and ask for all you want.'[1]

In the interlude between the evacuation of central Norway and the opening of the German offensive in the West, a new formulation of the Government's objectives was beginning to appear in Cabinet discussions and in orders to military commanders. The need to stifle the flow of iron through the port of Narvik remained prominent, as did the larger ambition of dominating (perhaps occupying) the Swedish mining areas as well. (Churchill had spoken in terms of having 50,000 men 'on or over the Swedish border' by the summer.[2]) But there was now the further purpose of preserving part of Norway as 'a seat of Government for the Norwegian King and people'. It was becoming clear, as never before, that the Narvik commitment was going to extend into the indefinite future. Moves were afoot to provide the ordinance and supply depots, the hospital space and the hutted accommodation that would be needed for the longer term. A specialist naval base construction unit was leaving for Harstad to install the coast defence artillery that Lord Cork had specified, and to lay the defensive minefields and anti-submarine nets that would defend the approaches to ports and anchorages.

But with the terrible example of central Norway before them, staffs were giving first priority to air defence. London had promised forty-eight heavy AA guns and a total of sixty lighter weapons for, like Namsos and Åndalsnes before it, the port of Harstad was attracting an increasing weight of air attack. Heavy emphasis was now being placed on the development of airfields in the far north and this seemingly mundane task would soon assume overriding priority. The airfield at Bardufoss, known from Norwegian sources to be capable of taking Gladiators, was absorbing most of the effort available. But it was 50 miles north-east of Harstad and difficult to supply; fuel, ammunition and anti-aircraft weapons, everything needed to support an air campaign, had to be ferried to Sørreisa on the Solbergfjord and then carried up 17 miles of narrow and crumbling road. Skånland at the head of the Tjeldsundet (the narrow sound linking Harstad with the Ofotfjord and a site much closer to the scene of action) was also receiving attention, though its peaty soil was to prove incapable of taking the necessary loads and it was never brought into effective use. A good deal of effort (also nugatory) was expended in preparing a forward airstrip at Bodø, 100 miles to the southward. Until Bardufoss finally opened for business on 21 May the *Ark Royal*'s Skuas did what they could to prevent the Luftwaffe from bombing and strafing at will.

In this trackless wilderness with its fjords and islands, and scattered populations, water transport set the tempo for every operation. A handful of landing craft (four load-carrying motor landing craft and four armoured assault craft) arrived in theatre at the end of April and soon proved themselves indispensable, if not always reliable.[3] But the fleet of 'puffers', hired when the expedition first arrived, remained the backbone of the transport service, ferrying men and materiel from the base areas to forward positions in the Vågs and Ofotfjords and, as the campaign developed, to points much further afield. The British command resented its dependence on this happy-go-lucky organization and, with the passage of time, the easygoing habits of Norwegian skippers became a source of mounting irritation. (There were moves to recruit people in Britain to man and run the service.) For their part, the skippers resisted regimentation and the system came, on occasion, to the verge of breakdown. It was part of a wider problem. The extent of the Army's authority over the civil population remained wholly unclear. In the end, Lord Cork was persuaded to speak to Norwegian Ministers about it but the matter was never fully resolved and the need to put things on a 'proper political footing' was later seen as one of the abiding lessons of the campaign.[4]

The Chasseurs Alpins arrived off Harstad on 26 April. They were the men of the 27th demi-brigade (formerly the reserve for 'Maurice') and were the leading edge of the French Light Division that was now on its way to Narvik. The 13th demi-brigade of the French Foreign Legion (two battalions) was following a few days behind and, after them (an unexpected addition to the total), the four battalions of the Polish 'Carpathian' Brigade.[5] Like their comrades at Namsos, the 27th Chasseurs were trained and equipped for operations on the Maginot Line. They had retained a limited ski capability (seventy men per battalion) and despite the parsimony of the Commissariat some, though not all, of their mules. They

142

arrived in theatre with a battery of Colonial Artillery and a section of light tanks.

Relations between the Admiral and the General had remained frigid and plans for the employment of the Chasseurs had opened up new differences between them. Some feel for the state of affairs can be guaged from an exchange of telegrams between Mackesy and the War Office on 27 April. Narvik was a position of great natural strength, Mackesy told Sir John Dill, the newly appointed VCIGS, and an assault from boats would be like 'attacking the Messines Ridge without adequate artillery support'. He knew of no single fact to support the Admiral's contention that, once the snow had cleared, Narvik could be taken in a matter of days. He was, on the other hand, well qualified to judge the state of the Admiral's military knowledge – it was 'exactly NIL'. He hoped that Lord Cork could soon be replaced by 'an officer of less exalted rank who would be ready to co-operate with, rather than dictate to, the military forces'. At present, the situation was 'simple lunacy'.[6] Dill's reply was soothing but firm. Mackesy should tender his advice freely but then go all out to further the Admiral's plans whether he agreed with them or not.

The issue that had triggered the General's outburst was Lord Cork's reaction to proposals put out in the immediate aftermath of the curtailed bombardment. In these, Mackesy had declared that direct assault was impractical. Instead, the 24th Guards Brigade with a battalion of Chasseurs in support would advance along the shores of the Ofotfijord to occupy Øyjord and Ankenes, the two headlands overlooking Narvik from the north and south. The two remaining Chasseur battalions would relieve the Scots Guards in the Sagfjord and drive southwards towards Bjerkvik making use of 'such active co-operation, if any, as the Norwegians can give'. Thereafter, things would depend on circumstances, but prominent in Mackesy's mind was the possibility of establishing the Chasseurs across the railway east of Narvik and thus of completing the isolation of the town.[7] Cork's response was dismissive. He suggested that too much attention was being paid to 'outlying enemy detachments'. (The Norwegians could deal with these.) The judgement, he told Mackesy, would be that 'we allowed ourselves to be diverted to secondary objects when the primary object was clear before us'. Further, Mackesy was failing to make use of the 'mobility that the sea confers'. Amphibious operations would save the French 'an arduous march and much wear and tear'. He (Cork) was so certain that he was right that unless he had a written assurance of co-operation he would have to give further consideration to the steps he would have to take to further the Government's policy.[8] This thinly veiled threat was not lost on its target but Mackesy made few concessions to the Admiral's views. He continued to stress that a direct attack on Narvik had to be 'ruled out absolutely' and that the establishment of shore artillery on

143

the Øyjord peninsula was an essential preliminary to the capture of the town. With the arrival of the French now imminent, existing arrangements for disembarkation and deployment would, he declared, have to stand.[9]

A conference was held on the morning of 28 April to brief Brigadier General Béthouart who had just arrived from Namsos to take charge of the French contingent.[10] It was an ill-tempered affair. Cork had attempted (quite brazenly) to elicit Béthouart's support for his views and Mackesy had responded with the assertion that command of land forces was vested in him. (The Frenchman, soul of discretion, had refused to commit himself to either camp without first seeing the ground.) It was agreed that Béthouart would accompany Lord Cork on an immediate reconnaissance of Narvik and the Øyjord peninsula. If he agreed that Mackesy's proposals represented the best and quickest route to the capture of the town he (Cork) would be willing to reconsider the stance that he had taken. He was insistent, however, that the issue should be looked at again after the reconnaissance had taken place.[11]

Cork and Béthouart set off in the destroyer *Codrington* that afternoon. They looked at the town under its pall of smoke (German demolition teams were blowing up the ore terminal) and gazed at the 'apocalyptic spectacle' in the harbour. They had then nosed into the Rombaksfjord, attracting a burst of automatic fire from the shore, before coasting up to the head of the Herjangsfjord at Bjerkvik. The Frenchman had leant towards Lord Cork's viewpoint and had established himself in the Admiral's mind as 'a live wire'. He had been prepared to accept that a direct assault on Narvik might be unwise. (The place was well defended and the shoreline outside the harbour steep.) But elsewhere, the German defenders would be short of heavy weapons and widely dispersed. It was thus 'inconceivable' that a force supported by the guns of the Fleet could not establish a foothold somewhere on the coastline north and east of Narvik and thus occupy the Øyjord peninsula which Mackesy had identified as the essential first step. An assault on Narvik could then be launched across the narrow entrance of the Rombaksfjord in conjunction with a simultaneous attack from the direction of Ankenes.[12]

Mackesy was unmoved. His operation order No. 3, issued next day, tasked the 24th Guards Brigade with the 12th Chasseurs in support to advance along the southern shore towards Ankenes. The 6th and 14th Chasseur Battalions would land at Salangen and in conjunction with Norwegian forces push southwards towards Bjerkvik. When that position was taken, German resistance north of Øyjord would collapse. Béthouart protested that his men would face a 30-mile march over snowbound mountain roads before reaching the front line, and that the problems of supply would be formidable. His objections were overruled. The South Wales Borderers, Mackesy told him, had already made a successful

144

landing at Håkvik, a village only 4 miles short of Ankenes and the 12th Battalion of Chasseurs was on its way to help them. The other battalions had already left for the Sagfjord; he was to go there and take command. It was, as he later observed, 'useless to argue'; he was given a destroyer and set out for Salangen with a Norwegian liaison officer and a member of Mackesy's staff.

The patronizing tone adopted by Mackesy in his remarks about Norwegian help was hardly justified for, while his British allies had been arguing about how to proceed, General Fleischer (GOC Norwegian 6th Division) had opened his attack on Dietl's northern salient. Strengthened by the arrival of two fresh battalions from the Finnish border, he had struck southward towards Bjerkvik during the night of 23/24 April, sending two infantry battalions against Deitl's forward positions in the high fell country around Lapphaugen, while a third (I/12th Infantry) had tried to turn the German flank by making a night march on Gratangen across the hills. His timing was inauspicious. His battalions had met the same (unseasonal) blizzard conditions that had accompanied Lord Cork's bombardment. The main attack had stalled and the I/12th Infantry Battalion, isolated beyond reach of support and weakened by a bitter night in the open, had been savaged by the German counter-attack. It had pulled back from Gratangen with the loss of half its number. But the strength of the Norwegian offensive had forced Dietl to review his dispositions. By 27 April, he had withdrawn his outposts from Lapphaugen and consolidated on a new and shorter line in the hills above Bjerkvik.

Mackesy's attempt to exploit this new situation met exactly the obstacles that Béthouart had feared. The move had started well enough. Béthouart had made contact with Fleischer (the Norwegian had complained bitterly about the lack of liaison with the British) and the two men had settled their respective boundaries of responsibility. He had then set off in his destroyer to investigate the fjords to the south of Salangen and at Foldvik, a tiny village at the entrance to the Gratangenfjord, he had learnt from a Norwegian gunboat that the Germans had left. He had signalled Lord Cork at once and, on the morning of 30 April, he had led a fleet of 'puffers' into Foldvik bringing the 6th Chasseur Battalion and as many pack-mules as his small ships could carry. By evening he had pushed a company of Chasseurs up to the head of the fjord and made contact with the Norwegians; next day, a combined ski patrol had surprised and captured a German outpost in the Labergdal, the valley leading south-eastward towards the Bjerkvik road. But his original misgivings had soon been confirmed. The snow in the Labergdal was deep and soft, and every small advance had demanded immense labour. The Germans were well supplied with automatic weapons and, in this open treeless landscape, the

Chasseurs had suffered constant harassment from the air. By 2 May, Béthouart was demanding a landing at Bjerkvik to 'unblock' his battalion in the Labergdal and offering a battalion of Légionnaires to conduct the operation. (Mackesy had been in bed with flu and had declined the offer.[13]) By 4 May the Chasseurs were reporting the first cases of frostbite and, soon afterwards, of snow-blindness. When, four days later, the 14th Battalion relieved their comrades in the Labergdal, they had advanced a mere 3 miles in six days of fighting.

The story on the southern shores of the Ofotfjord was little better. Supported by the guns of the Fleet (including those of the *Resolution*, the battleship that had relieved the *Warspite* on the Narvik station), the South Wales Borderers had pushed forward along the coastal road to positions within a mile of Ankenes village. But they had been stopped by a barrage of mortar and artillery fire and further progress had proved impossible. Brigadier Fraser had been wounded during a reconnaissance of enemy positions and command of the brigade had passed to Lieutenant Colonel T.B. Trappes-Lomax of the Scots Guards. Thereafter, the tip of the Ankenes peninsula had remained in dispute. The 12th Chasseurs had made modest progress up the valley towards the Storvatn Lake and finally, on 9 May, had occupied the ridge overlooking the port of Narvik from the south. But Ankenes and both shores of the Beisfjord had remained firmly in German hands, and any further advance on Narvik from this quarter had begun to seem increasingly problematical.

Cork had long since been forced to recognize that London would never be satisfied with the stately progress of Mackesy's campaign. 'Every day that Narvik remains untaken,' Churchill told him on 2 May, 'imperils the whole enterprise. I must regard the next six or seven days as possibly decisive.' (He had intimated too that the Government was ready to accept heavy costs to achieve a result.) Cork replied that improving weather and increasing troop numbers made it possible to progress from encirclement to attack and that he had set Wednesday, 8 May as the date for the transition, 'accepting all responsibility'.[14] His orders produced a new command crisis in the far north, matching the political crisis that was already brewing in the corridors of Westminster.

Trappes-Lomax, the acting Brigade Commander, was already familiar with the coastline and topography of the Herjangsfjord. He had examined the area in the *Aurora* on 2 May to assess the feasibility of seizing Bjerkvik and breaking the stalemate to the northward. His report had been adverse. There were two suitable beaches on the western shoreline but the nearby villages seemed full of women and children, and he would 'shrink from ordering bombardment' on humanitarian grounds. The area was also deep in snow and suitable only for mountain troops. The eastern shore was even more difficult – the beaches were rocky and access restricted. And this sector would, he thought, be heavily defended since it lay close to the enemy's line of retreat. A landing in the Herjangsfjord seemed to add nothing to Mackesy's plans.[15]

Cork issued his new orders the following day; he envisaged that the existing movements of the Chasseurs to the north and the Borderers to the south would continue, but he expected a direct attack on the Narvik peninsula either from the sea or across the mouth of the Rombaksfjord, whichever was thought best. Time was of 'primary importance' and preparations were to be complete by 8 May.[16] Trappes-Lomax set out that evening to examine a beach on the north-western shore of the Narvik peninsula, a site selected by the Navy. The beach appeared suitable for landing craft but the front was unacceptably narrow. A further reconnaissance followed on the night of 4/5 May, to identify landing sites where 'puffers' could get close inshore. This time the battalion commanders of the Scots and Irish Guards went along as well; indeed there were so many army officers on the bridge of the *Aurora* that it was thought wise to provide them with naval caps to avoid alerting the enemy. None of the beaches seemed capable of accepting a force larger than a platoon. Next day, Mackesy sent Cork a comprehensive summary of Trappes-Lomax's findings. (It was said to represent the views of Brigadier Fraser and of all military officers experienced in war.) Among the issues brought to the Admiral's attention were the shortage of assault landing craft, the uncertainty about beach gradients, the steep inclines that men would face on leaving the beaches ('they could barely clamber let alone assault'), the impossibility of surprise (there was no darkness, only a short period of twilight) and, not least, the growing danger from the air.[17] The report was so critical that Cork felt obliged 'to refer the matter to the judgment of HM Government'. He was careful to add that Mackesy had done nothing to inspire the report, that the General had been doing his best to carry out the orders given to him but that he too regarded an opposed landing without the benefit of air superiority as 'absolutely unjustified'. [18]

The Chamberlain Cabinet was (as usual) in two minds as to how best to proceed. But it approved the line suggested by the Chiefs of Staff. The reply, sent from the Admiralty during the afternoon of 6 May, acknowledged that the military view could not 'lightly be set aside' but pressed Lord Cork to reveal his own opinion. It added that General Auchinleck, who would 'ultimately command the troops' in northern Norway, would be arriving in a few days' time.[19]

The exchanges between London and Lord Cork's flagship continued into those critical days when the Chamberlain Government was fighting for its life. Something of the dilemma faced by the Admiral in forcing through an operation against the entrenched opinion of his military experts is revealed

147

in this exceptionally cautious reply. 'I do not consider success certain,' he told London during the early morning of 7 May, 'but believe that there is a good chance of success, whereas it is quite certain by not trying no success can be gained.' He had gone on to suggest postponing the operation until Auchinleck's arrival. But the crisis was beginning to generate those wild swings of opinion common at such moments. Late that evening, in a return to his characteristic bullish tone, Cork proposed anchoring the *Resolution* within 50 yards of the Narvik pier 'in order to get over the soldier's aversion to exposing men in boats to machine-gun fire'. He added, 'Her bulk at that range would scare enemy troops while her guns would blast them to Hades.'[20]

The War Cabinet examined the question again at noon on 8 May before returning to the Commons for that critical debate on the conduct of the war. They looked at the chances of holding and using the port of Narvik in the face of a determined German air offensive and at the likely outcome of a war of attrition in the air. Cork was told that HMG would support him 'in taking any risks that [he considered] it necessary to accept'. He was told to leave Auchinleck out of the reckoning since the General could not arrive before 12 May and would then need several days to get to grips with the situation. That afternoon the Admiralty approved the use of the *Resolution* in the way that Cork had suggested, provided that the ship was anchored (not beached), and that maximum protection from fighters and air defence ships was provided. But Cork had reached the conclusion that forcing soldiers to undertake operations to which they were wholly opposed was a certain recipe for disaster. He was looking for an intermediate step that would break the deadlock in the hills to the north of Narvik and pave the way for a later assault on the town. And he was looking for someone who would shoulder the risk and do so willingly. That night, at about the time that Churchill was rising in the House of Commons to defend the Government's record, he told the Admiralty that he was now committed to an alternative plan, a landing by French troops at Bjerkvik and the capture of the Øyjord peninsula. The landing would take place during the night of 10/11 May; if it failed he would prepare for a direct assault on the lines that he had already proposed.[21]

The landing at Bjerkvik followed a further reconnaissance of the Herjangs-fjord by Béthouart, by Colonel Raoul Magrin-Vernerey, the Foreign Legion commander, and the officers of the (French) tank unit that had recently unloaded in Harstad. It provides a remarkable (if belated) example of inter-service and international co-operation and was conceived as part of a concerted drive on Bjerkvik by the Franco-Norwegian forces to the north of the town, and by two Polish battalions from the direction of Bogen Bay. It was to be accompanied as well by a drive south-eastward into the uplands of the border region by the Norwegian 6th Brigade to threaten the line of the railway. In its use of landing craft (albeit in penny numbers) to land tanks and infantry of the first wave it foreshadowed the far larger assault landings of later years. In its use of open boats to land the rest, it looked back to Gallipoli, Tenerife and the Seven Years' War.

Although Mackesy remained in nominal command of Anglo-French land forces and gave Béthouart his directions for the coming operation, he seems never to have regarded the plan as anything other than a desperate gamble. According to Béthouart, Mackesy wished him good luck when he called at Force Headquarters on 9 May, but reminded him that an opposed landing was the most difficult of all operations, and that he himself had been unwilling 'to provoke a hecatomb to save the political fortunes of Mr Churchill'.[22] And even allowing for the fact that he was increasingly preoccupied with developments further south (the product of Carton de Wiart's failure to defend the road to Mosjøen), it is surely significant that neither Mackesy nor any member of his staff was present to witness the unfolding of this historic event.

The ultimate success of the operation should not blind us to the deep anxieties that tormented the men who had now to turn concept into reality. It was hard to assess the quality of the defence. Elements of the 3rd Battalion 139th Mountain Regiment were known to be at Elvegård. There had been reports (from Norwegian sources) of friction between Austrian troops and their German officers, but the significance of such information was uncertain. Elsewhere, the coastal defences were said to be manned by German 'marines' wearing Norwegian uniforms.[23] There could be no doubt whatever about the threat posed by the Luftwaffe. Air attacks on the Narvik flotilla had been exceptionally heavy during the first week of May; the Polish destroyer *Grom* had been sunk and a direct hit on the *Aurora* had 'ripped open a turret like a sardine tin'; casualties had been heavy.[24] The landing would have the support of the *Ark Royal*'s fighters and the operation would be timed for midnight when darkness over German bases would bring a brief lull in enemy air activity. But Béthouart had pleaded with Mackesy to do everything that he could to speed the distribution of anti-aircraft weapons and to press for raids on German bases on the day before the landing. The five light tanks (13-ton Hotchkiss H39s), which were to be carried to Bjerkvik on the decks of the *Resolution* and lowered into landing craft by crane, became an additional source of anxiety. The loss of a tank and a landing craft at the Tjeldsund ferry had called the whole concept into question and had delayed the entire operation. But the tanks had a vital role to play in suppressing enemy defences and were deemed indispensable. Occasionally, suppressed anxieties broke out into open dissent. Captain Maund recalled a desperate meeting in the flag-ship when the officers of the Foreign Legion had declared the plan

149

'unworkable' and when 'criticisms, ejaculations and impossibilities [had] simply poured out'. He had feared a mutiny but the outburst had died away as quickly as it had begun.[25]

The landing force assembled off Ballangen during the evening of 12 May. (Frenchmen knew by now that their country was under attack and were anxious for news from home.) The 'puffers' were missing and the troops were brought out in landing craft instead. Embarkation was completed ahead of schedule despite the unexpected addition of 200 bloody-minded Légionnaires who had refused to stay behind. The force sailed under a grey, drizzly sky with the cloud hanging low on the mountain slopes, conditions that forced the naval fighters to return to the carrier. After making an initial feint to the westward, it passed Narvik at 2300 (all appeared quiet although German radio circuits seemed unusually busy) and arrived off Bjerkvik at midnight, the destroyers leading the way and taking up their bombardment stations within a few cables of the shore. They were followed by the four assault landing craft carrying the 120 men of the first wave, and then by the *Vindictive*, the *Protector* and the two cruisers *Effingham* and *Aurora* with their booms extended and towing the lines of boats that would land the men of the second echelon. The *Resolution* with five tanks embarked brought up the rear. Lord Cork directed operations from the *Effingham* with Béthouart beside him and, in a gesture that made a deep impression on the Frenchman, delegated to him the order to open fire. It was light enough to take photographs. As the blast of the guns whipped the faces of the onlookers on the *Effingham*'s bridge, tearing the cigarettes from their mouths, houses on the foreshore burst into flames and a church that had been used as an ammunition dump exploded in a cascade of stars.[26]

As Mackesy had long predicted, naval gunfire proved incapable of silencing the German machine guns. Aerial photography had failed to identify the enemy's strongpoints and the fire plan had been drawn up on the basis of best estimates, first priority being given to buildings on the foreshore and then to the woods behind them. Even now, the sound of the enemy's guns was often the only clue to their whereabouts. The landing had thus gone ahead in the face of what General Auchinleck (an observer in Lord Cork's flagship) described as 'appreciable opposition from enemy machine guns ashore'.[27] Again as predicted, the unloading of tanks from the decks of the *Resolution* proved difficult and time consuming, and the Légionnaires of the first wave had waited in a fever of suspense for the landing craft carrying the tanks to clear the battleship's side. Eventually they could wait no longer and set off for the shore behind a single motor landing craft, a modern variant that had sailed from Ballangen under its own power. The tank went ashore close west of the village pier and was seen soon afterwards moving to and fro among the burning houses searching out the remaining pockets of resistance. The Légionnaires landed 1,000 yards to the left at a place where a small promontory sheltered them from the enemy's fire. They were seen soon afterwards, crossing the promontory and advancing into the village. The rest of the Battalion and two more tanks followed them. They landed, still under spasmodic fire though without appreciable loss, and could be seen later advancing behind the village with the tanks in support in the direction of the Gratangen road. The sound of French 75s in the hills above Bjerkvik, showed that the attack from the northward had already begun.

Attention now turned to the village of Meby a mile or so east of Bjerkvik where the second battalion was to go ashore and drive eastward towards Elvegård and the Hartvigsvatn. At 0200 the naval bombardment resumed, concentrating once again on target areas close to the shore. Béthouart was astonished to see a man running along the beach carrying a child and waving a white flag. There had been reports of civilians in Bjerkvik too. He was *bouleversé* – Fleischer had assured him that the area would be evacuated. The tanks were late and so, this time, were the assault craft. The boats of the second wave, gathering round the *Effingham*'s bows and impatient to get going, attracted a burst of machine-gun fire from shore and quickly retreated under the lee. After what seemed an interminable delay, two assault craft and two motor landing craft set out for the shore. Onlookers on the *Effingham*'s bridge heard the crunch of their ramps on the rocky beach. The first tank drove straight across the boulders and gained the grassy slope above, moving left to deal with a troublesome machine gun; the second slid sideways as it drove ashore and ended up broadside on. After several minutes of desperate manoeuvring it got itself square and followed its consort inland towards the first of the battalion's objectives.

At Meby, as at Bjerkvik, the Battalion landed without appreciable loss. It went on to storm the military depot at Elvegårdsmoen, fighting its way into the complex block by block. It found a hundred machine guns, eighty horses, sixty wounded (mostly Austrian) and a courier with a sackful of mail for General Dietl, most of it offering congratulations on his recent promotion. Its success was attributed in part to an act of conspicuous gallantry. Three Spanish Légionnaires (Spaniards formed the largest national group in the 13th demi-brigade) had scaled a 500-foot bluff to silence a nest of machine guns perched on the summit. (The sole survivor of this feat had later received the *médaille militaire*.) Although the cloud had lifted and from the small hours of 13 May the Fleet Air Arm had been able to resume its patrols, the landings had passed without interference from German aircraft.

At about seven o'clock in the morning, with the beachhead seemingly secure, Lord Cork withdrew from the Herjangsfjord and returned post haste to Harstad, leaving a force of three destroyers to support operations ashore. Béthouart transferred his headquarters to the *Havelock* and shortly afterwards landed at Bjerkvik to assess progress for himself. (He was wearing an elegant blue cloak.) He was delighted to find that his men had made contact with the Polish battalions which, after an epic march across the hills, were now approaching Bjerkvik from the west. He ordered them to join the Légionnaires in the drive northwards up the Gratangen road. But Øyjord was also in his sights and, determined to exploit his success to the full, he ordered a Foreign Legion motorcycle platoon to push southward along the coastal road. He had then returned to the *Havelock* to give his motorcyclists covering fire.

The road distance along the eastern shores of the Herjangsfjord was only 8 to 10 miles, but the progress of the platoon seemed painfully slow. At one stage the Légionnaires had seemed to engage in a lengthy conversation with a woman in red. The destroyer went on to Øyjord to assess the situation from seaward and arrived off the village to find that the whole population had taken to the streets. A party was sent ashore to find out what was going on and reported that the German garrison had pulled out. As Béthouart landed the Légionnaires presented arms. When the counterattack came, two companies of Poles were firmly established and the Germans were forced back by the way they had come. Béthouart had achieved his objectives at a cost of thirty-six casualties.

The landings at Bjerkvik unhinged Dietl's northern front and opened the way to an attack on the Narvik peninsula across the mouth of the Rombaksfjord. They did not, as had been hoped, succeed in blocking the German line of retreat since a small force of mountain troops had defended the approaches to the Hartvig Lake and kept an escape route open. The two battalions in the hills above Bjerkvik (1st and 3rd Battalions of the 139th Mountain Regiment) had retired through this gap and occupied a new perimeter running north-east from the shores of the Rombaksfjord to the Kuberg plateau on the Swedish border. But the future looked bleak and for the first time since his arrival in Narvik, Dietl faced imminent defeat. He had already warned Falkenhorst that he could only hold his northern salient if he received substantial reinforcements; he now told him that, if the enemy offensive continued, he would have to abandon Narvik altogether and withdraw to a final bridgehead close to the Swedish border. Group XXI reported the situation as critical and pressed OKW to prepare the ground for a retreat into Sweden. On 15 May, two days after the Bjerkvik landings, Falkenhorst asked Hitler for a parachute battalion to reinforce his beleaguered garrison in the far north. The loss of Narvik, he told the Führer would represent a damaging blow to German prestige.

Some saw in the Bjerkvik landings the vindication of the amphibious strategy that they had advocated from the first. Cork for one was convinced that an earlier landing could have succeeded 'always supposing that the same leadership and resolution as the French troops displayed would have been forthcoming'.[28] These views need qualification. Bjerkvik was not some single masterstroke but the culmination of a series of operations (inspired in part by Mackesy) that had put the German defenders under increasing pressure and fixed two mountain battalions (the backbone of the German force) in Dietl's northern salient. Without these preliminary moves the landings might have faced sterner opposition. Nor should we, after an interval of seventy years, be too ready to question the judgment of those who had looked on this and similar operations with the gravest misgivings. Memories of Gallipoli were still vivid and Mackesy's ideas were models of Staff College orthodoxy.[29] It was safe to assume that, with the Allied armies pressing in on Narvik from every quarter, German manpower would be stretched to the limit. But few could have predicted with any certainty that the landing force would encounter a makeshift naval battalion rather than a trained body of mountain troops, or that the German sailors would give ground easily and, in some cases, abandon their positions without firing a shot. (Dietl was appalled at their dismal performance.[30]) And no one could have counted on the complete absence of the Luftwaffe during the critical hours of 13 May. Auchinleck was much impressed by the 'businesslike efficiency of the French Foreign Legion' but he had been forced to concede that an air attack 'might well have turned the operation from a success into a failure'.[31]

Yet the apparent contrast between the enterprise of Béthouart's troops and the lethargy of their British counterparts left many contemporaries (and many later commentators) uneasy.[32] When every allowance is made for the difficulties presented by the Norwegian climate and for the administrative muddle that had dogged the expedition from the start (and both these factors affected the French expeditionary force to a comparable degree), the unpalatable fact remains that, at the date of the Bjerkvik landings, the Scots Guards had been ashore for almost a month without making any measurable impact on the course of the campaign. The same was largely true of the Irish Guards. Between 24 April (the date of Lord Cork's bombardment) and 14 May when they embarked for Bodø in a belated attempt to stem the German advance northward from Mosjøen, the Battalion had remained inactive among the scattered villages of the Bogen inlet, sunbathing, holding skiing lessons and fishing competitions, and exchanging elaborate courtesies with the Royal Navy.

Chapter 11

Trouble on the Road North

General Auchinleck arrived at Harstad during the morning of 11 May. (When he left London, Narvik was at the top of the Government's agenda – it was now being reduced to near irrelevance by far larger events in France.) His instructions named him GOC-in-C (Designate) of Anglo-French land forces and of the British air component with the immediate task of reporting to the Chiefs of Staff on the resources needed to meet the Government's objectives. When and in what circumstances he might assume command was left unstated for, despite its reservations about Mackesy's qualities, the War Office had been reluctant to upset the status quo until existing plans had either succeeded or failed. In his pocket, however, Auchinleck carried a secret directive from Sir John Dill authorizing him to take command immediately (under Lord Cork) if, in his judgement, local conditions made it necessary.

He met Mackesy on arrival; he had known him before as a Staff College instructor in Quetta and had a high opinion of his abilities. He explained that his mission was exploratory and received in return a detailed assessment of the military situation. (Mackesy was, he later reported, 'uniformly helpful and informative'.[1]) Two major developments were then in train. The Germans were on the move north from Namsos. They had advanced 90 miles over roads that had been declared impassable and were already threatening Mosjøen. The Scots Guards were moving to Mo (the next significant port to the northward) to block any further advance, and the Irish Guards were at short notice to follow them. But of more immediate significance, were the French landings at Bjerkvik, then in the final stages of preparation. Hearing that Lord Cork was planning to direct this latter operation in person, and that he was embarked in his flagship at Skånland, Auchinleck set out there and then to meet him. No detailed record survives of the conversations that took place in the flagship that evening. Cork seems not to have pressed for Mackesy's removal although Auchinleck did, according to his biographer, emerge from the meeting with the distinct impression that the differences between the two men were too deep to

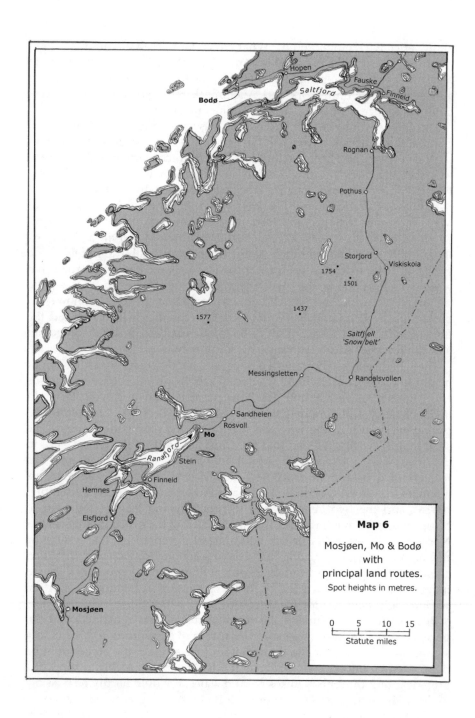

Map 6

Mosjøen, Mo & Bodø
with
principal land routes.

Spot heights in metres.

0   5   10   15

Statute miles

155

allow effective co-operation.[2] What is certain is that late that night Auchinleck sent Dill a personal telegram from the *Effingham* asking him to recall Mackesy for consultation. There, however, the matter rested for almost two days until Cork and Auchinleck returned from the Bjerkvik landings to face a situation of mounting complexity.

The defence of the stretch of coastline between Namsos and Narvik had claimed the attention of the staffs in London as soon as the evacuation of central Norway had been decided on. The main concern, initially at least, was that the Germans might seize an airfield in the region and bring Harstad or even Bardufoss within the radius of their dive-bombers, a point reemphasized by Ruge and Fleischer when they visited Harstad in mid-May. Factors of distance and terrain had seemed to preclude any rapid overland advance. It was 300 miles from Namsos to Narvik as the crow flies, and by road half as much again. The railway, still incomplete in the spring of 1940, extended no further than Grong, and the single road that wound its way along the river valleys and, north of Mo, crossed the mountain plateau of the Saltfjell with its permanent covering of snow, was broken in the Rana and Saltfjords by ferry crossings which reduced the flow of traffic to a trickle. North of Bodø, the road disappeared altogether and the traveller had to continue his journey by sea.

There had been no shortage of advice on what defensive measures might be put in place. Churchill had wanted to sell the ground between Namsos and Mosjøen 'as slowly and dearly as possible' and in a typically vivid flight of fancy had conjured up the vision of 300 or 400 Chasseurs disputing every inch of the way and tearing up the road behind them. 'We shall look very silly,' he had told the Chiefs of Staff, 'if the enemy slip up the road with a handful of armoured vehicles and make themselves masters of this strip of coastline.'[3] But Massy had failed totally in his attempts to convert Carton de Wiart and Audet to the notion of a fighting retreat, and the two generals had left for England leaving the road to Mosjøen open. Gamelin, never fully reconciled to the evacuation of central Norway, had urged his British colleagues to prepare for the systematic defence of the region arguing that delaying action (*détachements retardeurs*) could never be enough. And on 7 May, following first reports of German movement, he had instructed his military mission in London to offer the second Light Division for the purpose.[4]

But for practical planners the uncomfortable facts remained that the ports on this stretch of coast were incapable of supporting a force of any significant size, and for the immediate future at least, the area would be dominated by the enemy's air force. If it had been impossible to support a brigade group through Namsos or Åndalsnes, it would hardly be possible to do so through Mosjøen, Mo or even Bodø. A few precautionary moves had been easy to agree on. Just before the evacuation of Namsos, the *Janus* had delivered a company of Chasseurs to Mosjøen. (The Captain had reported afterwards that supply by sea lay outside the limits of justifiable risk.[5]) And on orders from the War Office, General Mackesy had sent C Company 1st Scots Guards to Bodø to secure that port and its airstrip against a descent by German paratroops. But what was to be done next? After several days of earnest debate, the Chiefs of Staff came down in favour of 'independent companies' – light mobile units with a strength of 300 officers and men, capable (supposedly) of operating for several weeks with the minimum of external support.[6] On 2 May, Colonel Colin Gubbins (architect of the independent company scheme and better known later as Director of Operations, SOE) was called to Massy's headquarters in Buckingham Gate and given his orders. He was to take command of 'Scissorsforce' (five independent companies in all) and secure Mosjøen, Mo and Bodø. He was not expected to engage the enemy head to head; his job, Massy told him, was to harass and delay. Gubbins left for Mosjøen on 4 May with Independent Companies 4 and 5. Number 1 had already left for Mo. 'Scissorsforce' headquarters (equivalent to that of an infantry brigade) and two more independent companies (3 and later 2) were going to Bodø. The Admiralty explained the reasoning behind these moves to an anxious Lord Cork who had asked what was being done to protect his southern flank, and who had complained that current measures seemed 'hardly adequate for the purpose'.[7] It was impossible, the Admiralty told him, to maintain large forces beyond the radius of friendly air cover. Independent companies were being placed in Mosjøen and Mo to delay the enemy's advance and to prevent landings by sea and air. He was told soon afterwards that 'Scissorsforce' was to come under his command.

The history of these embryonic commando formations was short. The German 181st Infantry Division took Grong and Namsos on 4 May (the day after Carton de Wiart's departure) and, driving a demoralized battalion of Norwegian reservists ahead of them, occupied positions in the southern approaches to Mosjøen only four days later. Gubbins had landed during the night of 8/9 May to find the Chasseurs waiting to embark – on orders from Paris apparently – and the exhausted Norwegians holding the Germans at Fellingfors, 20 miles south of the town. He had moved forward to cover the Norwegian retreat and, on the morning of 9 May, had scored a significant success against the German vanguard. But he had been in no position to counter the flanking movement that had followed or to conduct a protracted rearguard action. By nightfall he had been forced to conclude that Mosjøen was untenable although he and his Norwegian colleague had been planning to establish a new defensive line north of the town.

But next day, in a breathtaking feat of operational virtuosity, the Germans landed 300 mountain troops on the Hemnes peninsula 50 miles north-east of Mosjøen and only 20 miles short of Mo. Caught on the hop and with his flotilla already at full stretch, Lord Cork had diverted the *Calcutta* from the tail of the Lofotens and the *Zulu* from the Skjelfjord, but too late. The two ships sank the coaster *Nord Norge* while she was still unloading at Hemnesberget and helped to evacuate a platoon from No. 1 Independent Company which had fought a brisk action at the quayside, but the Germans had established themselves ashore and next morning they had started to rush in stores and reinforcements by flying boat. The position of their lodgement was extraordinarily well chosen. It threatened the line of retreat from Mosjøen, by-passed the Elsfjord ferry crossing, a natural bottleneck on the road northward, and posed an immediate threat to Mo. It was a move that could not be ignored. London warned Cork that Bodø had to be held at all costs. Mackesy ordered the Scots Guards to embark and put the Irish Guards at short notice to follow. In Mosjøen, the Norwegian Battalion abandoned its heavy equipment and pulled out, some by sea and some along the road to Elsfjord. Gubbins had little choice but to pull out too; he chartered a ferry and at six o'clock on the morning of 11 May, sailed for the mouth of the fjord, calling for a naval escort to come and meet him. London's experiment with light forces had failed at the first test. As a result, the Narvik command had been forced to commit a significant land force to a position 200 miles south of Narvik in circumstances that the Whitehall staffs had been trying so sedulously to avoid.

The ships carrying the Scots Guards (*Enterprise*, *Hesperus* and *Fleetwood*) left Skånland in the small hours of 11 May under the escort of the AA cruiser *Cairo*. Artillery, ammunition and stores accompanied them in the Norwegian coaster *Margot*. A final decision in favour of Mo was taken during the afternoon following an urgent appeal from the defenders, and the force arrived off its objective at 0400 on the morning of the 12th, the *Enterprise* having conducted a bombardment of German positions on the way past. The risks attached to the operation were soon apparent. The troops landed without mishap but the Luftwaffe arrived overhead while the unloading of stores was still in progress. Losses were trivial (the *Margot* seems to have done more damage to the jetty than German bombs) but the landing of guns, provisions and ammunition lasted a full nine hours and by the time the ships were ready to leave, the AA sloop *Fleetwood* had emptied her 4-inch magazines. (The *Margot*, Auchinleck told Dill, had escaped 'only by a miracle'.[8]) But the deciding factor was the character of the Ranafjord itself. The cruiser *Enterprise* (first to leave) had faced a 40-mile passage through narrow waters under constant attack by German aircraft. She had emerged unscathed but the emphatic message from her captain at the end of the ordeal was that no large ships, with the possible exception of AA cruisers, should enter the Ranafjord, and that in future 'puffers' or small coasters (or destroyers in the case of troop reinforcements) should be used instead.[9]

His message had grave implications for the Army's reinforcement plans. Lord Cork had returned from the Bjerkvik landings to find Brigadier Fraser (seemingly recovered from his wound) and Colonel Arthur Dowler, Mackesy's Chief Staff Officer, seeking urgent decisions on the deployment of the Irish Guards who were embarked at Skånland waiting to depart. Mackesy was absent; he was said to be ill again. The conference that followed faced an option of evils; no course open to them was without its risks. Auchinleck felt that the time had come to invoke Dill's secret directive and, with Lord Cork's agreement, announced that he was taking command. On Fraser's advice, he came down in favour of Bodø. He was sending no more troops to Mo, he told Dill in a letter the following day. The Navy was strongly averse to supplying the Army via the Ranafjord and the road from Bodø was still a doubtful factor because of snow. He was sending Fraser and the Irish Guards to Bodø with orders to hold the area Bodø–Saltdalen permanently, work south and get in touch with Mo if he could – but in any event to hold Bodø. He was sending the South Wales Borderers to reinforce the Irish Guards and putting 'Scissorsforce' at Fraser's disposal as well. (He had little time for independent companies – guerrillas were best employed in their own countries not in someone else's.) He hoped, he told the VCIGS, that he had time to 'pull this chestnut out of the fire'. This southern front was becoming 'a relatively serious commitment'.[10]

An unsuspecting Trappes-Lomax, meanwhile, had been doing what he could to organize the defences of Mo. Time was pressing and resources meagre. At Finneid (the northern terminal for the Elsfjord ferry) No. 1 Independent Company and a detachment of Norwegian Dragoons were holding the neck of the Hemnes peninsula, containing the German lodgement and keeping open the line of retreat from Mosjøen. An attempted counter-attack across the isthmus had failed. Prolonged resistance by these forward units seemed unlikely. Closer in, Norwegian reservists were preparing defences at Ytteren in the western approaches to Mo to guard against an attack along the opposite bank of the fjord. The Scots Guards, meanwhile, had taken up position at Stein, 7 miles short of Finneid, at a point where a river (the Dals) poured down from the mountains to join the upper reaches of the Ranafjord. The position dominated the river crossings and had much to commend it. Protected by the fjord on the right and by the mountain torrent in front, its most notable area of weakness lay on the left where the ground rose steeply to the mountain heights and where a thick covering of trees obscured the field of fire. The obvious remedy was to extend leftwards up the river valley but, with the endurance of the troops at Finneid in doubt, Trappes-Lomax had been forced to give first priority to the bridges and the road. Yet even here it had been hard to achieve an adequate concentration of force. C Company was still in Bodø, and after a joint reconnaissance with Lieutenant Colonel Roscher Nielsen (sent down from Ruge's headquarters to enliven the Norwegian defenders), he had been obliged to withdraw B Company from Stein in order to stiffen the close defences of Mo. With two rifle companies left to hold the line of the river the position had seemed precarious. Reinforcements were needed as a matter of urgency.

First intimations that all might not be well reached Trappes-Lomax on 14 May when the *Somali* arrived at Mo bringing Brigadier Fraser to review the situation and to explain the decisions that had been made in Harstad. Absolute priority, it was now clear, was being given to Bodø. Gubbins and his independent companies had already arrived there and the Irish Guards would be leaving from Skånland in a matter of hours. Trappes-Lomax was being asked to hold the enemy in a position that was inherently unsound and with a force that was (on any reasonable reckoning) unequal to the task. Yet relief was a distant and uncertain prospect. The command had ruled out reinforcement by sea – hence the decision to route everything to Bodø. Yet Bodø was 140 miles away. And at the halfway point loomed the treeless plateau of the Saltfjell where for a 20-mile stretch traffic moved in single file between steep walls of snow. The air threat on that long and open stretch of road could not be ignored. While the enemy's command of the air remained unchallenged, Mo was untenable. Fraser agreed and reported as much when he returned to the *Somali*. But the essential elements for a further debacle were already in place and there was little that could be done about it.

A difficult situation was made worse by accident of war. During the afternoon of 14 May, the liner *Chobry* (first used at Namsos and since then a regular on the Narvik run) sailed for Bodø via the Tjeldsund with 1st Battalion Irish Guards, HQ 24th Guards Brigade and a troop of the 3rd Hussars with three small tanks. The *Wolverine* and the *Stork* acted as escorts. Dive-bombers hit her just before midnight when she was about 30 miles short of her destination and left her with a fierce blaze amidships which soon spread beyond all possibility of control. This melancholy episode was relieved only by the exemplary conduct of the Irish Guards. Isolated in the forepart of the ship where boats could not be lowered they fell in as for a parade in Wellington Barracks and waited calmly for the *Wolverine* to take them off. (Eyewitnesses drew parallels with that exemplar of stoic courage – the loss of the *Birkenhead*.[11]) Almost 700 men had then filed across the narrow gangway to the destroyer's deck. By 0900 on the morning of 15 May the Irish Guards were back in Harstad awaiting the arrival of the *Stork* which had stayed behind to recover the

160

rest of the passengers and crew. The sloop brought in a further 300 survivors but not the Battalion Commander (Lieutenant Colonel W.D. Faulkner MC) and three of his most experienced officers, all of whom had perished in the attack. For the rest of the campaign the Battalion had a Captain in command.

The *Somali*, which had taken Brigadier Fraser to Mo for his conference with Trappes-Lomax, was making for Bodø during the early hours of 15 May when she got news of the *Chobry*'s plight. While closing the scene she came under heavy attack herself and was severely damaged by a near miss. She returned to Scapa Flow direct, taking the Brigadier with her. That day, Auchinleck put Colonel Gubbins in command of 24th Guards Brigade.[12]

Lord Cork saw the need for a firm hand on the tiller. 'We have to hold our own for six days,' he told Auchinleck that afternoon, 'then we shall have our own squadrons installed. If we give up now, we shall hand a success to the enemy. If we hold on there seems no valid reason why this setback should not be a prelude to success.'[13] Auchinleck ordered the South Wales Borderers to embark. He sent an immediate message to Gubbins saying that a firm stand was to be made at Mo and prepared an explanatory letter for delivery by James Gammell, his Brigadier General Staff, who was travelling to Bodø with the Borderers. It was important not to give further ground, he told Gubbins. He hoped that the arrival of the Borderers would allow him to reinforce Mo. He recognized that the Scots Guards were isolated and that the Germans were superior, but they too would be 'groping in the dark'. When they came up against really determined resistance, he hoped that they would 'sit back and think about it'.[14]

The letter was not delivered. Since his return from Bjerkvik, Lord Cork had been prevailed upon to move his headquarters ashore and the Borderers had sailed for Bodø in his former flagship the *Effingham*, with the AA cruisers *Cairo* and *Coventry* and an escort of two destroyers. (There was to be no gambling with the security of this second expedition.) They had sailed west of the Lofotens to defeat German reconnaissance (thought to be a factor in the loss of the *Chobry*) and had approached Bodø by a little-used route to reduce the risk of U-boat attack. The *Effingham* had run onto an uncharted reef while travelling at high speed. The *Cairo* and the *Matabele* had touched bottom as well though neither had been seriously damaged. But the *Effingham* had stuck fast and no amount of towing could get her free. The other ships, helped by local craft, took the troops off without loss and succeeded in salvaging some of the equipment from the cruiser's decks including four of the ten Bren carriers that she was carrying. But like the Irish Guards before them, the Borderers returned to Harstad to refit, and so did HQ 24th Guards Brigade, the latter for the second time.

161

The situation at Mo meanwhile had been moving quickly towards its denouement. The Norwegian column from Mosjøen withdrew through the Stein position during the night of 13/14 May in what seemed to the Scots Guards an endless stream of lorries. Later that day the forward position at Finneid was abandoned. With covering fire from the artillery and with the help of a Scots Guards platoon, the men of the Independent Company fell back through Stein to the reserve position, formerly occupied by B Company.

The next twenty-four hours brought a lull as the Germans assembled their forces at Finneid. (There was disturbing news from abroad. 'Damn it the Dutch have surrendered,' the battalion diarist recorded. 'A nasty blow.'[15]) But of more immediate concern was the German build-up 7 miles to the southward. Most of the new arrivals were reported as crossing from Elsfjord where engineers had improvised a replacement ferry service, but some had used a mountain route which bypassed the ferry altogether. More German columns were reported moving north from Mosjøen. (Although their identity had yet to be established, they were the leading battalions of Valentin Feuerstein's 2nd Mountain Division, withdrawn from 'Gelb' on the personal order of the Führer and charged with the relief of Narvik.[16]) Throughout 15 May, German aircraft probed and strafed the Scots Guards positions almost at will. One was brought down by anti-aircraft fire and the pilot and gunner captured. The overall position was assessed as 'anything but satisfactory' and at noon on 16 May, sappers blew the main bridge over the Dals using 1,000lb of gelignite. The second (wooden) bridge in front of the left flank position followed later in the day.[17]

In the early afternoon of 17 May it became clear that the Germans were massing for an attack along the coastal road. Despite heavy supporting fire, the attempt made little headway and the right flank frustrated a German attempt to lay planks across the girders of the broken bridge. Developments on the left proved much less easy to deal with. Signs that the Germans were, as predicted, using the unguarded mountain slopes to encircle the British left became evident early on, but little could be done to counter them. The Bren could not range far enough and the artillery had difficulty picking out a target against a background of rock and patchy snow. In early evening, anxieties were raised further by reports of a parachute landing on a frozen lake (the source of the Dals) 7 miles south-east of the Stein position.[18]

Late in the evening, the Germans launched a heavy attack down the river valley against the British left. Heavy fighting, much of it at close quarters, continued into the semi-darkness of the arctic night, Guardsmen having frequently to abandon prepared positions to counter some new attempt at infiltration or encirclement. A platoon was transferred from right to left across the rear of the British position but to little effect and by midnight the situation was judged critical. The left flank was virtually surrounded and there were reports from the rear of an attack by German paratroops at Lundenget, some 4 miles back on the road to Mo. Trappes-Lomax ordered B Company forward to a covering position behind the front line and, at 0200 on the morning of 18 May, the withdrawal began. It had all the hallmarks of those earlier withdrawals in the Gudbrandsdal; transport was limited to five rickety lorries. All that could be carried back were the wounded, of which there were seventy or eighty, and the supplies of food and small-arms ammunition.[19] Much of the rest, including the soldiers' kit was left behind. At 0430 on the morning of 18 May, the tail of the retreating column passed through B Company lines and took up a position overlooking the coast road in the immediate approaches to Mo.

Reports from Mo had done little so far to alert Brigadier Gubbins to the growing crisis. But during the evening of 17 May, Trappes-Lomax had reported the threat to his left flank and entered a new plea for the prompt return of C Company. Gubbins had put C Company on the move and, at 2030, had set off by car from his headquarters at Hopen on the Saltfjord to assess the situation for himself.

He met Trappes-Lomax and Roscher Nielsen at 0500 the following morning, was persuaded that Mo was untenable and agreed to take the matter up with Force Headquarters. Auchinleck proved much less amenable to persuasion. (He stressed the need to hold the line at Mo until the airfields were ready but when presented with the stark facts of the situation, gave his reluctant consent.[20]) 'The Mo detachment is being out-flanked and must retreat,' he told Dill, later in the day. 'Why our soldiers cannot be as mobile as the Germans I don't know, but they can't apparently. Anyway, I have to accept Gubbins's recommendation but have told him to resist all the way and fight hard.'[21] Satisfied that Trappes-Lomax understood the General's intentions, Gubbins set out to return to his head-quarters leaving his Brigade Major to settle the details of the withdrawal.

At nine o'clock that morning the Norwegians pulled out in a fleet of buses to begin the long journey to Bodø. Roscher Nielsen thought that his reservists were 'quite hopeless in present conditions'; he needed to pull them back to a quiet area and restore them to some semblance of military effectiveness.[22] Other non-effectives were sent back as well: specialist troops, the field ambulance and the Independent Company, judged to be a spent force after four days of sporadic fighting at Finneid. The British units moved off at 1000, but their withdrawal was poorly concerted. B Company, still in contact with the enemy and therefore most at risk, got no orders to move and was left to its fate. (It was fortunate to catch up with the rest of the Battalion forty-eight hours later after crossing hills still deep in snow and fording a turbulent river 'about the size of the Thames at Putney'.[23]) Other units left their positions in indecent haste, abandoning vital equipment. The artillery troop left its drums of telephone cable and much of its signals equipment behind, severely restricting its ability to provide supporting fire. Trappes-Lomax added it to the list of units being sent to the rear. The tail of the column cleared Mo in mid-afternoon. Sappers blew the bridges outside the town (the first of thirty that they were to destroy during the coming days) and the column set off on foot up the long valley of the Rana towards the Saltfjell and Bodø.

That evening, they met C Company which had crossed the 'snow belt' without mishap and had taken up a covering position at Rosvoll, 10 miles north-east of Mo. Trappes-Lomax finally called a halt at Sandheien, some 5 miles further on; the men were tired out after a fifteen-hour battle and a 'long weary march' of 18 or 20 miles under continuous surveillance and harassment by German aircraft.[24]

Was it was feasible for a single unsupported infantry battalion to hold the Germans in the Rana valley? The history of operations in the Gudbrandsdal suggests that the odds would have been heavily against. But in the wake of the *Chobry* and *Effingham* disasters time meant everything and there could be no doubt in Harstad that the attempt had to be made. News that Trappes-Lomax was continuing his retreat and offering no resistance to the German advance thus caused mounting indignation in Force Headquarters. By the evening of 19 May, Gubbins (now back at Hopen) was having to justify the actions of his subordinate; in a lengthy telephone conversation with Dowler, he explained that he had spent a good part of the previous day with the Scots Guards and that he was certain that Trappes-Lomax understood what was in the General's mind. At midnight Auchinleck came through to 'Scissorsforce' himself and told Gubbins that he was free to 'remove any officer not fit to command and replace him at his discretion'. Gubbins set off to visit the front line again. Trappes-Lomax had now reached Messingsletten, 40 miles from Mo, where the Rana valley narrows to a gorge and snakes south-east before the start of the ascent to the open plateau of the Saltfjell. That night Auchinleck sent the Battalion Commander a stiff signal: 'You have now reached a good position for defence,' he told him. 'Essential to stand and fight ... I rely on the Scots Guards to stop the enemy.'[25]

During his journey south Gubbins found large numbers of specialist troops making their own way to Bodø, among them the artillery troop whose guns by now were well out of range of the enemy. He turned them back. At Messingsletten, he found that Trappes-Lomax had replied to Auchinleck's signal, listing the reasons why he was unable to comply with the order to stand and fight, and explaining why further withdrawal was unavoidable. After further discussions with the Battalion Commander, Gubbins tried once again to put the General's mind at rest. Trappes-Lomax, he reported, had been anxious to get his force behind the snow-fields to excellent defensive positions on the other side, but that he should have no difficulty in holding the enemy where he was. Before leaving to return to his headquarters he handed Trappes-Lomax a written order telling him that he was to impede the enemy's advance by every means in his power. 'You will only withdraw from any position you hold,' he told him, 'if, in your opinion, there is a serious danger to the safety of your force. You must bear in mind that your object is to delay [the enemy] all you can, and that this can only be done by hitting him hard; this I wish you to do.' There was one slight hint of ambiguity in the message and one only. Trappes-Lomax could, if he felt he had enough troops, send one company across the snow to Storjord to prepare that position for all-round defence. He was, however, to refer to 'Scissorsforce' beforehand.[26] In the meantime the Battalion Second-in-Command, Major Lesley Graham, would recon-noitre an intermediate position at Viskiskoia, just north of the snowfields and at the start of the long descent into the Saltdal.

But by noon next day it was clear that Trappes-Lomax was abandoning Messingsletten. 'Just heard you are continuing retirement,' Gubbins's indignant message read. 'If so this is against my orders as cannot believe your force seriously endangered already in view no contact yesterday. You must hold the enemy as far south as possible. This is my final order.'[27]

At about the time this order was leaving 'Scissorsforce', a fleet of 'puffers' arrived in Bodø bringing two companies of Irish Guards that had been hastily re-armed from reserve stocks in Harstad and from materiel intended for the Norwegian Army. The rest of the Battalion came in by destroyer late that night and with them came Colonel Dowler for a con-ference with the Brigadier.

Gubbins's appreciation of the military situation was crisp and to the point, and Dowler told Auchinleck afterwards that the defence of Bodø 'could not be in better hands'. He had seen enemy mobility and his own lack of transport as among the most serious problems that he faced. He had to keep an adequate number of men on the Bodø peninsula to guard against turning movements by sea and air, and he had to adopt a dispersed disposition since he lacked the transport to respond rapidly to the un-expected. But he needed to hold Storjord at the head of the Saltdal at all costs and until this position could be occupied he had to stop the German advance as far forward as he could. The position of the Scots Guards in the Rana valley was 'precarious'. They were worried, Gubbins told Dowler, about fighting with their backs to the snowfields and depressed by their experiences at Mo. They felt that they did not understand the kind of warfare they were engaged in and looked on the Germans as superior. He (Gubbins) did not believe, however, that there was a case for replacing the Battalion Commander just yet. He was sending two good Indian Army officers with experience of mountain warfare to give a helping hand and he believed that the Battalion could hold south of the Saltdal plateau for a further four days. (Dowler took a less charitable view of Trappes-Lomax's performance. 'One is forced to the conclusion,' he told Auchinleck in his report of the meeting, 'that leadership has as much to answer for as lack of training.') In the meantime Gubbins needed infantry, transport, artillery and (particularly) naval support to prevent the enemy from using the Inner Leads. He was thinking in terms of two or three armed vessels to investigate shipping movements on his seaward flank and action by naval and air force units even if this could only be spasmodic. The enemy's mastery of the air and his apparent ability to advance unchecked by water was damaging morale. The Norwegians in particular had been unable to understand how the German coup at Hemnes had been allowed to happen.[28]

Later that day, Auchinleck told Cork that the Scots Guards would hold their position a few days longer and that Gubbins had things well in hand. But the situation could, he warned, turn nasty once again unless something could be done to offset German superiority at sea and in the air. On the strength of Dowler's report, Auchinleck formed 'Bodoforce' to defend the Saltdal and the Bodø peninsula, and placed it under Gubbins's command. The Irish Guards and half the South Wales Borderers had reached the area already, delivered piecemeal as soon as they had been re-equipped and in whatever shipping had come to hand. A squadron of Gladiators had arrived in Bardufoss and the forward airstrip at Bodø was reported ready. Other units – French, British and Norwegian – would become available within days. The imperative now was to hold the German advance in check until these assets could be deployed.

During the afternoon of 20 May, Trappes-Lomax selected three defensive lines in the upper Rana valley on which he could offer some temporary resistance to the enemy's progress. But the materiel and, increasingly, the moral shortcomings of his battalion, coupled with the daunting prospect of a rearguard action across the open plateau of the Saltfjell, weighed more heavily with him than the barely concealed strictures of his superiors. He had thus abandoned two positions in quick succession until by the afternoon of 22 May his force was concentrated at Randalsvollen at the foot of the long incline leading to the open fells. Here, demolitions and the pace of his retirement combined to give him a few hours of grace. The chartered buses that had carried Nielsen's Norwegians northwards had returned. (He had taken the precaution of putting a Scots Guardsman in each of them.) That evening the Battalion moved off section by section, covered at the last by two Bren-carriers salvaged from the *Effingham* and manned by men of No. 3 Independent Company. They crossed the snowfields without interference from the enemy and by midnight had taken up the positions at Viskiskoia that had been reconnoitred by Major Graham. But the long retreat had done little to prepare them for what lay ahead. The Battalion War Diary recorded that the men were 'utterly exhausted' and that 'a certain demoralisation had set in', the result of fatigue, loss of kit, the succession of rearguard actions and the ever-present menace from the air.[29]

News that Trappes-Lomax was intending to continue his withdrawal reached 'Scissorsforce' during the afternoon of 22 May. (Gubbins had sent a staff officer to ensure that his orders were being complied with and to demand the return of the transport that he needed to move troops to the head of the Saltdal.) He decided to accept the retirement as a fait accompli, fearing that any attempt to reverse it would lead to disaster. His plan to establish his main defensive position at Storjord was now at serious risk. Time was against him. He had little alternative but to concentrate the Irish Guards at Pothus at the lower end of the valley and a mere 10 miles in front of the Rognan ferry. He sent orders to Trappes-Lomax to hold at Viskiskoia until 27 May and ordered No. 3 Independent Company to occupy a commanding feature on the right of the position to counter any flanking movement.

The German attack on Viskiskoia opened in mid-afternoon. Trappes-Lomax had been called back to Storjord to answer a telephone call from Headquarters, and there he had met Brigadier Gubbins, armed with a letter from Auchinleck. He had returned to the front line with the news that he had been recalled to Harstad on the ground that he had failed to carry out his orders. The description of what followed is best left to the battalion diarist. 'This crushing blow took place in the middle of an attack,' the entry read, 'and it is scarcely to be wondered at that the morale of both officers and men was still further shaken by the loss of a C.O. for whose personality and ability everybody had the highest respect and in whom everyone had the greatest confidence.'[30]

The regimental historian found a certain irony in the fact that, when Gubbins came forward with Graham to witness the progress of the battle, he came under heavy mortar and machine-gun fire from the dominant feature on the right that the Independent Company had been unable to hold. He quickly rescinded his order to defend Viskiskoia and authorized an immediate retreat.[31]

The defence of the Saltfjord and of the Bodø peninsula now depended on holding the Germans at Pothus, the final river crossing in the long descent from Viskiskoia before road and river reached the head of the fjord at

Rognan. Gubbins put the defence of the area in the hands of Major Hugh Stockwell, an experienced infantryman and former commander of No. 2 Independent Company,[32] and 'Stockforce', pushed forward piecemeal by road and ferry, took up its positions during the afternoon of 24 May, unaware that momentous events in France had been reshaping government policies in fundamental ways. People remembered it as a perfect summer's day, although pleasure was tempered by apprehension of what lay ahead and by the swarms of ants and midges.

The Pothus position centred on a girder bridge which, viewed from British positions, carried the road from left to right across the swollen Saltdal river. Beyond the bridge and on the left the land rose steeply from road and river to a spur of high ground, overlooking the southern approaches to the crossing. No. 1 Company Irish Guards was sent to occupy this spur and to delay the enemy's advance. (When their position became untenable, they were to retire over the tributary immediately behind them and cross to the right bank by means of a footbridge a mile or so downstream.) Below the girder bridge and on the right bank of the river, the road crossed a stretch of gently sloping and heavily forested ground referred to generally as Pothus Wood. Stockwell put two companies of Irish Guards to cover the river crossing with his artillery (the half battery of 25-pdr guns from Mo) and a Norwegian mortar and machine-gun section in support. These had a clear field of fire across the river in the direction of the enemy's approach. His headquarters and his reserves (No. 2 Company Irish Guards and Independent Companies 2 and 3) were concealed in the plantations of Pothus Wood.

The Scots Guards retreated through Pothus in the small hours of 25 May. The Irish Guardsmen heard the 'shuffling tramp of tired men' as they passed through and there was none of the banter that usually marked a meeting of the two battalions.[33] Shortly afterwards, sappers blew the girder bridge leaving No. 1 Company isolated on its spur. At about eight o'clock in the morning, German scouts came pedalling down the road, seemingly unaware of what awaited them. Norwegian machine gunners 'shot them into a tangled heap of bicycles and bodies'.[34] But by late morning the Germans were pushing hard on the British left and gathering for an attack on the spur. A first attempt to storm this feature met fierce resistance and was driven back. A second attempt in the early afternoon, covered by a heavy air raid on Pothus Wood, failed as well but soon afterwards it became clear that the Germans were working round the ridge to the east of the company position. In late afternoon, therefore, No. 1 Company began to pull back across the tributary to new defensive positions downstream. The last platoon to leave found the suspension bridge already blown and forded the torrent under fire using a chain of rifle slings to help themselves across. Stockwell sent No. 3 Independent Company across the river to help stabilize the situation.

On the opposite side of the valley, meanwhile, No. 4 Company Irish Guards, with the Norwegians on their right, had frustrated a succession of German attempts to cross the river near the site of the girder bridge. But during the night German engineers rigged a pontoon bridge 1,000 yards upstream and men began to filter into the woodland on the opposite bank. By morning, it was clear that the weight of the German attack had shifted to the British right. Stockwell had few reserves left to counter this development. No. 3 Independent Company was already committed and following reports of a wide flanking movement by German mountain troops he had sent No. 2 Company Irish Guards to occupy a high point overlooking Pothus from the east. In the early hours of 26 May he committed the last of his reserves (part of No. 2 Independent Company) in an attempt to stop the enemy's advance and to prevent encirclement.

But behind the scenes, important decisions were being made. During the night, Gubbins had been summoned back to Bodø for an urgent meeting with Dowler. He had declared that he was 'hopeful but not confident' of holding Pothus, and had spoken of his plans for a further withdrawal and for new defensive positions on the Saltfjord.[35] But Dowler had told him in the strictest confidence that the Government had decided to abandon northern Norway – his task now was to prepare for the evacuation of Bodø beginning on 1 June. Gubbins had returned to Rognan to find Stockwell threatened with encirclement and, at 1130 on the morning of 26 May, he had given the order to withdraw.

Stockwell set the time of withdrawal for 1900 that evening. He had hoped to recall his troops from the east bank of the river to form a rearguard on the road to Rognan, but since he was wholly dependent on runners to get the message through, few got the word in time. No. 2 Company Irish Guards and No. 3 Independent Company thus retired down the east bank of the river and only reached safety after a long and arduous march across trackless mountain territory. The situation on the right bank, though easier, was by no means straightforward. No. 4 Company was still heavily engaged at the girder bridge as the time for withdrawal approached and it was only the sudden intervention of a Gladiator fighter that had given them their opportunity to break contact. This aircraft (one of three that enjoyed a fleeting, meteoric career at Bodø) had shot down two Heinkels in quick succession and then machine-gunned the astonished Germans in their trenches. No. 4 Company had loaded its stores and wounded, and followed the rest down the road to Rognan. They later boasted that they had left Norway without losing a man and with one more Bren than they had started with.[36]

By midnight 'Stockforce' was gathering at Rognan waiting to embark. The Norwegian ferry crew had long since left but soldiers were attempting to work the ferry and Gubbins had assembled a dozen 'puffers', all manned with naval crews, to help ship his men to the northern shore of the Saltfjord. The embarkation remained tense to the last. Demolition teams set their charges to destroy the jetty when the last ship was clear. But as the appointed time approached, the ferry with nearly 1,000 men on board was still alongside, immobilized by a fire in the engine room. Attempts to extinguish the fire and start the engine failed and in the end a 'puffer' was called in to tow her off. This was done with seconds to spare and as the ferry drew clear of the jetty she was showered with flaming debris. Ashore, German cyclists were already arriving in the village.

Chapter 12

The Storm Clouds Gather

The Commons met during the afternoon of 13 May (the Monday following Churchill's summons to the Palace) to give its blessing to an administration pledged to do its utmost to prosecute the war to a successful conclusion. In his brief statement to the House, the new Prime Minister said nothing about Norway and little about the great battle that was opening on the other side of the Channel (there was little to say), but he delivered one of those lines which has since become embedded in the national consciousness. 'I have nothing to offer,' he told his listeners, 'but blood, toil, tears and sweat.' His promise was fulfilled all too quickly.

Within hours Churchill was stemming the flood tide of disaster that had followed the German breakthrough on the Meuse, and wrestling with the dilemma that was to dog British decision-makers for the rest of this brief campaign – whether to risk Britain's metropolitan air force in an attempt to win the battle for France, or whether to preserve it for the onslaught against Great Britain that would surely follow. Reynaud's early appeals for air support were treated with reserve (on the Wednesday morning he had seemed seriously overwrought), but by the Thursday the need to 'do something to bolster up the French' had become paramount and the War Cabinet had agreed to the immediate despatch of four fighter squadrons, with two more at short notice to follow them.[1] The Prime Minister had left for Paris that afternoon.

The informal meeting of the Supreme War Council which followed has been fully described elsewhere. It is mostly remembered for Gamelin's response to Churchill's question: '*Où est la masse de manoeuvre?*' He had answered with a shrug and a shake of the head: '*Aucune.*' Outside, in the garden of the Quai d' Orsai, 'venerable officials' were burning the state papers.[2] After the meeting, Churchill telegraphed London describing the situation as 'grave in the last degree' and asking the War Cabinet to sanction the despatch of further fighter squadrons (beyond the four already agreed), and to switch Bomber Command's offensive from the Ruhr to the mass of the German Army flowing into what he called 'the Bulge'. His personal view was that France might go the way of Poland unless this critical battle was won, and that all available British and French aviation should be concentrated above the battlefield to give the French Army a last chance to 'rally its bravery and strength'. Late that night the War Cabinet agreed to make six Hurricane squadrons available as early as possible and to switch the bombing offensive to the Meuse crossings.[3]

It was inevitable in these changed circumstances that the future of the campaign in arctic Norway should be called into question. The point of decision still lay some way ahead but Cork had been warned as early as 12 May not to expect anti-aircraft or fighter reinforcements beyond those already authorized. On the 17th, the Chiefs of Staff had put precise figures to this guidance and asked him to report on the implications for his campaign. And on his return from Paris, Churchill had demanded a review of the situation to determine whether Narvik was absorbing resources that might better be used elsewhere.[4]

By now, attention was shifting from the Meuse to dangerous developments in Flanders where the BEF, flanked by the French First and Seventh Armies, was retreating from the advanced positions that it had occupied under Plan D, Gamelin's great scheme for shortening the front and stopping the Germans on Belgian soil. Churchill had gone down to Chartwell on the Sunday (19 May) hoping for a few hours of recreation, but he had returned to London post-haste following news that a 'vast gap' had opened on the British right and that Gort was considering a retreat to the Channel coast. Ironside told the War Cabinet that night that he had vetoed Lord Gort's proposal and that he had urged him to withdraw south-west towards Amiens and the Somme, and regain touch with the French there. The Defence Council had endorsed this proposal but the future had looked full of uncertainty and Churchill had ordered the first precautionary moves for the evacuation of the BEF.[5] A resolution of the situation in the far north had seemed more urgent than ever and on the Monday Churchill had invited the War Cabinet to consider sending a direct order to Lord Cork 'to take Narvik by assault'. Anthony Eden (Secretary of State for War) and A.V. Alexander (the new First Lord) dissuaded him; but that night he told Cork that he was disappointed by the 'stagnation' which appeared to rule at Narvik. 'It is necessary to reach a decision in this theatre,' he went on, 'in view of larger events ... I should be much obliged if you would enable me to understand what is holding you back.'[6] But a withdrawal from northern Norway had still seemed premature. Commitments had been made to the Norwegian Government; there was Sweden to consider; and there was still the hope that a miracle might intervene as had happened on the Marne in 1914.

The 'Weygand Plan' had offered just such a glimmer of hope. Prompted by frustration, by signs of a leadership vacuum in Flanders and by news of changes in the French High Command, Churchill had flown to Paris for a second time. Gamelin had gone and Maxime Weygand, the new military Supremo, had just returned from a lightning tour of the front. Churchill and Reynaud had driven to his headquarters at Vincennes to hear his findings. The veteran General, once Chief of Staff to Marshal Foch, the great apostle of the offensive, had urged that there could be no question of the Anglo-French armies on the Belgian frontier simply retreating south-west to rejoin the rest. 'Such a movement would be bound to fail and the forces would be condemned to certain disaster.' Instead they should strike southwards towards Cambrai and Arras and take the German incursion in the flank. Churchill and Dill gave their enthusiastic support. It was agreed that the Anglo-French armies would begin their drive southwards by the next day at the latest. They would have the 'utmost possible help' from the British air force; and the new French army group forming south of the German incursion would strike north to join hands with them.[7]

Churchill returned to London in buoyant spirits, but by the following morning (23 May) the German threat to the Channel ports (and hence to Gort's line of supply) was looking so serious that he confined the CIGS to the War Office so that he could give his undivided attention to events across the Channel. (Ironside's days as CIGS were numbered – he stepped aside on 25 May in favour of Sir John Dill and was given command of Britain's Home Forces.) There was no sign that the French were taking the offensive. Churchill told Reynaud that the salvation of the northern armies depended on the immediate execution of the Weygand plan and demanded that the commanders concerned be given 'stringent orders' to comply. In Cabinet that morning Churchill warned his colleagues that, if the Weygand plan failed, the next step would have as its object the evacuation of the BEF with as little loss as possible.[8]

By now, Narvik was in the balance too. The Chiefs of Staff had just received Auchinleck's reaction to the cap that had been placed on his numbers. Replying on behalf of the command as a whole, Auchinleck reported that the land forces offered by London were probably adequate provided that additional artillery and engineer units could be provided. But with barely half the aircraft and half the anti-aircraft guns that he judged necessary, he could not hold himself responsible for the security of the forces under his command, or offer any reasonable certainty of achieving the objectives he had been given.[9] For the Chiefs of Staff the issue was now clear-cut – capture Narvik and withdraw. Churchill ex-pressed reservations about asking troops to 'incur heavy losses' for no obvious purpose, but he too had little doubt that the forces 'at present devoted to the Norwegian project' would soon be needed at home. He expected that it would be some weeks before the withdrawal could be organized and hoped that, in the interim, effective action could be taken to block the port of Luleå, and strike that final blow against Germany's ore supplies. It was agreed that the staffs should be given immediate instructions to prepare plans for a complete withdrawal from northern Norway.[10]

The directive from the Chiefs of Staff reached Harstad in the early hours of 25 May. It made it clear that the Government had decided to evacuate the Narvik expeditionary force at the earliest possible moment, men and equipment being urgently needed at home. The capture of Narvik remained 'highly desirable' (the destruction of port facilities and the railway were given as the main reasons) and it was recognized that evacuation would be 'facilitated' if the German garrison was defeated first. But thereafter speed of evacuation would be of primary importance in order to limit the duration of the Navy's commitment. Plans were to give priority to the evacuation of personnel, anti-aircraft guns and ammunition, and field artillery. The signal emphasized that the Norwegian Government had *not* been informed and that the strictest secrecy was to be observed.[11]

In the Narvik backwater, the urgent need to stop the German advance on Bodø, and to provide a counter to the growing force and effectiveness of the Luftwaffe, had prevented any swift sequel to Béthouart's spectacular success at Bjerkvik. Despite the presence of the *Ark Royal* and her fighter squadrons, the toll in ships, lost and damaged, had continued to mount, and the air threat had become the foremost of Lord Cork's concerns. On 17 May, he had reported that air attacks during the previous twenty hours had been 'almost continuous', and that he was in urgent need of more anti-aircraft ammunition. Two days later, he had reported that the constant bombing was weakening the morale of merchant seamen, and that the ships' companies of the *Aurora* and the *Enterprise* were showing definite signs of strain.[12] He had thus dealt robustly with Churchill's charge of stagnation. The issue, he told the Prime Minister, was not whether he could capture the town (that could be done at leisure once the air problem was solved) but 'whether or not we can establish ourselves in this country'. Bringing the airfields into operation was an essential first step. He was waiting for landing craft and these were necessarily engaged in lifting stores and guns to the airfields. 'Nothing holds me back but the desire to get fighters established,' he continued. 'I assure you [the] desire not to fail you is uppermost in my mind. I do not require spurring for I am doing my best in order to obtain the object and do not doubt achieving it.'[13]

By now the chance of progress was tantalizingly close. On 21 May, three weeks of intense labour had finally borne fruit and the *Furious* had delivered the first of sixteen Gladiators to Bardufoss. (Most of the pilots were veterans of Lesjaskog with a score to settle and one of them had appeared over Pothus in the final stages of the battle.) At its height the airfield project had employed a reserve battalion and 600 Norwegian labourers working in

174

two shifts, clearing snow and ice, draining floodwater, extending the runway and constructing blast-proof shelters at the forest's edge. (There had been a determined effort to learn the lessons of central Norway.) A pack train of 200 mules had been used to bring a million rounds of ammunition and half a million gallons of aviation spirit from the coast, and a battery of twenty-four anti-aircraft guns had been installed. Skånland (deemed vital because of its central position) had continued to frustrate the best efforts of the engineers and a first attempt to install the Hurricanes of 46 Squadron had failed. But Skånland too was now becoming ready. Auchinleck and Béthouart met during the morning of 23 May to set the first (tentative) date for the assault on Narvik. They selected the night of 25/26 or, failing that, the nights immediately following, and Lord Cork, who had spent the day in Tromsø calling on King Haakon and settling a number of outstanding difficulties with Norwegian Ministers, endorsed their decision on his return.

The Chiefs of Staff directive added new complications to their plans. It was immediately clear that with Allied forces in contact with the enemy in the Narvik area and in the Saltfjord, a withdrawal would prove difficult and dangerous. Cork and Auchinleck were in full agreement that secrecy was paramount and that knowledge of the Government's intentions had to be confined to those with an imperative need to know. Béthouart who, as commander of the Narvik sector, had been perfecting his plans for the assault on the town, was an obvious exception. They called him in on 26 May to break the news and to enquire whether in all the circumstances he would be willing to continue the attack. He retired briefly to confer with his staff and returned with an affirmative answer, warning only that he could never consent to abandoning the Norwegian Army on the field of battle. It was agreed that pressure on the enemy would be maintained to the last, that the attack on Narvik provided the best possible cover for Allied intentions and that the evacuation of non-essential HQ elements could begin at once on the pretext of a move to new and safer positions.[14]

In the uneasy interlude between the landings at Bjerkvik and the Allied assault on Narvik, the German command had been making desperate attempts to reinforce Dietl's hard-pressed battalions. The airdrop of supplies had continued – Lord Cork's ships had tried, without any real expectation of success, to disrupt the process. But the trickle of men who arrived from Germany during the first month of the occupation (mostly specialist troops) had arrived by seaplane to the Beisfjord and the Rombaksfjord, both safe from British interference. There had been comings and goings by rail as well, generally on some humanitarian pretext. (The total number of arrivals through Sweden during the campaign is usually put at 200 or 300.[15]) But Falkenhorst's urgent appeal to Hitler, made in the aftermath of the Bjerkvik landings, had prompted initiatives which crossed all previous boundaries of risk taking. A plan to bring in a battalion of mountain troops by glider was overtaken by events and the gliders got no further than Ålborg. During the final weeks of May (and despite their heavy commitments in the West) the Germans managed to insert a parachute battalion and two companies of parachute-trained mountain troops (more than 1,000 men in all) to augment Dietl's meagre numbers. Béthouart's Chasseurs had watched some of these new arrivals from their vantage point above Ankenes and had soon been locked in combat with them.

The plan for the attack on Narvik was drawn up by Béthouart and his staff after careful observation of German positions. The 1st Battalion French Foreign Legion would lead the assault, embarking in landing craft at Sagnes (shielded from German eyes by the Øyjord peninsula) and striking across the narrow mouth of the Rombaksfjord to Orneset, a small headland overlooking Narvik from the north-east. Having scaled the rock-strewn and scrub-covered slope behind the beach, the Battalion would cover the landing of the General Fleischer's Narvik Battalion and the 2nd Battalion of Légionnaires. The force would then cross the railway and fan out to occupy the Taraldsvikfjell (the 1,500-foot plateau immediately east of the town) and the fringe of low wooded hills overlooking Narvik from the north and west. Supporting fire would be provided by the guns of the Fleet and by three artillery batteries (two French Colonial and one Norwegian) positioned on high ground above Øyjord and commanding the landing point from the northward. Naval gunfire would deny the Germans the use of the railway (the principal line of reinforcement and retreat) and put heavy pressure on the high points overlooking the town and the landing area. Two subsidiary operations would accompany the main assault. Drives by the 14th Battalion of Chasseurs along the northern shore of the Rombaksfjord and by the Poles on Ankenes, and thence towards the head of the Beisfjord, would isolate the defenders of the Narvik peninsula and converge on the railway at Hundalen (12 miles east of Narvik), confining Dietl to a shrunken enclave of mountain territory on the Swedish border.

Although the seizure of Øyjord and the later advance eastward to the narrows had extended the choice of landing beaches open to the Allies, and improved the chances of achieving tactical surprise, the main sensitivity of the plan was the one identified by Trappes-Lomax almost three weeks before – the shortage of landing craft, for accident and action damage had reduced the total to five.[16] This would limit the first flight of Légionnaires to 290 men who would have to maintain themselves, unsupported, for a full forty-five minutes until the second batch arrived. And thereafter, the build-up would become slower still if (as was intended)

176

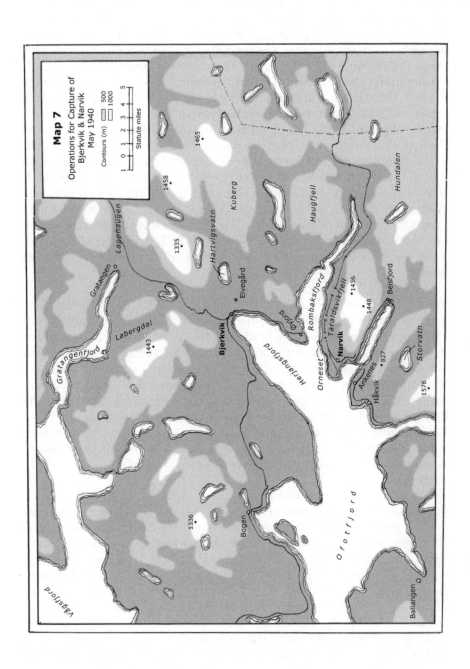

Map 7

Operations for Capture of
Bjerkvik & Narvik
May 1940

Contours (m) 500 / 1000

Statute miles
1 0 1 2 3 4 5

Lapphaugen

Kuberg

Haugfjell

Hundalen

1465

1458

1335

Hartvigsvatn

Gratangen

Labergdal

Gratangenfjord

1443

Elvegård

Bjerkvik

Øyjord

Rombaksfjord

Beisfjord

1436

Taraldsvikfjell

1448

Narvik

Storvatn

Ankenes

827

1576

Håkvik

Herjangsfjord

Orneset

1336

Bogen

Ballangen

Orotfjord

Vågsfjord

177

tanks were to be put ashore to support the landing. This early phase of the operation was recognized as critical. Reflecting on it later, Auchinleck described the operation as having been conducted with the 'barest margin of safety'. Cork thought that a lesser man than Béthouart might well have made the shortage of landing craft 'an excuse for inaction'.[17]

Continuing worries about German airpower dogged decision-makers to the end. Skånland was at last becoming ready and the *Glorious* was due to return on 26 May with the long-awaited Hurricanes. Cork and Auchinleck elected to postpone the assault on Narvik until the night of 27/28 May in the hope that they could exploit this new and valuable asset. And they held to their decision despite the crisis in the Saltfjord and mounting evidence that the Narvik flotilla would have to begin the evacuation of 'Bodoforce' in a matter of days. In the event Skånland was to prove a sorry disappointment: the first of the Hurricanes ended nose down in the soggy ground and the rest of the squadron, eleven aircraft in all, had to be sent to join the Gladiators at Bardufoss. During the 24-hour period of the operation the combined squadrons flew a total of ninety-five sorties over Narvik.

The bombardment opened at 2340 on night of 27/28 May. (The Dunkirk evacuation had just begun and that night the King of the Belgians sent plenipotentiaries to Germany to discuss the terms of an armistice.) Four destroyers took station in the Rombaksfjord to control the railway and watch the tunnel entrances, while the *Cairo*, *Coventry* and *Firedrake* lay off to suppress enemy fire positions in the hills around Narvik. The *Southampton*, the only 6-inch gun ship remaining now that the *Aurora* and the *Enterprise* had left, supported the Polish battalions at Ankenes. Cork flew his flag in the *Cairo*, his intended flagship, the AA cruiser *Curlew*, having succumbed to dive-bombers off Skånland the day before. Auchinleck and Béthouart were with him and the Frenchman had again given the order to open fire.

The first wave of Légionnaires landed promptly at midnight. They met minimal resistance and quickly established themselves on the ridge looking across the railway to the lower slopes of the Taraldsvikfjell. The slow and nerve-wracking build-up had then started, and despite interference from a German gun that frustrated attempts to embark the second wave at Øyjord and forced a return to the more distant (but sheltered) embarkation point at Sagnes, the movement of troops to Orneset had continued on schedule. By four o'clock on the morning of the 28th, two full battalions (I/13th and Fleischer's Narvik Battalion) were ashore, heaving weapons and ammunition up the slope behind the beach, and preparing to cross the railway and work up the shoulder of the hill in front of them. The first elements of the II/13th were beginning to land as well, but the two tanks were stuck beyond hope of recovery in soft clay on the beach at Taraldsvik.

The crisis of the operation was not long in coming. As the two battalions with the sun in their eyes began to work their way forward up the slopes of the Taraldsvikfjell, the German defenders launched a powerful counter-attack from broken ground on the left and swept the Norwegians and the Légionnaires back across the railway to the cover of the ridge beyond it. The German thrust gained positions overlooking the beach at Orneset and the landing of the II/13th was seriously disrupted. The Battalion was forced to shift to a beach on the other side of the promontory and it was almost seven hours before the last man was ashore. At the height of the crisis, Commandant Paris, Béthouart's Chief of Staff, sent forward in a landing craft to assess the cause of the delay, was killed.

Pierre Olivier Lapie, who observed these events from Margin-Vernerey's command post on the ridge above Orneset, attributes this near disaster to the snail's pace of the Allied build-up and subsequent advance. (In the warm morning sun, the climb up the slopes of the Taraldsvikfjell demanded immense physical exertion and the defenders had ample time to gather their strength.) British sources have tended to emphasise the role of the Luftwaffe. Just after four o'clock that morning, fog had brought operations at Bardufoss to a standstill and, from 0430 onwards, German bombers (about thirty were reported) had enjoyed a free hand over Narvik for two full hours. Their attacks, conducted at high and low level, had forced Cork's ships into spasms of evasive action and their gunnery had suffered accordingly. Whether naval gunfire had a genuine role to play in the close support of troops must be open to doubt, however. Broken ground, birch scrub and rocky outcrops were making accurate observation impossible and, by the time of the German counter-attack, the Navy's job was largely done. The effect of the Luftwaffe's intervention on the transit and landing of the second Legion battalion must of course be acknowledged. In the end, it was the physical endurance and raw courage of men on the ground that determined the outcome. Lapie provides a glimpse of Margin-Vernerey standing on the ridge above Orneset in sword and medals, rallying his men and calmly dictating the order of the day that eventually stopped the rot. It was, however, well into the evening before the I/13th took the plateau and pushed the Germans eastwards along the railway towards Forneset.[18]

During those difficult morning hours, Cork's ships had faced a crisis of their own. For some time their anti-aircraft fire and their high-speed man-oeuvres had saved them from damage, but at 0620 a whole pattern of bombs had erupted in the water around the *Cairo* and two had hit. One went through the deck just aft of 'B' mounting, bursting among the ammunition party, killing eight men and wounding twenty more. The second exploded on the signal deck, not far from where Cork and Béthouart were standing, knocking out a 0.5-inch machine gun and setting fire to ready-use ammunition. Only one of the cruiser's eight 4-inch AA guns was still in action, the rest having experienced 'dangerous prematures' caused by continuous firing.[19] Cork called the *Havelock* alongside to take off Béthouart and his staff, intending to transfer his own flag to the *Stork*. Béthouart seems to have concluded, however, that with the bulk of the army ashore, he could manage from now on with the help of one or two destroyers. After an exchange of courtesies between the two men, Béthouart went ashore to direct operations from the gun batteries above Øyjord, while Cork withdrew his squadron leaving only the *Coventry*, the *Firedrake* and the *Beagle* to support operations on the Narvik peninsula.

The Polish battalions had faced a stiff fight as well. The weight of their initial attack, launched at midnight with the help of the *Southampton*, two batteries of artillery (one French and one British) and two light tanks, had carried them into the outskirts of Ankenes. But in the morning, the German counter-attack had driven them out and reoccupied positions not held since the British landings almost a month before. They had launched a second attack, however, from the heights above the village, and by noon they had expelled the last of the Germans from Ankenes and pushed eastward as far as Nyborg. A fourth Polish battalion meanwhile had been working up the valley past the Storvatn towards the head of the Beisfjord. Late that night it made contact with a Foreign Legion motorcycle patrol that had made its way from Narvik along the opposite shore of the fjord. The southern flank was now secure.

Fleischer entered Narvik at the head of his troops at 1700 on 28 May. (It was forty-nine days since Dietl had landed.) Béthouart crossed to Orneset late that evening and at 2200 reported to Cork that Narvik was in Allied hands. Cork sent his report next day and it was handed to Churchill during the morning meeting of the War Cabinet. He had recommended a KCB for Béthouart and a CB for Fleischer, both awards to have immediate effect.[20] Allied casualties on the Narvik peninsula numbered 150 of which sixty were Norwegian. The Poles (full of drive and hatred for the enemy but lacking in proficiency)[21] took a further 100 casualties at Ankenes. Between 300 and 400 prisoners were in Allied hands.

Chapter 13

Evacuation and a Final Tragedy

When Béthouart's troops went ashore at Orneset, plans for their eventual evacuation were already in hand. The task was a challenging one. A multi-national force of more than 25,000 men, which had arrived piecemeal over a period of weeks, had now to be taken off in a matter of days together with as much of its impedimenta as Harstad's limited port facilities allowed. The French naval auxiliaries which had delivered Béthouart's Light Division to Norway were now in the Mediterranean lifting colonial troops to Metropolitan France, and the force assembled for the operation was predominantly British. It included thirteen fast transports (some like the *Franconia*, *Lancastria* and *Georgic* household names) and a total of twelve stores ships, four of which went to Tromsø. The Admiralty set the earliest date for their arrival off the Lofotens as 2 June. The two carriers *Ark Royal* and *Glorious* were to join them.

Did Churchill have second thoughts? There is the merest hint that he did. In the mood of near euphoria which had followed the Army's miraculous escape from Dunkirk, his mind had returned once again to the importance of Swedish iron. On 2 June he had told Ismay that the evacuation of the BEF had 'revolutionised the Home Defence position', making it possible to keep a garrison at Narvik 'for some weeks on a self contained basis'.[1] But it was the most fleeting of second thoughts. A new and critical battle for the defence of Paris was taking shape and French demands for men and aircraft were becoming more insistent than ever. That evening, he told the War Cabinet that he had considered the question of Narvik once again but that the decision to abandon northern Norway must stand.[2]

The evacuation of Bodø presented a separate and more immediate challenge. Initial hopes that 24th Guards Brigade, reinforced now by the Norwegian I/15th Infantry Battalion, could hold its own in the Saltfjord until the transports and carriers arrived on station proved illusory. The Gladiators that had appeared over Pothus in the final stages of the battle had survived to cover the withdrawal of Stockwell's force from Rognan. But they had been swept away in the savage reprisal that had followed. At eight o'clock on the morning of 27 May, a pack of dive-bombers and long-range fighters had attacked the weakly defended airstrip, destroyed one aircraft and driven the other (badly damaged) back to Bardufoss.[3] That night, the Luftwaffe raided Bodø with 100 bombers, a force scarcely credible at that stage of the war. They reduced the town to ash and rubble, and put the airstrip, never more than a makeshift affair, beyond possibility of further use. It was clear following this onslaught that 'Bodoforce' would have to pull out in a matter of days even if, in doing so, it risked compromising the larger evacuation plan. Gubbins pressed for evacuation by 31 May and plans were laid accordingly. The first 1,000 men would leave in two destroyers during the night of 29/30 May, with the rest of 'Bodoforce' following in equal batches of 1,500 on the two succeeding nights. The use of destroyers for the evacuation (there was no practical alternative) meant leaving artillery and transport behind.

It proved impossible to conceal these intentions from the I/15th Infantry Battalion. The Norwegians had taken up a strong defensive position at Finneid, protected on the right by the fjord and on the left by the string of lakes leading eastward to the Blåmannsis Glacier. The transfer of the Irish Guards to Fauske (less easily defended but giving easier access to Bodø), and the reluctance of the British command to move reinforcements forward to advanced positions on the Saltfjord, invited immediate suspicion. The intention to abandon Bodø was thus admitted, the move being presented as a sensible adjustment to Allied dispositions following the capture of Narvik. It had seemed nonetheless to put the safety of the I/15th at risk and an angry Fleischer had demanded an immediate rethink. He was told merely that the withdrawal would be phased over a period of three days; and with that he had to be content. As the Irish Guards began their move westward along the road to Bodø, the Norwegians retired northwards towards Røsvik. After fighting a sharp rearguard action in the approaches to the town, they embarked in a fleet of local craft and crossed safely to the Lofotens.[4]

Despite these unpromising beginnings, the evacuation of Bodø continued according to plan and with minimal interference from the German Army. The weather helped as well. A timely 'Scotch mist' descended on the Saltfjord and kept enemy air activity to a minimum. Just before midnight on 29 May the first 1,000 men (Nos 1 and 4 Independent Companies and administrative echelons) left Bodø in two destroyers and were transferred offshore to the fleet repair ship *Vindictive*. Next day the 1st Irish Guards and Nos 2 and 3 Independent Companies fell back through a covering position at Hopen (12 miles east of Bodø) and embarked that night for Harstad, leaving it to the 1st Scots Guards and 2nd South Wales Borderers to hold the Germans off, demolish what materiel could not be carried away and complete the evacuation on the night of the 31st. There was a brisk action with German cycle patrols at the Hopen bridge after the last of the Irish Guards had passed, but the pursuit was not pressed strongly. After a further brush with enemy patrols at Lake Soloi (the first really good defensive position that the Scots Guards had occupied)[5] the two remaining battalions and HQ 24th Guards Brigade retired, company by company, through the ruins of Bodø to the waiting destroyers. By midnight 31 May the town was deserted and the ill-conceived campaign launched in Mosjøen three weeks earlier was finally at an end.

Preparations for the main evacuation were meanwhile continuing apace under the fiction that base facilities were being moved to the greater security of Tromsø. The deception, driven by suspicions of loose talk and even of treachery among the civil population, was bare faced and deliberate, and was practised on all but the narrow circle of officers in Force Headquarters. To lend plausibility to the story, the naval base construction unit, among the first to leave, was loaded for Tromsø, diverted to British waters when at sea and held incommunicado at Scapa Flow until the news was out. Even in the final stages of the evacuation, men found out about their destination only after they had embarked. Leaders found the deceit distasteful but they justified it on the grounds of necessity. 'The secret was well kept,' Auchinlech wrote afterwards, 'and even those who might have suspected were kept constantly confused by conflicting rumours and instructions sedulously circulated by those staff officers in the know.'[6]

The fiction could not be preserved indefinitely, however, and with the start of the evacuation from Bodø, Cork called for the decision on how and when to break the news to the Norwegian authorities to be left to him. He then invited Sir Cecil Dormer and Colonel R.C.G. Pollock (Head of the British Military Mission in Tromsø) to a conference at Harstad to discuss ways and means. A message from London invited him to brief Sir Cecil Dormer in the following sense. He was to tell King Haakon and the Norwegian Minister of Defence that the Allied Governments had reviewed the situation in the light of events in France and that it was no longer possible to defend northern Norway against German attack. What had just happened at Bodø where he (Cork) had been forced to evacuate at short notice was an example of what would happen elsewhere when that defence was no longer available. The message went on to say that the restoration of Norwegian independence rested on the ability of Britain and France to resist the attack that was taking place on them, that they were obliged to make arrangements for the early withdrawal of their forces and that they were prepared to bring away the King of Norway, his Government and as many Norwegian troops 'as may wish to ... continue the fight with the Allies on other battlefields'. The message said in conclusion that if

183

the Norwegian Government felt that there was any chance of reaching agreement on the 'Mowinckel Plan' (a scheme designed to preserve Norwegian independence on the basis of neutrality under Swedish protection) the British Government would see no objection. The message ended with a warning that any hint to the Germans about Allied intentions would destroy any chance of an agreement and that the evacuation plan could not be delayed.[7]

Time was already short. On 30 May it was reported from Tromsø that the evacuation of Bodø was common knowledge and that Norwegian ministers were discussing the possibility of an armistice. The position was 'obviously precarious'. It was agreed on 1 June that Sir Cecil Dormer would return to Tromsø and sound out members of the Norwegian Government individually. If he was confident of their continued loyalty he would break the news of the evacuation to King Haakon on the following morning, and then to the Norwegian Cabinet and General Ruge. On 2 June (the day that the evacuation force was due off the Norwegian coast) Dormer rang through to Force Headquarters urging a postponement pending the outcome of negotiations on the Mowinckel Plan. After consulting Béthouart, Cork and Auchinleck agreed reluctantly to a 24-hour delay. The fears that they had entertained about the reaction of the Norwegian High Command, however, proved unfounded. 'They might with some justification,' as Auchinleck later observed, 'have decided to lay down their arms at once and so gravely prejudice our withdrawal.' Instead, despite much 'soreness and disillusion' they 'continued to co-operate loyally to the end'. It is perhaps to the lasting credit of Cork, Auchinleck and Béthouart, and of Dormer and Pollock in Tromsø, that in spite of all that had passed, and in spite of the deliberate falsehoods of recent days, cordial relations with the Norwegian authorities were preserved, and that on 7 June, Haakon VII, Crown Prince Olav and a large party of ministers and officials left Tromsø in the cruiser *Devonshire* to establish a government in exile in London.

An unsuspecting German High Command, meanwhile, had been pressing ahead with plans for Dietl's relief.[8] A force of handpicked mountaineers from the 2nd Mountain Division was preparing to leave the Saltfjord and cross the 150 miles of broken and trackless coastal terrain between Sørfolda and Narvik. They were to be supplied by air and were expected to reach their objective, fit to fight, in fourteen days. Hitler had ordered Göring to make elements of the 7th Air Division available and by 4 June it had been agreed that two parachute battalions would be inserted within the week, with a further 1,000 parachute-trained mountain troops to follow.[9] And by 4 June, Grand Admiral Raeder had been ready to report on the Navy's contribution to this supreme effort. The conditions were right, he told the

Führer, for a major surface operation against British naval forces and transports en route to Norway and, if air reconnaissance was favourable, for a raid on Allied bases in the Narvik area as well. This operation was already beginning and would involve the use of the two battleships. Trondheim was fully stocked and available as a base. Subsequent operations would eliminate enemy light forces between Trondheim and Bodø and secure the supply lines to the Feuerstein Group.

He went on to report, a little guardedly this time, on discussions with the Luftwaffe about a landing in the Lyngenfjord, a deep cleft in the Norwegian coastline, east of Tromsø and 100 miles north and east of Narvik. Operation 'Naumberg' involved the use of the fast liners Bremen and Europa to deliver a complete mountain division to the area although it was clear that one or two serious difficulties had yet to be resolved. (Hitler had demanded tanks and artillery yet the liners were incapable of handling heavy loads, and little was known about unloading and landing facilities at the far end.) Raeder suggested that 'Naumberg' was unlikely to 'change the difficult situation existing at present', and that it would be quicker and easier to land troops by glider and seize the airfield at Bardufoss instead. More troops could then be brought in by air. Hitler told him that the two operations would take place simultaneously.[10]

The Luftwaffe had continued its offensive against the base areas albeit under conditions of increasing difficulty. In the days following the capture of Narvik, bombing had been sporadic but on 2 June wave after wave of bombers and dive-bombers, often with fighter escort, had arrived over Narvik and Harstad, and attacked shipping in the nearby fjords. They burnt out Narvik's commercial district but inflicted little damage elsewhere. That day the two squadrons at Bardufoss flew seventy-five sorties between them, conducted forty-four air-to-air engagements and shot down nine German aircraft for no loss to themselves.[11]

Lord Cork's evacuation plan involved the assembly of troop transports at one of two offshore rendezvous 180 miles off the Norwegian coast and their despatch, in pairs and under anti-submarine escort, to an appointed anchorage inshore. There each transport would embark its quota of troops, usually from destroyers, before returning to the distant rendezvous to await the formation of a convoy for the return passage. The only exceptions to this general rule were the three Irish Sea packets (Royal Ulsterman, Ulster Prince and Ulster Monarch) which could berth alongside in Harstad.

The embarkation programme, a complex schedule spread over five nights and involving a dozen embarkation points, was managed by a combined headquarters in Harstad. Rear areas were to be cleared first, troops mustering at their embarkation points during the night hours when enemy air activity was at its lowest. The bulk of the ferrying work went to Cork's small destroyer force acting under the orders of Captain E.B.K. Stevens of the *Havelock*. The use of destroyers was inevitable if the pace of the evacuation was to be maintained; the decision meant, however, an acute shortage of these vessels for patrol and escort duty. Despite Lord Cork's appeals, there were no more to be had and he had been forced to manage with his own resources.

Fears that enemy action might throw this intricate mechanism into chaos were very real. Raids on the scale of 2 June could well have dire consequences. Auchinleck gave orders that fighters and anti-aircraft guns should be kept in action until the last soldier was embarked. They would then inevitably be destroyed. As a further precaution, every embarkation point would have its alternative and a 'puffer reserve' would be kept in each main area. There were concerns too that the Germans might establish themselves on the southern shores of the Ofotfjord and interfere with the transfer of troops from Narvik to embarkation points in the Vågsfjord, or even make a landing on Hinnøy and pose a direct threat to Harstad. Naval aircraft mounted extensive patrols from Bodø northwards and an armed steamer, the *Ranen*, waged a campaign of disruption on the same stretch of coast, destroying oil tanks and cutting telegraph cables that might serve the purposes of the advancing Germans. On the island of Hinnøy, motor patrols kept watch for signs of a German landing.

Few of these expected problems arose. Instead, the embarkation of troops and the loading of stores went ahead with 'the greatest smoothness and celerity' aided by low cloud, rain and drizzle which reduced enemy air activity to a minimum. Troops embarked at the rate of 5,000 men per night until by the morning of 7 June only 4,600 remained – French and Polish troops on the Narvik peninsula still in contact with the enemy, a rear party at Harstad disposing of damaged and disabled ships, and, 50 miles to the northward, the RAF ground staff at Bardufoss. Béthouart returned to Narvik on 7 June to oversee the final withdrawal of his troops. Fleischer, reconciled to the inevitable, had already withdrawn his battalion to the northern shore of the Rombaksfjord to put space between himself and the Germans. Most of the civilian population of Narvik had left. That day the two Foreign Legion battalions and the 1st Polish Battalion withdrew into the town and were transferred by 'puffer' to the waiting destroyers. A 'kind of suppressed fury' at the waste of life and effort lay heavily on them.[12] Béthouart waited while a party of engineers blew up a tunnel and last 300 metres of railway track. Only a few mules were left wandering the streets. There was no sign of the enemy. Béthouart left at midnight having penned a final telegram to Ruge, swearing to liberate Norway on final victory and commending to him 250 French dead as a gauge of eternal friendship. At about the same time, Auchinleck went down to the quay in

Harstad where he had landed four weeks earlier to witness the loading of the rear parties into the *Ulster Monarch* – a company of Chasseurs, a few Sappers and a section of Military Police. Fighters were still overhead. Having seen the last man on board, he joined Lord Cork in the *Southampton* to await the formation of the final convoy and the arrival of Béthouart from Narvik.

The exodus from Norwegian waters began in the early hours of 7 June when the six fast transports of Group I, *Monarch of Bermuda, Batory, Sobieski, Franconia, Lancastria* and *Georgic* left the distant rendezvous under the escort of the *Vindictive* to begin the 1,000-mile passage to the Clyde; they were carrying the first 15,000 men of the expeditionary force. They were followed some twenty hours later by eight stores ships from Harstad under the charge of the *Stork*, the *Arrow* and ten anti-submarine trawlers, and by a second slow convoy from Tromsø, part British and part Norwegian, with an escort of trawlers only. Also leaving Tromsø during the late evening of 7 June was the cruiser *Devonshire* (Vice Admiral Cunningham) with 461 passengers, mostly British servicemen but including the King of Norway, the Crown Prince and members of the Norwegian Government. By the morning of 8 June evacuation was complete and, towards noon, the seven transports of Group II, *Oronsay, Ormonde, Arandora Star, Duchess of York* and the three Irish Sea packets left for British waters with the final 10,000 men of the expeditionary force, under the escort of the *Coventry* (Admiral Vivian), the *Southampton* (Lord Cork) and the five remaining destroyers. The strict secrecy that Cork and Auchinleck had imposed had served its purpose; although the weather had cleared on 7 June and intermittent bombing had resumed, the enemy had made no discernable attempt to exploit Allied vulnerabilities during this long and delicate operation.

The protective arrangements put in place to cover the passage of this mass of shipping were, in retrospect, remarkably light. The acute shortage of destroyers in the aftermath of Dunkirk and the priority now being accorded to anti-invasion precautions were certainly contributory factors. But so was wishful thinking. The German surface fleet had remained quiescent since its pummelling in mid-April and, since then, Allied shipping had crossed and recrossed the North Sea with apparent immunity, fostering the illusion that control of the open sea, if not of Norwegian coastal waters, was firmly in Allied hands.[13] Indeed, the Admiralty had initially proposed that the transports of Group I (urgently needed for operations elsewhere) might sail for the United Kingdom without any escort at all. Cork had demurred. He had considered holding them at the distant rendezvous until his destroyers had completed their ferrying task, but he had relented following assurances of adequate protection further south. He had thus sailed the convoy under the charge of the *Vindictive* knowing that the *Valiant* with a screen of four destroyers was on her way northwards to meet it.[14]

Admiral Forbes had originally tasked the *Renown* and *Repulse* to support the returning convoys but other priorities had intervened. On 5 June he had received warning of 'two unknown ships, possibly raiders' steering, apparently, for the Iceland-Faeroes gap and, concerned for the security of the ships of the Northern Patrol, he had sent Admiral Whitworth with the two battlecruisers and a small fleet of escorts to investigate.[15] Whitworth had found nothing (the report had later proved false) but on 7 June he had turned towards Iceland in response to rumours of a German landing.[16] On 8 June, the Admiralty had recalled the *Renown* on precautionary grounds (they wanted an additional heavy ship at short notice to meet the threat of an invasion in the south and there were additional fears about an invasion of Ireland), but the sorry fact remains that at this critical time, when the convoys were leaving Norwegian waters, key elements of the Home Fleet were 1,500 miles to the south-west and in no position to intervene.

The two carriers had been operating off the Lofotens since 2 June. The *Glorious* had been tasked to re-embark the Gladiators of 263 Squadron and she had left Scapa on 31 May with a reduced air group sufficient for her own protection, but hardly enough to make a significant impact on events ashore. While the *Ark Royal* had kept up an intensive flying programme off the coast of Norway, protecting embarkation points and base areas, and raiding German positions at Hundalen, Sildvik and Fauske, the *Glorious* had spent much of the period loitering to seaward and conserving fuel until the time for re-embarkation arrived. During the afternoon of 7 June, Captain Guy D'Oyly-Hughes DSO* DSC, a submariner with a remarkable record of personal gallantry, received new proposals.[17] A Walrus amphibian brought the CO of 46 Squadron on board with the suggestion that the *Glorious* should attempt to re-embark the surviving Hurricanes as well, an evolution that had never been tried before and which professional opinion had always judged impossible. D'Oyly-Hughes agreed to make the attempt and a flight of three Hurricanes made a test run that evening, demonstrating that, with 30 knots of wind over the deck and a sandbag in the tail, this high-performance monoplane could be recovered to the carrier's deck without undue risk. A message was sent to Bardufoss that the rest of the squadron was to follow and in the small hours of 8 June, ten Gladiators and seven more Hurricanes were safely embarked. D'Oyly-Hughes had then (for reasons which are still disputed) sought and received permission from Admiral Wells in the *Ark Royal* to proceed independently to Scapa Flow. He left the coast of Norway in the early hours of 8 June with the destroyers *Ardent* and *Acasta* to screen him, leaving the *Ark Royal* to embark the six Walrus aircraft of 701 Squadron and to cover the departure of the second troop convoy.

During the night of 6/7 June, Admiral Wilhelm Marschall, the German Fleet Commander, had been refuelling his destroyers from the tanker *Dithmarschen* in a remote and unfrequented area some 350 miles west of the Lofotens, relying on reports from Group West in Wilhelmshaven and on his embarked B-Dienst (radio intelligence) team to build up a picture of British activity in the Norwegian Sea. He had under his command the battleships *Gneisenau* (flag) and *Scharnhorst*, the *Hipper* and four destroyers.

His operation ('*Juno*'), the first by the battleships and the *Hipper* since their hasty retreat to German waters nearly two months before, had been under discussion since 14 May. It had been conceived as a raid into the fjords to provide relief for the Narvik garrison but it had been extended, at Hitler's behest, to include the guarantee of sea-borne supplies to Group Feuerstein, an addition that was recognized as turning what had been conceived as a brief sortie into a commitment of weeks, if not of months. (It was the protracted nature of the operation as well as Raeder's desire for a naval spectacular that had justified the use of the battleships.)[18] Trondheim, fully stocked and well protected, was the designated base of operations; Admiral Boehm (Flag Officer Norway) had been instructed to move there for the duration and to act in close co-operation with Falkenhorst's XXI Corps Headquarters and Air Fleet 5.[19]

Throughout 7 June Marschall had continued to assess enemy strengths in the northern area of operations with a view to mounting an attack on Harstad during the night of 8/9 June. Radio intelligence had established the presence of the *Valiant*, the *Ark Royal* and the *Glorious*, but Group West had assured him that there was nothing in the patterns of enemy signal traffic to suggest that the British were aware of his presence. He was now looking to air reconnaissance to add to his understanding of what lay between him and his objective. He was informed of a southbound convoy of seven ships passing 100 miles south-east of his position (he assumed that it consisted of 'empties' returning home) but, otherwise, information remained sparse. 'Air reconnaissance in the northern area,' he noted a little sourly, 'is, as previously, not available.'[20] But late that evening during a conference with his commanding officers a report reached him which pointed to significant naval activity off the mouth of the Andfjord. Just after midday, an aircraft had sighted a light cruiser, two destroyers and two large ships on a westerly course; north of these were the *Ark Royal*, the *Glorious* and two more destroyers apparently stopped. 'It occurs to me,' Marschall recorded, 'that the noticeable westward movement may indicate a British evacuation of Norway and that the westbound convoys will now offer valuable targets.' At 0300 on 8 June, he told Group West that he intended to operate against the convoys. He was instructed to 'proceed with main task Harstad' and to leave the convoys to the *Hipper* and the destroyers, an order later amended at Naval Staff insistence to the simple statement that 'the main object is, as before, the destruction of enemy naval forces in the area Harstad–Narvik', a formula that seemed to allow him a measure of discretion in how he conducted his business.[21]

Marschall spread his force in search formation and swept across the convoy routes between Harstad and the Scottish coast. The wind was light to moderate north-westerly and the air gin-clear. In the early hours of 8 June he sighted and sank the 5,000-ton tanker *Oil Pioneer*, homeward-bound from Tromsø with the trawler *Juniper* as escort. Neither ship was able to transmit a distress signal. His floatplanes had then reported two large ships to the north of his position and what appeared to be a heavy cruiser, a destroyer and a cargo ship to the south. He sent the *Hipper* and two destroyers to find the first group while he set off with the rest of the force to search for the second. He found nothing (it was later concluded that the aircraft had been reporting his own ships) but the *Hipper* found the hospital ship *Atlantis* and the 20,000-ton transport *Orama*, both returning home independently. The *Atlantis* was spared and she for her part made no report; but the *Orama*, returning empty except for 100 German prisoners, went to the bottom. Her SOS was jammed. Marschall's destroyers recovered 275 survivors.

Certain now that the enemy must be aware of his presence and that he would have no further opportunity to fuel his escorts undisturbed, Marschall despatched the *Hipper* and the four destroyers to Trondheim with orders to replenish, and then to support supply convoys on the route to Bodø. His own intention was first to warn his tanker to clear the area, and then to operate against the carriers that had been reported off the Norwegian coast. Luck was on his side for at 1545, while he was steaming northwards to meet the *Dithmarschen*, a lookout in the *Scharnhorst* reported a wisp of smoke on the eastern horizon. Marschall turned to investigate and worked his ships up to a speed of 28 and finally 30 knots. Soon after four o'clock he established that the target was an aircraft carrier with an escort of two destroyers.

As the battleships settled on their closing course with their quarry broad on the port bow, the nearest destroyer turned to head them off, put down smoke across the line of sight and opened fire. The *Scharnhorst*, leading the formation in the early minutes of the action, met the destroyer with salvoes from her secondary (5.9-inch) batteries and moments later engaged the carrier, now identified as the *Glorious*, with her 11-inch guns. The time was 1632; the range 28,000 yards. Her gunnery was lethally accurate. Her first salvo was short, the second a straddle. The third produced a hit and soon a telltale pall of smoke was hanging in the air above the carrier's wake.

Further hits had followed. But the destroyer had continued to place herself across the line of sight, fouling the range with smoke and emerging from the murk now and again to fire torpedoes. Some of these had passed uncomfortably close. Both battleships had been forced to take evasive action and both had checked their fire until the smoke had cleared sufficiently to provide another glimpse of the carrier.[22]

The *Scharnhorst*'s secondary batteries had taken their toll, however, and by 1700 the destroyer (the *Ardent*) had fallen astern and taken on a heavy list. But the second destroyer had taken her place, zigzagging across the line of sight, laying smoke, obstructing the work of German spotters and range-takers and closing from time to time to attack with guns and torpedoes. At 1733, lookouts in the *Scharnhorst*'s foretop reported a new attack developing from the starboard bow. The battleship responded with 5.9-inch salvoes and a barrage of flak. An evasive manoeuvre was ordered but, at 1734, the ship was shaken by a heavy explosion aft. The extent of her injuries became clear as the minutes passed. At 1743, it was reported that 'Caesar' turret was out of action and that the starboard engine had failed. By 1746 there was a marked list to starboard. At 1805 it was reported that the centre engine was running down and that a propeller was vibrating badly. Two officers and forty-six ratings had been killed.

The action, however, was over. The *Glorious* was stopped, burning like a torch and listing 40°. Men were abandoning ship. The second destroyer (the *Acasta*), also well ablaze, was sinking. Marschall withdrew towards Trondheim at the best speed that the *Scharnhorst* could manage. He suspected the presence of a submarine and did not stop to pick up survivors. His welcome was not a warm one. He got few plaudits for the sinking of the *Glorious* and her escorts – that was dismissed as 'an extraordinary stroke of luck'. Instead he faced censure for his mishandling of '*Juno*' and for the tactical errors that had resulted in damage to the *Scharnhorst*.[23] He reported sick and, ten days after these events, was relieved by Vice Admiral Günther Lütjens, the intense and ascetic Deputy Fleet Commander, who had commanded the battleships during '*Weserübung*' and who, in May 1941, was to lose his life in the *Bismarck*.

Group II and its escort had left the distant rendezvous at midnight 8 June and set course to the south-west unaware of the fate of the *Glorious*. The first hint of trouble reached them during the forenoon of the 9th. The *Valiant* was returning northwards after escorting Group I to the latitude of the Faeroes when she met the hospital ship *Atlantis* and learnt from her the fate of the *Orama*. The *Valiant* broadcast the news at once and continued northwards at her best speed. The C-in-C diverted the *Repulse* and her escorts to join the returning convoy and instructed the *Glorious* to do the same if she had enough fuel. The *Valiant*'s signal drew new information from Admiral Cunningham in the *Devonshire* who reported hearing what appeared to have been 'a mutilated amplifying report' that had been addressed to the Vice Admiral (Air) at 1720 the previous afternoon.[24] Reception had been 'very doubtful' but the signal had referred to an earlier message (not received by the *Devonshire*) and had mentioned two pocket battleships.[25] During the afternoon of the 9th a German communiqué reported that a battle group had sunk the British carrier *Glorious* and an enemy destroyer while a second combat unit had sunk the *Orama* and the *Oil Pioneer*. Many prisoners had been taken. The sighting of wreckage by aircraft from the *Ark Royal*, and of bodies from the bridge of the *Southampton*, lent weight to these claims and next day the Admiralty issued a statement saying that repeated attempts to make contact by W/T had failed and that the ships had to be presumed lost. Admiral Forbes left Scapa with the *Rodney*, the *Renown* and a screen of six destroyers.

Late on 10 June and into the early hours of the 11, almost two and a half days after the sinking of the *Glorious* and her escorts, a small Norwegian motor vessel en route from Tromsø to the Faeroes fished a total of thirty-nine survivors out of the water in an area 5 miles in radius centred on 68° 08′ North, 4° 00′ East. They were in the last extremities of hypothermia. One man died while on passage to Thorshavn and two more within days of their arrival, but on 16 June the destroyer *Veteran* embarked the remainder for the passage to Rosyth. During the twenty-four hours that followed, the Captain of the *Veteran* (Commander J.E. Broome) began to put together the first account of what had happened to the *Glorious* and her escorts. It was a disturbing story and the Admiralty immediately convened a Board of Inquiry to collect detailed evidence from the survivors.

The Board interviewed twenty-nine witnesses in all, twenty-eight from the *Glorious* and one from the *Acasta*. (There were no known survivors from the *Ardent* although two were in fact in German hands as were four more from the *Glorious*.) The senior survivor was Lieutenant Commander R.C. Hill of the *Glorious*, an off-duty officer of the watch whose action station had been the starboard aft director. There were two Sub Lieutenants (Air) from the Swordfish Squadron, Squadron Leader Cross, CO of the Hurricane Squadron,[26] and a handful of senior rates and NCOs; the rest were junior ratings and Royal Marine other ranks. Their evidence raised awkward questions about the ship's state of readiness and about the conduct of its gallant captain. It became clear during the course of the enquiry that, following the recovery of the RAF squadrons from Bardufoss, the carrier's Swordfish and Sea Gladiator squadrons had been put at ten minutes' notice (an unprecedented relaxation in vigilance) and struck down to the hangar. There had been no aircraft in the air during the twelve hours prior to the action and no aircraft ready to respond to an emergency. Action stations had been piped at about 1600 – most people had been thinking about a cup of tea – and soon afterwards 823 Squadron had been piped away. Three Swordfish had been brought up from the hangar but none had been armed and their engines had never started. The aircraft and the men tending them had been swept away by a salvo of heavy shells that had plunged down on the flight deck. Minutes later the hangar was an inferno; one survivor remembered the order 'Flood "A" Hangar' being given; but the fire had never been brought under control. A second salvo had hit the superstructure and the bridge. It was widely thought that D'Oyly-Hughes had perished early in the action and that the Commander had assumed command of the ship at the emergency conning position. It had been Commander Lovell who had given the final order to abandon ship.[27]

There were other signs that the ship had been caught in holiday mood. Despite the unlimited visibility, the crow's nest had not been manned. A Petty Officer sent aloft to identify the enemy shortly before the first salvoes fell had reported a Hipper and a six-inch cruiser, an impression that was widely shared among survivors. (They were certainly not pocket battle-ships.) There had been no surface ammunition at the guns; no bombs had been fused and ready. More understandably, perhaps, a number of boilers had not been connected.

Several survivors from the Glorious had seen the destroyers laying smoke but they could say little about their fate. Able Seaman Carter of the Acasta, however, gave the Board a graphic account of what had happened to his ship. He had been manning the after tubes and had been told that the ship was closing to 8,000 yards to fire torpedoes. They had been told to set tubes 2, 3, 6 and 7. They had fired to port; the ship had then turned and they had fired to starboard. He was sure that they had got a hit with the first salvo because the captain had congratulated the Torpedo Control Officer. Soon after the second salvo, the Acasta had taken a hit in the engine room and had come to a stop with a heavy list to port. The forward guns had still been firing. He had abandoned ship when ordered.

The tale that survivors had to tell of their two and a half days in the water were harrowing. Estimates varied widely. Lieutenant Commander Hill put the original number of men on the floats at 400; Sub Lieutenant Baldwin of 823 Squadron thought double that figure. They had been happy enough to start with, but after six hours or so they had started to die. They had seen a Walrus and a Swordfish passing by and a cruiser on the horizon. Hill thought there had been fifty men on his float at the start; when they were picked up there were five left alive. Men on other floats had survived the final hours alone.[28]

The Board issued its report on 22 June. It could offer no satisfactory explanation for the apparent absence of precautions. It was satisfied that the Glorious had transmitted an enemy report, albeit on low power, and was sure that a report of the ship's sinking had been originated. There was insufficient evidence, however, to show that it had been sent. On 26 June Admiral Pound raised the question of court martial. The advice from Sir Charles Little (Second Sea Lord) was an emphatic 'No'. None of the survivors were senior enough to be held responsible for the ship's state of preparedness although a court might, he suggested, take evidence on the 'external aspect' – the apparent absence of surface cover and the lack of intelligence warning. (He understood that this was being 'dealt with separately'.) Pound accepted that charging the survivors could serve no purpose, but described the absence of precautionary measures as 'deplorable'. Knowing Captain D'Oyly-Hughes and the ship's fine record, he could not understand it. The ship, he supposed, was being used as a transport and had 'forgotten that it was a man o' war'. He hoped, however, that the gallant conduct of the *Ardent* and *Acasta* would be suitably rewarded.[29]

Roskill's verdict on the loss of the *Glorious* seems admirably balanced fifty years after it was written.[30] He expressed surprise at the absence of air patrols and at the failure to keep a striking force prepared (omissions clearly attributable to the Captain of the ship), but he pointed equally to the unfortunate dispositions adopted by the Home Fleet and to the 'excessive secrecy' which had kept the staff of Coastal Command (and incidentally of the OIC and of the GC&CS as well) in ignorance of the evacuation, able neither to initiate sensible precautionary measures nor to react intelligently to events as they unfolded. (On 10 June the Director of (Naval) Plans complained that the whole world had known about the evacuation except the British and there is at least some evidence that ignorance led to important clues being missed.)[31] If the admirals of the day were inclined, like Pound, to point the finger at D'Oyly-Hughes, opinion outside the Admiralty tended to look elsewhere. Churchill composed two minutes on the 'loss of a certain ship', both saying (rightly) that the protection of the convoys from Harstad was, or should have been, the 'first charge on the Home Fleet' and calling for reports by the Naval Staff on a matter that was sure to be taken up in Parliament. '[I]t will be felt,' he told the First Lord (A.V. Alexander), 'that the Navy has bungled this and certainly the Germans have had a remarkable success.'[32]

But there was little appetite in Parliament or elsewhere for a detailed investigation into the origins of the tragedy. It is certainly true that the admirals kept their heads below the parapet. Cork for instance declined to comment on the report of the Board on the grounds that the *Glorious* had been acting under the orders of Vice Admiral (Air). But those who hint at a deliberate conspiracy of silence fail to appreciate the spirit of the times. Weygand's attempt to hold the German offensive on the line of the Somme was failing. The French Army, the central pillar on which the Allied war effort had rested, was giving way; strident and increasingly unrealistic demands on British airpower were reaching London daily. On 8 June, the day the *Glorious* went down, Churchill told Reynaud, 'We are giving you all the support we can in this great battle short of ruining the capacity of this country to continue the war.' His aim, he told the French Premier, was to prolong the war until the United States could enter the conflict and 'thereby in the long run save France as well as ourselves'.[33] On 10 June, months of patient (if anxious) diplomacy came to nought with Italy's declaration of war and, on the 11th, Churchill flew to the French GQG near Orléans in a desperate attempt to strengthen Reynaud's hand against the forces of despair and defeatism. The battle, Weygand told this penultimate meeting of the SWC, had been raging along the whole front for six days. The last reserves had been committed. If the line broke, there was nothing left with which to form another; Paris and every other city in France would be occupied and coherent defence would cease.[34] Back in London on the evening of the 12th, Churchill told the War Cabinet that the end was in sight, though the possibility remained that the French Government might continue the fight from the Colonies or by supporting a massive guerrilla movement. The French Fleet might offer resistance too.

During the night of the 12th, Churchill was summoned back to France for a final meeting with Reynaud at Tours, the French Government's transitory pied à terre. The signs of dissolution were plain to see. The SWC met in the *préfecture* during the afternoon of the 13th. Weygand reported that the French Army was at its last gasp and that it would soon be necessary to 'plead for an armistice to save the soil and structure of France'. Reynaud was hoping against hope for some pledge on the part of the United States that he could present to his colleagues and to the people of France. Yet since France had nothing left to offer to the common cause, he asked to be released from the commitment that the two governments had agreed to three months before, not to conclude a separate peace. Churchill replied that he would not waste time in recrimination but declined to give his consent. In a last and desperate attempt to stave off the forces of defeatism, he offered that day his famous declaration on the indissoluble union between the two peoples and the two Empires.[35]

Nor was there any relief from the constant pressure of events. The collapse of French resistance and the certainty that the French Government was exploring the possibility of an armistice brought new and urgent concerns about the future of the French Fleet, concerns that would lead, in early July, to the seizure of French warships in British home ports, to protracted negotiations for the neutralization of French ships in Alexandria and, at Oran, to the painful decision to use force against the warships of an erstwhile ally. Seen against the background of these events, a detailed inquest into the loss of a carrier held few attractions. The loss of life, however regrettable, had not on the broad scale of things been remarkable. On 17 June, a mere eight days after the loss of the *Glorious*, the 20,000-ton liner *Lancastria*, which had brought the Irish Guards home from Narvik and which was now evacuating the remnants of the BEF from the Atlantic coast of France, was bombed and sunk off St Nazaire with the loss of 3,000 lives. For Churchill this was a disaster too far. All news of the sinking was withheld for six weeks.

The Parliamentary pressure that Churchill had alluded to never materialized. A few stout hearts were prepared to take up the cudgels on behalf of the bereaved, Richard Stokes (Labour member for Ipswich) being among the best informed and the most persistent. During the summer and autumn of 1940 he asked a succession of questions on the loss of the *Glorious* to establish whether Coastal Command had been informed of the convoy movements (and if not, why not), and why 1,000 men had been left in the water for forty-eight hours with no effective steps to save them. At an adjournment debate on 7 November he added the Admiralty's intelligence arrangements to his list of targets and asked whether the Board of Inquiry had commented on the adequacy of the carrier's escort.[36] But the truth of the matter was that the Commons had no more appetite than the admirals for a probe into the matter, and the climate of the day made it all too easy for ministers to refuse answers on the grounds of national security. His persistence was seen as obsession, as lacking a sense of proportion. The matter was best forgotten; it was time in that tiresome modern phrase 'to move on'. This collective amnesia extended to the Norway campaign as a whole.

Chapter 14

Norway in Retrospect

It will always appear extraordinary that, during the weeks that preceded the German offensive in the West, the Allied Governments should have focussed so much of their attention on a minor campaign on Europe's arctic fringe. The explanation is to be found in the aspirations, illusions and sensitivities of the 'Twilight War'. Fears of a lengthy stalemate in the West, and even of a protracted war of attrition on the pattern of 1914–1918 made a campaign on the European periphery highly attractive to governments in London and Paris. It was fully consistent with the broad thrust of a strategy which sought to postpone the onset of a general European war pending a relative improvement in the military balance, and it seemed likely to divert German attention from sensitive regions close to home to remote areas where Allied forces could engage the enemy on terms of relative advantage. It had even appeared possible that a successful campaign in the far north might have a decisive influence on the course of the war.

Yet the case for an Allied initiative in the region was never sufficient to outweigh the legal, moral and practical objections advanced by influential voices in the Chamberlain Cabinet. The result was prevarication, delay, friction within the alliance and a succession of forlorn attempts to engage the co-operation of reluctant Scandinavian governments. When a mounting crisis in Anglo-French relations finally forced Chamberlain's hand, it was too late. Hitler, less susceptible to legal and moral pressures (and less given to half measures) had already made his move. The Allies now had the pretext that had eluded them (indeed, a response of some kind had become imperative), but they had ceded the military initiative to Germany. And thanks to the foresight of German planners and to the drive of German commanders, they were never able to regain it.

Many of the troubles experienced by Allied forces in Norway had their origins in the three or four days of manic activity that followed the German coup. It was during this time of executive turmoil that the Narvik expedition left for Norway, its naval and military commanders holding 'diametrically opposite views' as to what was required of them. It was at this time when scarcity of resources should have dictated the most careful setting of priorities that the Chamberlain Cabinet found itself torn between its Narvik strategy (relatively well defined) and a new, urgent and largely open-ended commitment to support an imperilled Norwegian Government, and to provide a counterweight to German pressure on Sweden. Unable to determine which course to follow, the War Cabinet decided (by default) to do both.

Churchill's role during these critical few days is of particular interest. Chamberlain's seemingly casual decision in the wake of the Finnish crisis to promote Churchill to the Chairmanship of the MCC allowed this energetic but turbulent subordinate to extend his influence over the full range of British military strategy. In the policy vacuum that followed the German coup, Churchill's dominating personality, his grasp of military theory (if seldom of practice), his air of conviction, his sudden intuitions and his determination to have the last word enabled him as the agent of the War Cabinet to force from weak Service Ministers and from overburdened Chiefs of Staff (some like Ironside never comfortable in the Whitehall bedlam) concessions that, on mature reflection, they would never have agreed to – hence the division of the Narvik convoy and the opportunistic though ill-considered landings at Namsos, Ålesund and Åndalsnes. But in his advocacy of 'Hammer' (the direct assault on Trondheim) Churchill overreached himself. Military opinion, hitherto unorganized and divided, came together to oppose this adventure and succeeded, for the moment at least, in setting limits to his growing influence over the direction of the campaign. But by then the damage had been done.

The practical consequences of a rash of directives coming from White-hall during these days are visible in the despatches of the commanders who had to put them into effect. Warnings against 'improvisation' form a recurring theme, although the precise meaning of the term varies from author to author. For General Massy the term meant expeditionary forces cobbled together at the last moment and command arrangements put in place *after* those forces had been committed to action.[1] For Carton de Wiart, it meant plans 'concocted from hour to hour' by staffs with little understanding of the situation on the ground and the deployment of troops 'totally unfitted' for the task at hand.[2] For Paget it meant sending forces into action without first investigating how they were to be supplied. For the most part, criticism was directed against anonymous targets in Whitehall, but Paget's report included a direct and personal attack on General Riddell Webster, the then DMQ, who, during pre-embarkation briefings in the War Office, had stated that he was 'prepared to take a chance' on maintaining three infantry brigades through Åndalsnes. 'I do not know the assumptions on which he made this statement,' Paget wrote, 'but the facts proved that there was no such chance, and these facts should have been ascertained before Sickle Force was disembarked.' He then put his finger on the single factor that had done more than anything else to embarrass the Allies in central Norway. The possibility of maintaining any force through the single port of Åndalsnes, he wrote, depended primarily on whether 'local air superiority could be established and maintained. Since the necessary degree air superiority was scarcely to be expected, the project was not administratively practicable. Operationally therefore it was doomed to failure.'[3]

How could this vital factor have been overlooked? It is too easy to portray the officers who had succeeded to positions of high responsibility in 1939 and 1940 as a generation of sauropods, ignorant of the advances in military aviation that had occurred since their formative years. The lessons of Spain and Poland were too stark to have escaped their attention. And while 'Avonmouth' and 'Stratford' were being planned, it had become abundantly clear that operations in southern Scandinavia would mean a dangerous disparity in the air. The Chiefs of Staff had argued for a lifting of the government veto on raids on German territory; they had seen no other answer to the problem.[4] But 'Maurice' and 'Sickle' had their origins in late-night crisis meetings and bureaucratic horse-trading, and not in the tried and tested processes of military appreciation. Paget seems to have glimpsed the truth when he described 'Sickle' as being in breach of every military norm. The outstanding lesson of the campaign, he told the War Office, was the need to 'apply in the field what we have practised in peace, to foresee events by means of careful appreciation ... and thus go a long way towards the avoidance of "ad hoc" plans and improvisations'.

In defence of the Chiefs of Staff who (with Churchill and the other members of the Chamberlain Cabinet) must shoulder the blame for the central Norway fiasco, it can be said that the weight of the German air offensive, and the degree of co-operation established between German air and ground forces, surprised even the most 'air-minded' of serving officers. It was only in the Fleet, with its first-hand experience of the problem, Admiral Forbes told the Admiralty, 'that the scale of air attack that the enemy could develop over the Norwegian coast was properly appreciated'.[5] And the degree of integration achieved was something new. That a tactical air force could engage in anti-ship operations, attack base areas with devastating effect, provide reconnaissance and fire support in the battle area, deliver parachute troops to key objectives and supply forces in the field for weeks at a time lay beyond their professional horizons. Something comparable had to be achieved, Massy noted enviously, if the Allies were not 'to remain at a dangerous disadvantage'. Paget put it more strongly still. Unless the decisive effect of the air arm was fully appreciated, he told the War Office, the war might not be won. But the bombing of enemy bases was not enough; if troops were to be given a 'fair chance' there had to be the 'close co-operation between the ground and the air, as practised so effectively by the Germans'.[6] His remarks still have resonance for Britain's armed forces today.

Yet we need to look further than the disparity in the air and the material deficiencies that followed from it if we are to explain the extraordinary ascendancy achieved by the German Army in this remote theatre. The twenty-first century observer will be struck, firstly, by the scale of the psychological and moral adjustment that the Britain of 1940 had to make if it was to compete with an enemy that had already come to terms with the idea of total war. The gulf still to be crossed is visible in the proceedings of a Cabinet in which realpolitik competed uneasily with moral rectitude and in the tender consciences of soldiers whose opponents were already working to a code of brutal realism. War seems always to involve an element of moral compromise. It may well be that Churchill's supreme service to the nation was to have forced a liberal-minded establishment to cross that moral divide. Behind that benign even homely image, the uplifting rhetoric and the inspiring presence lay a ruthlessness (even sometimes a vindictiveness) worthy of Al Capone. In Norway, these traits were visible in his treatment of individuals who (for good reasons or bad) had failed to meet his inflated expectations. (It must surely be admitted that his bullying of military commanders whose judgement was in conflict with his own was a deeply unpleasant facet of his character.) They would soon manifest themselves in the ruthless destruction of French warships at Oran, and in due course in a strategic air campaign of unequalled savagery.

But other, more strictly military factors were at work too. In Norway, as later in Flanders and on the Meuse, we see Allied commanders struggling to understand the methods of a new kind of enemy. The term 'blitzkrieg' is usually associated with the use of mechanized forces on a large scale, something that Norwegian topography made impossible, but German commanders had adapted the concept to local conditions. In the Norwegian highlands, their turning movements proved a constant embarrassment to their opponents, while at Steinkjer and later at Hemnes, they demonstrated that they could practise the art of littoral manoeuvre to decisive effect. In contrast, the British Army had remained in the grip of a suffocating orthodoxy, many of its woes stemming from outmoded assumptions (based on First World War experience) about the strength of the defensive. These assumptions underpinned the overblown expectations of what could be achieved by a single infantry battalion in the upper Rana valley. And they are clearly visible in the dourly conservative campaign at Narvik where, as Mackesy's correspondence shows, memories of

Flanders and Gallipoli lay over the proceedings like a dark cloud.[7] These ghosts would have to be laid before the British Army could prove itself in the field.

Some commanders looked beyond outmoded doctrines and lack of moral purpose to signs of a deeper malaise. In his correspondence with Dill, Auchinleck spoke of the need for a 'new Army' that would be markedly different from the old one. It was 'lamentable', he thought, that, in a wild and undeveloped country like Norway, which should have shown the British soldier at his best, he had been outmanoeuvred and outfought on every occasion. The French (surprisingly in light of what was happening elsewhere) seemed to be 'real soldiers'.[8] He returned to the theme in his official report to the War Office. 'By comparison with the French or the Germans for that matter,' he wrote, 'our men ... seemed distressingly young, not so much in years as in self-reliance and manliness generally.' Prospects were not reassuring, he thought, unless training for war could be made 'more realistic and less effeminate'.[9] His views were not widely shared. Though deeply critical of the state of training of the troops under his command (many men had 'hardly fired a rife and very few really knew the Bren'), Carton de Wiart had few doubts about their potential.[10] And Paget described 15th Infantry Brigade as being 'highly trained and admirably led', and as having 'done magnificently' in very difficult circumstances.[11] These variations in opinion reflected the truth of the situation. The Britain of 1940 had the army that it deserved. The weapon forged at huge cost and sacrifice twenty years before had been frivolously cast away and it was now being rebuilt almost from scratch. It contained one or two units of high quality, toughened physically and morally for the demands of war. But there was little depth. 24th Guards Brigade, despite the huge expectations placed on it by Churchill and others, was a scratch formation that had never exercised as a single entity. (The two Guards battalions had gone straight to Narvik from public duties in London.) The battalions of 146th Infantry Brigade, diverted from Narvik to Namsos, had not completed company training; they had received their mortars only a day or two before sailing. It would take several years of patient endeavour (in which General Paget as a future C-in-C Home Forces was to be intimately involved) to overcome the decades of neglect.

There were glimmers of hope amid the encircling gloom. When present, British pilots had shown something of the dash and gallantry that would soon prove decisive in the Battle of Britain. And co-operation between the Army and the Navy had been of the 'highest standard possible'. 'No words of mine,' wrote General Massy in his final report, 'can adequately express the gratitude and admiration I feel for the skill in planning and efficiency in execution of the tasks which the Navy have carried out in support of the forces in Norway.'[12] The campaign in Norway had helped to forge a bond of trust that would prove highly significant in the years to come.

Where did it all lead? A cursory reading of the balance sheet suggests that with the Allied evacuation of Narvik Hitler had achieved his stated aims in full. He had secured his access to Swedish iron, equipped himself with 'expanded bases for the war against England', and, for the moment at least, removed the threat of interference on his northern flank. And he had done it all at modest cost. German casualties (5,583 in all) were trifling by the standards of the day, and materiel losses were easily sustainable. (It was only in Admiral Raeder's surface fleet that losses had any significant impact on future operations.) [13]

Yet with the triumph in the West, German gains in Norway began to lose something of their lustre. The fall of France restored access to the ore fields of Lorraine and gave Germany a rich choice of naval and air bases stretching westwards from the Hook of Holland to the Biscay coast. These new territorial gains had genuine war-winning potential. And the occupation of Norway brought the German leadership little peace of mind. By the winter of 1941–2 Hitler had convinced himself that Norway would become the scene of future Anglo-Saxon adventures and had ordered substantial reinforcements to the region. The German garrison had reached a total of 300,000 men and a reluctant Raeder had been forced to accept that the defence of the Norwegian coast would become the principal role for the surviving heavy ships of his surface fleet. Some have seen further adverse consequences and concluded that, all in all, 'Weserübung' created more problems than it solved. Modern German scholars have seen this early and easy victory as concealing chronic defects in the German command system, and as encouraging Hitler's faith in audacity and surprise as the answer to every military problem.[14] And then, the final irony – that this sweeping German success should have sparked the upheaval which removed Chamberlain's hesitant and divided ministry, and opened the way for an implacable and uncompromising opponent, determined to see the war though to its bitter end.

For Britain the balance sheet was almost wholly negative. She had the continued adherence of the legitimate government of Norway to show for her pains and the more tangible asset represented by the Norwegian merchant marine. But by now Norway was an irrelevance. The cataclysm of May 1940 had taken the war in new directions leaving Norway stranded on the periphery of World events. It was never to regain the central position in British or indeed Allied thinking that it had occupied during those brief months, and it was to remain outside the mainstream to the last.

Notes

Chapter 1

1 The name came from the *Daily Mirror* cartoon strip 'Pip Squeak and Wilfred' and reflected the character's timid and innocent nature. Gilbert 1993, p. 780.

2 War Cabinet Minutes; Gilbert 1993, p. 119. See also WSC memo 29 September 1939, ibid., p. 181.

3 War Cabinet Minutes, 30 November 1939, ibid., p. 450.

4 Paper for War Cabinet, 12 December 1939; Gilbert 1993, pp. 523–4.

5 Bedarida 1977, p. 11.

6 Cited in Butler 1957, p. 100.

7 War Cabinet Minutes, 22 December 1940, Gilbert 1993, pp. 553–6.

8 War Cabinet Minutes, 12 January 1940, ibid., pp. 629–31.

9 Report by CoS, 28 January 1940, ibid., pp. 699–700. See also McLeod and Kelly 1962, pp. 211–13.

10 Ibid., p. 214.

11 Cited in Butler 1977, p. 107.

12 Minutes of Supreme War Council, 5 February 1940; Gilbert 1993, p. 719.

13 For an account of the *Altmark* incident see Roskill 1954, pp. 151–3.

14 War Cabinet Minutes, 23 February 1940; Gilbert 1993, pp. 795–6.

15 War Cabinet Minutes, 29 February 1940; ibid., pp. 824–7.

16 McLeod and Kelly 1962, pp. 217–18.

17 Dilks 1977, pp. 41–2.

18 McLeod and Kelly 1962, pp. 217–18.

19 Ibid., pp. 222–3.

20 Briefing note for Admiral Pound; Gilbert 1993, p. 850. The First Lord was visiting the Home Fleet.

21 Major General P.J. Mackesy, CB, DSO, MC, GOC 49th Division.

22 Admiral Sir E.R.G.R. Evans (1880–1957), first Baron Mountevans; Antarctic 1909–1912; legendary Dover Patrol destroyer captain WWI; *Repulse* in command, 1926–8; C-in-C African Station 1932–3; C-in-C Nore 1935–9. M. 1916 Elsa, d. of Richard Andvord of Oslo.

23 Butler 1957, p. 113.

24 Kennedy 1957, p. 49.

25 McLeod and Kelly 1962, p. 228. Churchill wanted to present the expedition as protecting Scandinavian neutrality against Russian expansion.

26 Colville 1985, p. 87. See also Nicolson 2004, p. 210.

27 Gilbert 1993, pp. 883–4.

28 Lord Chatfield (Minister for Co-ordination of Defence) and Lord Hankey (Minister without Portfolio) left the War Cabinet on 3 April 1940. Churchill took Chatfield's former

role as Chairman of the MCC while retaining his departmental responsibilities as First Lord of the Admiralty.

29 Bedarida 1977, p. 20.

30 McLeod and Kelly 1962, p. 237.

31 At this conference the two premiers declared that neither would accept an armistice or initiate peace negotiations without the consent of the other.

32 Gilbert 1993, pp. 930–1.

33 Churchill's apparent conversion to the French cause was the subject of wry comment. Chamberlain provoked laughter in Cabinet by telling the story of the pious parrot sent to convert a foul-mouthed neighbour but which returned home swearing like a trooper. Colville 1985, p. 96.

34 Ibid., pp. 96–7; remarks attributed to R.A. (Rab) Butler, then Under-Secretary at the Foreign Office.

Chapter 2

1 Raeder 1960, p. 278.

2 Führer Conferences, pp. 41–3.

3 Ibid., p. 47.

4 Report to Führer, 8 December 1939, Ibid., pp. 61–3.

5 Text in Führer Conferences, pp. 63–5.

6 Ibid., pp. 65–6.

7 Ibid., pp. 66–7. OKW (Oberkommando der Wehrmacht) or Supreme Command of the Armed Forces, was responsible under Hitler for the higher direction of the war.

8 Diary entry for 13 January 1940, Naval Staff War Diary, vol. 5, pp. 62–4 (USN translation).

9 For an account of the Naval Staff's preliminary thoughts, see Ziemke 1959, p. 9.

10 Memorandum from Keitel dated 17 January 1940, cited in Churchill, I, 1950, p. 504.

11 The extraordinary circumstances of von Falkenhorst's appointment, made without reference to the Army General Staff, are described in Warlimont 1964, pp. 72–3.

12 Trevor-Roper 1964, pp. 23–4 (original emphasis).

13 Diary entry 1 March 1940, Naval Staff War Diary, vol. 7, p. 8.

14 The Lützow was the former Deutschland, recalled from the Atlantic at Hitler's behest in November 1939.

15 Conference with the Führer, 5 March 1940; ibid., p. 28 (original emphasis).

16 Ibid., p. 10.

17 Ibid. p. 28. Raeder made a similar point when reporting to Hitler on 9 March 1940, Führer Conferences, p. 86.

18 Staff discussions, 5 March 1940, Naval Staff War Diary, vol. 7, p. 27.

19 Report to Führer, 9 March 1940, Führer Conferences, p. 86.

20 Ibid.

21 Naval Staff War Diary, vol. 7, p. 36.

22 Ibid., p. 83.

23 Ibid., pp. 137–8.

24 Führer Conferences, pp. 87–8. See also, Naval Staff War Diary, vol. 7, p. 161.

25 This summary of Group XXI plans is based on Ziemke 1959, pp. 32–5.

26 Kaupisch was to be subordinate to XXI Corps until W+3. His forces (XXXI Corps) would then revert to the direct control of OKW. This outline of XXXI Corps plans is based on Ziemke 1959, pp. 35–6.

27 Bekker 1994, p. 366. See also Ziemke 1959, pp. 36–8. I have used the term 'wing' to denote the German Air Force 'Gruppe'. They usually had a strength of thirty to thirty-six aircraft.

28 Ziemke 1959, p. 40.

29 Naval Staff War Diary, vol. 7, p. 76.

30 Ibid., p. 180.
31 Naval Staff War Diary, vol. 8, pp.10–11.
32 The ship was brought back through the Kiel Canal on 6 April.
33 Naval Staff War Diary, vol. 8, p. 41.
24 Ibid., pp. 60–2.

Chapter 3

1 The converted destroyers were *Esk, Impulsive, Icarus* and *Ivanhoe*; they were armed with two 4.7-inch guns and carried sixty mines apiece. They were escorted by the destroyers *Hardy* (D2), *Hotspur, Havock* and *Hunter*.
2 Sir Charles Moreton Forbes (1880–1960). Gunnery Specialist. Med Fleet in 1914; present at bombardment of Gallipoli forts. Flag commander to Jellicoe Oct 1915; Jutland (DSO) 1916. *Galatea* in command 1917–18. Alternate sea and staff appointments during inter-war years including 3rd Sea Lord (Controller) and V Adm second in command Med Fleet. C-in-C Home Fleet 1938–40. Modest and unassuming though much admired by those who worked for him. As C-in-C gained reputation for being unlucky.
3 VAdm Submarines signal 1931 of 4 April 1940; Brown 1999, p. 45.
4 For an assessment of the state of British Intelligence at this time, see Hinsley 1979, pp. 116–25.
5 NHB WIR of 5 April 1940, p. 13.
6 Derry 1952, p. 22.
7 Cited in Hinsley 1979, p. 125. Cryptography gave no help to British decision-makers before the invasion. But in mid-April GC & CS began to read operational traffic between Army and Luftwaffe headquarters in Norway. From then on 'Hydro' information begins to appear in War Office intelligence files.
8 NHB, Naval Staff Meeting, 7 April 1940, p. 177.
9 AT 1259 of 7 April 1940, Home Fleet war diary NA ADM 199/361.
10 Home Fleet signals 1546 and 1607 of 7 April 1940, ibid.
11 The strike leader filed his report on arrival at base; attack report by W/T was not received by any station.
12 Diaries of Captain (later Admiral Sir) R.E. Edwards; cited in Roskill 1977, pp. 101–2.
13 Brown 1999, pp. 12–13. The *Glowworm*'s reported position was 60 miles in error.
14 AT 1259 of 7 April, NA ADM 199/361.
15 McLeod and Kelly 1962, p. 248.
16 Gilbert 1993, pp. 979–80.
17 General Sir Ian Jacob, Military Assistant Secretary to the War Cabinet; cited in Roskill 1977, pp. 98–9.
18 Richards 1953, p. 80.
19 Forbes told the pilot to land in Norway and give himself up. He would be released in a few days since a German invasion was imminent. He was then to get hold of some fuel and fly to the Shetlands.
20 AT 1435 of 8 April; NA ADM 199/361.
21 AT 2102 of 8 April, ibid.
22 AT 0210 and AT0235 of 9 April; ibid.
23 BCS ROP 41/4 of 29 April; NA ADM 199/379.
24 The encounter between the *Renown* and the German battleships is described in Brown 1999, pp. 19–20 and Macintyre 1960, pp. 37–9. For the German account see BR 1840 (1), pp. 23–4.
25 McLeod and Kelly 1962, p. 249.
26 Ibid.
27 Gilbert 1993, pp. 987–90.

28 Colville 1985, p. 99.
29 Gilbert 1993, pp. 990–2. The assumption was not unreasonable; commercial traffic had been suspended.
30 801 Squadron (6 Skua) was disembarked at Evanton (Invergordon) and had been earmarked for convoy escort duty on the Scottish coast.
31 The aircraft were He-111s of KG26 and Ju-88s of KG30. Both formations were trained in attacks on ships. Radar (then RD/F) was fitted in a handful of major units only including, in this instance, *Rodney* and *Sheffield*.
32 C-in-C's 2231 of 9 April, NA ADM 199/361.

Chapter 4

1 The Foreign Minister, Dr Halvdan Koht, had reaffirmed that neutrality remained the keystone of Norwegian policy that same day.
2 Johan Nygaardsvold (1879–1952), former trade unionist and leader of the Labour Government.
3 Hambro 1940, p. 9.
4 Koht 1941, p. 62.
5 See Moulton 1966, pp. 123–6. Under the Norwegian military code, partial mobilization produced one field brigade (*felt brigade*) per Command District; call-up papers went out by post. Full mobilization produced additional reserve units of lower effectiveness and was announced by press and radio. For an account of the mobilization order and the confusion that followed, see Kersaudy 1990, pp. 68–72.
6 Koht 1941, pp. 68–70.
7 Ibid., p. 76.
8 Hambro 1940, p. 12.
9 Admiral Raeder's order of 1 April 1940, *Führer Conferences*, pp. 90–1.
10 Dickens 1974, p. 37; BR 1840 (1), p. 26; Bekker 1977, pp. 102–3.
11 Boats from other ships in the anchorage rescued ninety-eight men from the *Norge* including Commander Askim, her Commanding Officer; there were only eight survivors from the *Eidsvold*; 287 Norwegian lives were lost in these incidents. Ibid., p. 103.
12 Broch 1943, p. 80. Moulton 1966, p. 83, suggests that Sundlo was an elderly incompetent rather than a traitor.
13 Dickens 1974, p. 37; based on conversations with Bonte's subordinates.
14 BR 1840 (1), p. 27.
15 The forts had been put on a war footing. Their lack of success has been put down to the smoke and debris thrown up by the *Hipper*'s salvos and to a lucky hit on the cable supplying power to the searchlights. See Derry 1952, p. 40; Ziemke 1959, p. 48.
16 Naval Staff War Diary, vol. 8, pp. 74–5. See also BR 1840 (1), pp. 29–31.
17 Bekker 1994, pp. 87–9. Moulton 1966, pp. 90–1.
18 Zeimke 1959, pp. 59–62.
19 HM submarine *Trident* had narrowly missed the *Lützow* just north of the Skaw; the *Posidonia* had scuttled herself when challenged by the *Trident*.
20 Captain Lief Olsen was the first Norwegian to lose his life in this campaign.
21 British sources have tended to exaggerate the numbers; Rohwer and Hummelchen 1992, p. 15, gives numbers killed 125 Navy and 195 Army. Kummetz and Engelbrecht survived.
22 *Führer Conferences*, p. 92.
23 Naval Staff War Diary, vol. 8, p. 73.
24 Ibid.
25 Ibid., p. 74. This staff appreciation formed the basis of Raeder's report to Hitler at noon on 10 April, *Führer Conferences*, pp. 93–4.
26 Hambro 1940, p. 34.

27 Moulton 1966, p. 99, citing statements by Falkenhorst and Bräuer, suggests that Spiller was acting on his own initiative. There seems little doubt, however, that the arrest of King and Government was planned; the *Blücher* had been carrying a Gestapo company for that purpose.
28 Koht 1941, p. 85.
29 Ibid., p. 87.
30 Ibid.

Chapter 5

1 Gilbert 1993, p. 996. See also, McLeod and Kelly 1962, pp. 250–1.
2 Captain 2 DF signal 1751 of 9 April, NA ADM 199/361.
3 Gilbert 1993, pp. 999–1000.
4 AT 0136 of 10 April; ADM 199/361. Most historians have detected Churchill's hand in this message.
5 Brown 1999, p. 27; Dickens 1974, pp. 60–6.
6 *London Gazette* 38005, p. 3049. 160 members of the *Hardy's* ships company got ashore and made their way to the village of Ballangen. They were rescued by the *Ivanhoe* three days later. Warburton-Lee died on the beach. He was awarded a posthumous VC.
7 Gilbert 1993, p. 1004.
8 Mackesy's orders are in Derry 1952, pp. 247–8.
9 *London Gazette* 38011, p. 3167.
10 Derry 1952, pp. 248–9.
11 *Führer Conferences*, pp. 93–4.
12 Naval Staff War Diary, vol. 8, pp. 79–81.
13 Home Fleet War Diary, 11 April 1940, NA ADM 199/361.
14 Naval Staff War Diary, vol. 8, p. 94. The *Lützow* remained under repair for twelve months.
15 *Führer Conferences*, p. 94; Naval Staff War Diary, vol. 8, p. 81.
16 Brown 1999, p. 34.
17 Roskill 1954, p. 176.
18 German sources admit to splinter damage only. Brown 1999, p. 36; Derry 1952, p. 48.
19 AT1033 of 12 April, NA ADM 199/361.
20 Bekker gives a comprehensive account of these failures and of the controversy which followed in *Hitler's Naval War*, pp. 119–38.
21 *London Gazette* 38005, pp. 3051–2. There was believed to be a shore-controlled minefield between Tranøy and Barøy and aircraft from the *Furious* had reported seeing mines in the Ofotfjord.
22 The *U64* had been attempting to rectify a periscope defect and sank immediately. In his despatches, Whitworth wrote: 'I doubt if ever a ship-borne aircraft has been used to such good purpose as it was during this operation.' *London Gazette* 38005, p. 3056.
23 Ibid., p. 3053.
24 Ibid. See also Brown 1999, p. 38.
25 Dickens 1974, pp. 114–16.
26 Ten Swordfish arrived over Narvik at 1350. They dive-bombed several ships but inflicted no damage. Two were lost.
27 *London Gazette* 38005, p. 3054.
28 Ibid.
29 Naval Staff War Diary, vol. 8, p. 116.
30 *London Gazette* 38005, p. 3054. The *U25* had fired at the destroyers at 1315 but had been unable to get a shot at the *Warspite*. She had moved westward in the hope of catching the battleship on her way out. Dickens 1974, p. 153.

207

31 Ibid., p.148. The *Roeder* had shortly afterwards blown apart as her demolition charges went up.
32 *London Gazette* 38005, p.3055. Views differ as to whether a landing party might have succeeded. Broch 1943, p, 95, reports 'bands of beaten Germans drifting through the town'. Moulton 1966, p.116, hints that a landing party drawn from Home Fleet ships as a whole might have succeeded in gaining a lodgement and holding it until the main expedition arrived. Mackesy argues persuasively that Dietl's men were far from demoralized and that the 'beaten Germans' were survivors from the destroyers. Later events suggest that the odds against success would have been high.
33 Whitworth's 1027 of 14 April, ibid. Force B was the *Warspite* and her escorts.

Chapter 6

1 Gilbert 1993, pp.1011–13.
2 McLeod and Kelly 1962, pp.253–4. Maj Gen (later Lt Gen Sir) Adrian Carton de Wiart VC, DSO (1880–1963). DSO, Somalia 1914. Eight times wounded on Western Front including loss of left hand at 2nd Ypres. VC, Somme, July 1916 when leading 8th Battalion, Gloucester Regiment. British military mission, Poland, 1918. Resigns 1924 to become tenant of sporting estate, property of Prince Charles Radziwill, his Polish ADC. Recalled July 1939 to head new military mission to Poland; escapes via Romania. Appointed to command 61st Division (Midland Territorials) on return to England. April 1941 head of military mission to Yugoslavia but was captured by the Italians. 1943–5 Churchill's personal representative to Chiang Kai-shek.
3 Gilbert 1993, p.1041; Colville 1985, pp.102–3.
4 Notes for JPS, 12 April 1940, Gilbert 1993, p.1045.
5 Ibid., pp.1048–50, 1057.
6 Ibid., pp.1054–5.
7 The account of this incident is based on McLeod and Kelly 1962, pp.255–60; it has been accepted by most historians.
8 Gilbert 1993, pp.1061–2.
9 W.H.D. Boyle, Twelfth Earl of Cork and Orrery (1873–1967). Red Sea Patrol during the middle years of the First World War, supporting irregular operations on the Red Sea coast. (T.E. Lawrence described him as 'very professional, alert, businesslike and official; sometimes a little intolerant of easy-going things and people.') Grand Fleet in 1917 commanding battlecruisers *Repulse* and *Lion*. Second in Cmd 1BS (Atlantic Fleet) 1923, serving later as R Adm 1CS (Med). V Adm Reserve Fleet 1928; C-in-C Home Fleet in 1933–5 and C-in-C Portsmouth 1937–9.
10 FO Narvik's signal 1327 of 14 April, NA ADM 199/1929.
11 AT 2347 of 14 April, ibid.
12 *London Gazette* 38011, p.3168.
13 Maund 1949, pp.26–32. Brigadier C.G. Phillips had sailed in the Polish liner *Batory* and it had been impossible to transfer him at sea.
14 *London Gazette* 38011, p.3168.
15 Note by Chairman MCC and FO Narvik's 1813 both of 17 April, NA ADM 199/1929.
16 *Aurora's* 0943 of 19 April, ibid.
17 *Aurora's* 0514 of 21 April, ibid.
18 Churchill, I, 1950, p.572. The letter did not reach London until 6 May.
19 FO Narvik's 2229 of 21 April, NA ADM 199/1929.
20 AT 1429 and FO Narvik's 2332 both of 22 April, ibid.
21 FO Narvik's 2209 of 25 April 1940, NA WO 168/83.
22 Maier 1991, p.213.
23 Warlimont 1964, pp.79–80.

24 Ibid., p. 77.
25 Ziemke 1959, p. 64.
26 Brown 1999, p. 72.
27 Gilbert 1993, p. 1067.
28 C-in-C's signal 1157 of 14 April, NA ADM 199/39.
29 War Cabinet 15 April 1940, Gilbert 1993, p. 1067.
30 AT 0121 of 15 April, NA ADM 199/39.
31 C-in-C's 1733 of 15 April, ibid. See also Churchill, I, 1950, p. 559.
32 Gilbert 1993, p. 1071.
33 Note for PM by Chairman MCC, 16 April, ibid., pp. 1076–7.
34 MCC 16 April 1940, Ibid., pp. 1073–6.
35 War Cabinet 17 April 1940, ibid., p. 1082. Orders are in Derry 1952, pp. 249–53.
36 WSC to Forbes 17 April 1940, Gilbert 1993, pp. 1084–5.
37 Later Marshal of the Royal Air Force Sir John Slessor; long sceptical about Norway.
38 McLeod and Kelly 1962, pp. 262–3.
39 The worrying ineffectiveness of Fleet AA gunfire may have been an additional factor; on 17 April the DCNS had demanded 'urgent and drastic steps' to improve it. NHB Naval Staff Meetings, p. 196.
40 Churchill, I, 1950, pp. 563–4.
41 Gilbert 1993, p. 1100.

Chapter 7

1 War Cabinet 17 April 1940, Gilbert 1993, p. 1082. See also 146th Infantry Brigade War Diary, NA WO 168/25.
2 Ziemke, p. 78.
3 Brown 1999, p. 73.
4 Ibid., pp. 73–4.
5 Carton de Wiart 1950, p. 168. See also Hingston 1950, p. 62.
6 Carton de Wiart report; NA WO 196/1905.
7 Ironside's orders to Carton de Wiart are in Derry 1952, p. 249.
8 Carton de Wiart 1950, pp. 166–7.
9 Gilbert 1993, p. 1094.
10 For a critique of Phillips's dispositions, see Hingston 1950, pp. 63–6.
11 McLeod and Kelly 1962, p. 266.
12 Although nominally an Alpine unit the 5th demi-brigade was equipped for operations on the Maginot Line and was heavily dependent on wheeled transport. Each battalion had enough skiers to form a reconnaissance company. Béthouart 1968, p. 17.
13 Brown 1999, p. 75.
14 Béthouart 1968, p. 25.
15 For deployment of AA ships off central Norway, see Brown 1999, pp. 62–3.
16 Derry 1952, p. 90. That Phillips was conscious of his vulnerability is shown by his report of 20 April in NA WO 168/25.
17 146th Infantry Brigade War Diary, NA WO 168/25.
18 HMS Nubian's 2335 of 21 April 1940, cited in Brown 1999, pp. 76–7.
19 Moulton 1966, p. 172.
20 For the epic retreat of the KOYLI see Hingston 1950, pp. 68–77.
21 London Gazette 37584, p. 2601.
22 SWC 22 April 1940, Gilbert 1993, p. 1120.
23 McLeod and Kelly 1962, pp. 278–9.
24 Ibid., p. 280.

Chapter 8

1 Ziemke 1959, p. 66.
2 Moulton 1966, pp. 141–2.
3 Ibid., p. 144.
4 AT 1633/16 April 1940; cited in Brown 1999, p. 81.
5 Clarke 1948, pp. 89–92.
6 Ironside's instructions of 16 April, Derry 1952, p. 250.
7 AT 2217/17 April 1940; Brown 1999, p. 81.
8 Ibid., p. 82.
9 Clarke 1948, p. 106.
10 Ibid., p. 110.
11 148th Infantry Brigade War Diary, NA WO 168/26. See also Clarke 1948, p. 114 and Derry 1952, p. 105.
12 Clarke 1948, pp. 114–15.
13 The Brigade War Diary (NA WO 168/26) gives his effective strength at this point as 650 men.
14 Clarke 1948, p. 127.
15 NA WO 168/26.
16 Ibid.
17 Clarke 1948, p. 130.
18 King-Salter's description of this position and of his part in organizing the defences is in Ash 1964, pp. 163–5.
19 Though seriously wounded, King-Salter survived captivity and later took Holy Orders.
20 Derry 1952, p. 112.
21 Kersaudy 1990, p. 149.
22 *Führer Conferences*, p. 99.
23 Report of 22 April 1940, ibid., pp. 96–7.
24 Jodl diary cited in Kersaudy 1990, p. 150.
25 Ziemke 1959, p. 74; the groups took their names from Lt Gen Richard Pellengahr and Col Herman Fischer, CO of the 340th Infantry Regiment.
26 Gilbert 1993, p. 1129.
27 Colville 1985 (citing Cabinet Secretary), p. 107.
28 Major General (later General Sir) B.C.T Paget DSO, MC (1887–1961), third son of Francis Paget, theologian and Bishop of Oxford. Commissioned Oxfordshire and Buckinghamshire Light Infantry 1907. France 1915–18 including GHQ and staff of Sir Douglas Haig. Staff College 1920; Imperial Defence College 1929; later Staff College at Quetta as Chief Instructor. 4th Quetta Infantry Brigade in command 1936–7. Commandant Staff College 1938–9. 18th Infantry Division in command November 1939 whence selected for command of 'Sickleforce'. Later succeeds Alan Brooke as C-in-C Home Forces; often regarded as the best trainer of men since Sir John Moore.
29 *London Gazette* 37584, pp. 2598, 2610.
30 Hingston 1950, p. 86.
31 Ibid., p. 90.
32 Ibid., p. 92.
33 Derry 1952, p. 55, gives Bomber Command losses in the first month of operations as twenty-seven out of an inventory of 216.
34 V Adm L.V. Wells, Flag Officer (Air), cited in Brown 1999, p. 60.
35 C-in-C Home Fleet despatch, NA ADM199/39.
36 Moulton 1966, p. 207.
37 Appreciation dated 27 April, NA WO 168/93.

38 *London Gazette* 37584, p. 2604.
39 Sheffield 1956, pp. 35–6; Synge 1952, pp. 12–14.

Chapter 9

1 MCC, 26 April 1940; Gilbert 1993, p. 1140.
2 Gamelin 1947, pp. 366–7.
3 Air Marshal Sir Cyril Newall, Chief of Air Staff.
4 Massy's appreciation is in NA WO 198/9.
5 Instructions for Lt Gen H.R.S. Massy, 27 Apr 1940, *London Gazette* 37584, pp. 2610–11.
6 Roger John Brownlow Keyes, first Baron Keyes (1872–1945), man of action. *Britannia* 1885 followed by service in West Africa and China. Special promotion to Cdr 1900 during the Boxer uprising. Controversial Commodore Submarines 1912–14. CoS to successive naval commanders at Dardanelles 1915–16. VAdm Dover 1918 and driving force behind celebrated Zeebrugge raid. DCNS 1921–5. C-in-C Med 1925–8. Passed over for post of First Sea Lord and retired (embittered) 1931. Conservative MP for Portsmouth 1934–43. Appointed Director of Combined Operations in July 1940 but proved unable to work amicably with the Chiefs of Staff and was replaced by Mountbatten.
7 Churchill to Keyes, 25 April 1940, cited in Marder 1972, p. 50. Lady Keyes seems to have played a part in encouraging the Admiral's aspirations.
8 Carton de Wiart 1950, pp. 171, 175.
9 *London Gazette* 37584, p. 2601.
10 Ibid., p. 2607.
11 Moulton 1966, p. 212.
12 Clarke 1948, pp. 150–1.
13 WC 29 April 1940, Gilbert 1993, pp. 1161–2. Dormer had been in touch with Dr Koht, Norwegian Foreign Minister.
14 Captain M.M. Denny (NOIC Molde), cited in Brown 1999, p. 89.
15 'Sickleforce' report, NA WO 168/93.
16 Ibid.
17 *London Gazette* 37584, p. 2604.
18 Ibid., p. 2606; Hingston 1950, p. 103.
19 Ibid., p. 105. The account that follows is based on *London Gazette* 37594, Hingston 1950 and Synge 1952.
20 Brown 1999, p. 91.
21 Ibid.
22 Ibid., p. 89.
23 Ibid., p. 61.
24 This statement caused bitter resentment since the evacuation of Namsos was still continuing.
25 Colville 1985, p. 111.
26 Rhodes James 1996, p. 244.
27 *Hansard*, 5th series, vol. 360, cols 1073–86.
28 Ibid., cols 1086–94.
29 Ibid., col 1105; Colville 1985, p. 117.
30 Admiral Sir John (Jackie) Fisher.
31 Ibid., cols 1124–30.
32 Ibid., cols 1140–50.
33 Ibid., cols 1251–65.
34 Ibid., col 1283.
35 Rhodes James 1996, p. 246.
36 Hansard, 5th series, vol. 360, cols 1348–62.

211

37 Rhodes James 1996, p. 247.
38 See particularly Jenkins 2002, pp. 583–7; Stewart 1999, pp. 414–20 and Churchill, I, 1950, pp. 595–600.
39 McLeod and Kelly 1962, pp. 295–7.
40 NHB Naval Staff Meetings, 8 May 1940, p. 262.
41 Colville 1985, p. 122.

Chapter 10

1 AT 0148 of 28 Apr; NA ADM 199/1929.
2 Note to Pound, 26 Apr 1940, Gilbert 1993, p. 1147.
3 MLC and the lighter ALC had been developed in the late 1930s, but with the acceptance of the continental commitment in September 1939, construction had been suspended.
4 *London Gazette* 38011, pp. 3188, 3194–5.
5 Part of the Free Polish Army raised in France from veterans of the German invasion and from enthusiastic émigrés. They took their name from a brigade that had distinguished itself in September 1939; although nominally a mountain brigade they had minimal mountain capability. Zbyszewski 1940, p. viii.
6 Rupertforce message 1050 of 27 April (original emphasis), NA WO 168/83, paper 48.
7 Rupertforce proposals of 25 April, ibid., paper 42.
8 Cork memorandum 27 April 1940, ibid., paper 49.
9 Ibid., paper 51.
10 Antoine Béthouart, infantryman and Alpine specialist. Saint-Cyr with de Gaulle. Western Front 1914–18; Croix de Guerre, three citations. Selected Feb 1940 to command Finnish expedition. Later commands French contingents at Namsos and Narvik in rank of Brigadier General. On repatriation reluctant servant of Vichy authorities in North Africa. Later one of de Gaulle's principal lieutenants. Died, loaded with honours, in 1982.
11 Notes of meeting 28 April 1940, NA WO 168/83/3.
12 Béthouart 1968, pp. 39–41; FO Narvik's 2327 of 28 April, NA ADM 199/1929.
13 Béthouart 1968, p. 45.
14 Gilbert 1993, pp. 1187, 1189.
15 NA WO 168/83, paper 56.
16 Ibid., paper 60.
17 Ibid., paper 65.
18 FO Narvik's 2355 of 5 May to Admiralty and War Office, NA ADM 199/1929.
19 AT1418 of 6 May, NA ADM 199/1929. Lt Gen (later FM Sir Claude) Auchinleck. Commissioned Indian Army 1903. Mesopotamia 1916–18 (DSO). India 1919–39. GOC-in-C Norway 1940. GOC-in-C Middle East 1941–2; sometimes seen as architect of Alamein.
20 FO Narvik's 0631 and 2151 of 7 May, ibid.
21 FO Narvik's 2154 of 8 May, ibid.
22 Béthouart 1968, p. 49.
23 Norway Intelligence Log, 8 May 1940, NA WO 106/1845.
24 Fitzgerald 1949, p. 34.
25 Maund 1949, pp. 39–40.
26 These impressions of the Bjerkvik landings are based on ibid., pp. 40–4 and Béthouart 1968, pp. 50–3. Lapie, who observed the landings from the *Vindictive*, agrees in all essential respects.
27 *London Gazette* 38011, p. 3182.
28 Cited in Mackesy 1970, p. 32.
29 'I fear a "Narvik Royal Commission",' Mackesy had scrawled over one of Cork's missives, 'that will put the Gallipoli one in the shade.' NA WO 168/83, paper 68.
30 Ziemke 1959, p. 95.

31 *London Gazette* 38011, p. 3182.
32 See particularly Connell 1959, p. 141 and Moulton 1966, p. 225.

Chapter 11

1 *London Gazette* 38011, p. 3182.
2 Connell 1959, p. 110.
3 Gilbert 1993, p. 1173.
4 Gamelin 1947, pp. 373–5. This light division was already waiting in the Clyde.
5 Brown 1999, p. 104.
6 Independent companies were designed for raiding operations and had been raised from territorial battalions awaiting passage to France. Wilkinson 1993, pp. 50–1, describes the origins of the scheme.
7 *London Gazette* 38011, p. 3173.
8 Cited in Connell 1959, p. 115.
9 Brown 1999, p. 107.
10 Cited in Connell 1959, p. 115.
11 Fitzgerald 1949, p. 46.
12 Fraser returned to Harstad in the *Curlew* but a medical board declared him unfit and he was invalided home.
13 Cited in Connell 1959, p. 119.
14 Ibid., p. 120.
15 Erskine 1956, p. 38.
16 The full strength of the German push northward through Mosjøen did not become known for another week, NA WO 106/1845.
17 Erskine 1956, p. 38.
18 These impressions of the action at Stein are taken from NA WO 168/56, Erskine 1956, pp. 39–41 and Adams 1989, pp. 76–7.
19 Fatalities were very few; Erskine 1956, p. 40, attributes this to the German reliance on the sub-machine gun and to the 4-inch mortar bomb which appeared to produce blast rather than fragmentation.
20 Auchinleck had been looking for something more – the ultimate recapture of Mo. Ruge's plans had been more ambitious still; he had visited Harstad on 17 May with proposals for an offensive southwards into the Trøndelag. Anything less 'risked breaking the moral (sic) of the Norwegian people', memo by Ruge, NA WO 198/14.
21 Cited in Connell 1959, p. 123.
22 Report 21 May, NA WO 198/8.
23 Erskine 1956, p. 41.
24 NA WO 168/56.
25 Cited in Connell 1959, p. 123.
26 There is a copy of this message in NA WO 198/8; it was handed to Trappes-Lomax at about 1600 on 20 May.
27 'Scissorsforce' signal 1200 of 21 May, ibid.
28 Dowler's notes on visit to Bodø, 21–22 May, NA WO 198/8.
29 NA WO 168/56.
30 Ibid.
31 Erskine 1956, p. 45.
32 Later General Sir Hugh Stockwell, who in 1956 commanded British forces at Suez.
33 Fitzgerald 1949, p. 58.
34 Ibid.
35 Note by Dowler on visit to Bodø, 26 May 1940, NA WO 198/8.
36 Fitzgerald 1949, p. 60.

Chapter 12

1 War Cabinet, 16 May, Gilbert 1994, p. 32.
2 Churchill, II, 1950, p. 42.
3 Telegram to War Cabinet, 16 May 1940, Gilbert 1994, pp. 61–2.
4 AT 0107 of 12 May, NA ADM 199/1929; War Cabinet 17 May, Gilbert 1994, p. 67.
5 War Cabinet, 20 May, ibid p. 96.
6 AT 1848 of 20 May, NA ADM 199/1929; see also Gilbert 1994, pp. 95–8.
7 SWC 22 May 1940, ibid., pp. 110–14.
8 WC 23 May 1940, ibid., pp. 117–18.
9 Connell 1959, p. 128.
10 WC 23 May 1940, Gilbert 1994, p. 120.
11 *London Gazette* 38011, pp. 3175–6; Connell 1959, p. 133.
12 Cork's 1103 of 17 May and 1517 of 19 May; NA ADM 199/1929. Worries about 'neurasthenia' (nervous breakdown) among tired men exposed to constant air attack were exercising minds in the Admiralty at this time.
13 Churchill's 1848 of 20 May and Cork's 1456 of 21 May, ibid.
14 *London Gazette* 38011, p. 3176; Béthouart 1968, p. 61.
15 Ziemke says 230.
16 Two LCM and three LCA.
17 *London Gazette* 38011, pp. 3174, 3190.
18 Lapie 1941, pp. 85–7.
19 Cork, *London Gazette* 38011, pp. 3174–5.
20 FO Narvik's 1130 of 29 May 1940, NA ADM 199/1929.
21 Béthouart 1968, p. 77.

Chapter 13

1 Gilbert 1994, pp. 226–8. Churchill was influenced, by a letter from Hugh Dalton (the new Minister of Economic Warfare) pointing to the significance of the high-grade iron ore stockpiled at Narvik.
2 Ibid., p. 231.
3 The story of this Gladiator detachment is told in MacClure 1941, pp. 204–6.
4 Derry 1952, pp. 214–16; see also *London Gazette* 38011, p. 3188.
5 Battalion War Diary, NA WO 168/56.
6 *London Gazette* 38011, p. 3191.
7 Ibid., pp. 3176–7. Mowinckel, a former Norwegian Prime Minister, had floated the idea with the Swedish Foreign Ministry on 20 May. Derry 1952, p. 171.
8 The German Foreign Ministry began to suspect an Allied evacuation when Stockholm broached the Mowinckel proposals on 4 June; but OKW seems to have ignored the matter.
9 Ziemke 1959, pp. 101–2.
10 *Führer Conferences* 1990, pp. 107–9.
11 Richards 1953, pp. 102–3.
12 Lapie 1941, p. 127.
13 Roskill 1954, p. 193.
14 *London Gazette* 38011, p. 3178.
15 C-in-C Home Fleet despatch, NA ADM/199/39.
16 British forces had landed in Iceland on 17 May.
17 DSC, June 1915 following epic patrol in Sea of Marmara; DSO October 1915 after single-handed attack on Hejaz railway. Bar to DSO Sept 1918 when in command of *E.35*.
18 Maier et al. 1991, p. 215.
19 NHB BR 1840(1), p. 69.

20 Ibid., p.71.

21 Ibid., pp.71–2.

22 This account is based on the war diaries of the *Gneisenau* and *Scharnhorst* in NA ADM 1/19910. For the sake of consistency, times have been converted to British Summer Time (Zone − 1).

23 NHB BR 1840 (1), pp.74–5.

24 Minute by Director of Signals, NA ADM 178/201.

25 Brown 1999, p.130.

26 Later ACM Sir Kenneth Cross.

27 The evidence collected by the Board is in NA ADM 178/201.

28 The final total of killed and missing from the *Glorious* was 1,207; this figure includes fifty-nine RAF personnel; figures for the *Ardent* and *Acasta* were 152 and 160.

29 Minutes by Pound and Little on report of Board of Inquiry, NA ADM/178/201. RA (D) Home Fleet recommended both captains for the VC. The reward recommended by Pound was limited to a special letter of appreciation to next of kin.

30 Roskill 1954, pp.197–8.

31 Some authors have tried to make the case that traffic analysis provided clues to the German presence; there is little in OIC daily reports to support this view. But the report for 9 June refers to an unconfirmed report (received 0900 on the 8th) of a German battleship, two destroyers and a seaplane attacking a transport in 67° 44′ N, 03° 52′ E. This was later thought to be the *Orama*.

32 Gilbert 1994, pp.281–2, 355.

33 Ibid., pp.268–9.

34 SWC minutes 11 June 1940, ibid., p.290.

35 SWC minutes 13 June 1940, ibid., pp.312–13.

36 For a very readable account of the parliamentary proceedings see Winton 1986, pp.208–12.

Chapter 14

1 *London Gazette* 37584, p.2608.

2 Report, NA WO 106/1905.

3 Sickleforce report, NA WO 168/93.

4 CoS 28 January 1940, Gilbert 1993, pp.699–700.

5 C-in-C Home Fleet, NA ADM 199/39.

6 Sickleforce report, NA WO168/93.

7 NA WO/168/83, paper 68.

8 Cited in Connell 1959, pp.140–1.

9 Auchinleck's report, NA WO 168/9. These opinions were removed from the published version.

10 Carton de Wiart, NA WO 106/1905.

11 Paget, NA WO 168/93.

12 *London Gazette* 37584, p.2607.

13 Figure covers Norway and Denmark and includes killed, wounded and missing. Germany lost 242 aircraft, one third of them transports. Naval losses included 1 heavy cruiser, 2 light cruisers, 10 destroyers, 4 U-boats and 18 merchant ships, totalling 88,604 grt.

14 Maier et al. 1991, pp.218–19.

Bibliography

Unpublished

National Archives (NA)
ADM 1/19910, Translations of German Documents relating to loss of HMS *Glorious*.
ADM 178/201, Report of Board of Inquiry, Loss of *Glorious, Ardent* and *Acasta*.
ADM 187/7, Pink Lists, April–May 1940.
ADM 199 series (War History Cases and Papers)
   39, Despatch of C-in-C Home Fleet, 1 March to 15 June 1940.
   361, Home Fleet War Diary, April–May 1940.
   379, Battle Cruiser Squadron, War Diary April–May 1940.
   1929, First Lord's Papers.
WO 106/1845, Norway Intelligence Log, 14 April to 25 May 1940.
WO 106/1905, Report by Maj Gen A. Carton de Wiart.
WO 168/9, Report by Lt Gen C.J.E. Auchinleck.
WO 168/24, War Diary of 24th Guards Brigade.
WO 168/25, War Diary of 146th Infantry Brigade.
WO 168/26, War Diary of 148th Infantry Brigade.
WO168/56, War Diary of 1st Battalion Scots Guards.
WO 168/83, Rupertforce General Staff Papers including French attack on Bjerkvik.
WO 168/93, Sickleforce War Diary.
WO 168/103, Scissorsforce War Diary.
WO 198 series (North-west Expeditionary Force in Norway 1940).
   8, Reports and Notes on visits to Bodo–Saltdalen area.
   9, Appreciation by C-in-C NWEF dated 27 April 1040.
   14, Reports and notes from General Ruge.
   16, HQ NWEF conference records and decisions.

Naval Historical Branch (NHB)
BR 1840 (1), The German Campaign in Norway.
Naval Staff Meetings, 1 February to 31 May 1940.
OIC Daily Reports, April to June 1940.
Weekly Intelligence Reports April 1940.

US Naval War College
War Diaries of German Naval War Staff (Operations Division), January to April 1940 (USN
   Translation).

Official Publications

London Gazette (Supplement) No. 38005, Despatches of R Adm R.C.H. Hallifax, RA(D) Home Fleet, on First and Second Battles of Narvik.

London Gazette (Supplement) No. 38011, Despatches of Adm of Flt the Earl of Cork and Orrery (Flag Officer Narvik) with Appendices by Maj Gen P.J. Mackesy and Lt Gen C.J.E. Auchinleck.

London Gazette (Supplement) No. 37584; Despatches of Lt Gen H.R.S. Massy, C-in-C North Western Expeditionary Force.

House of Commons Debates, vol. 360 (Debate on the Conduct of the War, 7 and 8 May 1940).

Führer Conferences on Naval Affairs 1939–1945, Greenhill Books, 1990.

Other Published Sources

Adams, Jack, *The Doomed Expedition*, Leo Cooper, 1989.

Ash, Bernard, *Norway 1940*, Cassell, 1964.

Barnett, Correlli, *Engage the Enemy More Closely*, Hodder and Stoughton, 1991.

Bedarida, Francois, 'France Britain and the Nordic countries', *Scandinavian Journal of History* 2, 1977.

Beesley, Patrick, *Very Special Admiral (Life of Ad J.H. Godfrey)*, Hamish Hamilton, 1980.

Bekker, Cajus, *Hitler's Naval War*, Panda Books, 1977.

——, *Luftwaffe War Diaries*, Da Capo Press, 1994.

Béthouart, Général Antoine, *Cinq Années d'Espérance*, Plon, 1968.

Broch, Theodore, *The Mountains Wait*, Michael Joseph, 1943.

Brodhurst, Robin, *Churchill's Anchor: Biography of Admiral of the Fleet Sir Dudley Pound*, Leo Cooper, 2000.

Brown, David (ed.), *Naval Operations of the Campaign in Norway*, Frank Cass, 1999.

Brown, David, *Carrier Operations in World War Two*, II, Ian Allen, 1974.

Butler, J.R.M., *Grand Strategy*, II, HMSO, 1957.

Carton de Wiart, Lt Gen Sir Adrian, *Happy Odyssey*, Jonathan Cape, 1950.

Churchill, W.S., *The Second World War: The Gathering Storm*, Cassell, 1950.

——, *The Second World War: Their Finest Hour*, Cassell, 1950.

Clarke, Dudley, *Seven Assignments*, Jonathan Cape, 1948.

Colville, John, *Fringes of Power, Downing Street Diaries 1939–1945*, Hodder & Stoughton, 1985.

Connell, John, *The Auk: A Biography of Field Marshal Sir Claude Auchinleck*, Cassell, 1959.

Derry, T.K., *The Campaign in Norway*, HMSO, 1952.

Dickens, Peter, *Narvik: Battles in the Fjords*, Ian Allen, 1974.

Dilks, David, 'Great Britain and Scandinavia in the Phoney War', *Scandinavian Journal of History* (2), 1977.

Erskine, David, *The Scots Guards, 1919–1955*, Wm Clowes & Sons, 1956.

Fitzgerald, D.L.J., *History of the Irish Guards in WWII*, Gale and Polden, 1949.

French, David, *Raising Churchill's Army*, OUP, 2000.

Gamelin, Général Maurice, *Servir, Tome III*, Plon, 1947.

Gilbert, Martin (ed.), *The Churchill War Papers*, I, Heinemann, 1993.

——, *The Churchill War Papers*, II, Heinemann, 1994.

Haikio, Martti, 'The Race for northern Europe', see Henrik S. Nissen (ed.), *Scandinavia during the Second World War*, Oslo, 1983.

Hambro, Carl J., *I saw it happen in Norway*, Hodder and Stoughton, 1940.

Hingston, Walter, *Never Give Up (History of the KOYLI)*, Lund Humphries, 1950.

Hinsley, F.H. et al., *British Intelligence in the Second World War*, I, HMSO, 1979.

Howsley, C., *A History of the 8th Battalion Sherwood Foresters 1939–45*, Miliquest Publications, Nottingham, 1996.

Hubatsch, Walther, 'Problems of the Norwegian Campaign 1940', *RUSI Journal*, August 1958, pp. 336–45.

Ismay, *Memoirs of Lord Ismay*, Heinemann, 1960.

Jenkins, Roy, *Churchill*, Pan Books, 2002.

Kennedy, General Sir John, *The Business of War*, Hutchinson, 1957.

Kersaudy, F., *Norway 1940*, Collins, 1990.

Koht, Halvdan, *Norway, Neutral and Invaded*, Hutchinson, 1941.

Lapie, Pierre O., *With the Foreign Legion at Narvik*, Murray, 1941.

MacClure, V.A., 'Gladiators in Norway', *Blackwoods Magazine*, vol. 249, March 1941.

Macintyre, D., *Narvik*, Norton & Co, 1960.

Mackesy, Piers, 'Churchill on Narvik', *RUSI Journal*, CXV (Dec 1970).

McLeod R. and Kelly D. (eds), *Ironside Diaries 1937–40*, Constable, 1962.

Maier Klaus A. et al., *Germany and the Second World War: Germany's Initial Conquests in Europe*, Clarendon Press, 1991.

Marder, A.J., 'Winston is back: Churchill at the Admiralty 1939–40', *English History Review* (Supplement 5), Longman, 1972.

Maund, R Adm L.E.H., *Assault from the Sea*, Methuen, 1949.

Moulton, J.L., *The Norwegian Campaign of 1940*, Eyre and Spotiswood, 1966.

Mountevans, Admiral of the Fleet Lord, *Adventurous Life*, Hutchinson, 1946.

Nicolson, Nigel (ed.), *Harold Nicolson Diaries and Letters 1907–1964*, Weidenfeld & Nicolson, 2004.

Raeder, Erich, *My Life*, US Naval Institute Press, 1960.

Richards, Denis, *Royal Air Force 1939–45*, I, *The Fight at Odds*, HMSO, 1953.

Rhodes James, Robert (ed.), *'Chips': the Diaries of Sir Henry Channon*, Phoenix, 1996.

Rohwer, J. and Hummelchen, G., *Chronology of the War at Sea 1939–45*, Greenhill Books, 1992.

Roskill, S.W., *Churchill and the Admirals*, Collins, 1977.

——, *Naval Policy between the Wars*, II, Collins, 1976.

——, *The War at Sea 1939–1945*, I, HMSO, 1954.

Slessor, Marshal of the RAF Sir John, *The Central Blue*, Cassell, 1956.

Sheffield, O.F., *The York and Lancaster Regiment 1915–1955*, III, Gale and Polden, 1956.

Slessor, Tim, *Ministries of Deception*, Aurum Press, 2002.

Stewart, Graham, *Burying Caesar: Churchill, Chamberlain and the Tory Party*, Weidenfeld and Nicolson, 1999.

Synge, W.T., *The Story of the Green Howards 1939–45*, Richmond, Yorks, 1952.

Trevor-Roper, H.R. (ed.), *Hitler's War Directives*, London, 1964.

Warlimont, Walter, *Inside Hitler's Headquarters 1930–45*, Weidenfeld and Nicolson, 1964.

Wilkinson, Peter and Bright Astley, Joan, *Gubbins and SOE*, Pen & Sword, 1993.

Winton, John, *Carrier Glorious*, Leo Cooper, 1986.

Zbyszewski, Karol, *The Fight for Narvik, Impressions of the Polish Campaign in Norway*, Lindsay Drummond, 1940.

Ziemke, Earl F., *The German Northern Theatre of Operations 1940–45*, Dept of Army pamphlet No. 20-271, Washington DC, 1959.

Index

221